Lord, *Zèga* and Peasant:
A Study of Property and Agrarian Relations in Rural Eastern Gojjam

Habtamu Mengistie
Addis Ababa University

Forum for Social Studies
Addis Ababa

FSS Special Monograph Series 1

The opinions expressed in this publication are those of the author and do not necessarily reflect the views of FSS or its Board of Advisors.

ISBN: 1-904855-64-4
ISBN-13: 978-1-904855-64-6

Financial support for this publication has been provided by the FSS donor consortium which consists of the Norwegian Embassy, DFID and the Irish Embassy.

Copyright: © The Author and Forum for Social Studies 2004

Text Layout by Mihret Demissew

Table of Contents

Page

Key to the transliteration System..i
Acknowledgment...ii
Preface..iv
Abstract..viii

Chapter One: Introduction..1

1.1. *The Geographical Setting..1*
1.2. *Rest, gult and the Institution of zègenät..........................5*
1.3. *Delimiting and defining the meaning and the socio-economic scope of the term zèga or the institution of zègenät in Eastern Gojjam........9*
Notes...34

Chapter Two: Gult Lords, Zèga and the Balä-Rest, The Structure of the Society in Eastern Gojjam, c.1767-1874.....................41

2.1. *Property and the Institution of Zègenät, Main Features and Characteristics..41*
2.2. *Property, Surplus Appropriation and the Social Structure of the Society..71*
Notes...82

Chapter Three: Land Tenure and the Redistribution of Land: Peasants, Lords and the State, 1874-1901................................86

3.1. *Land Grants during the Reign of Täklä-Häymanot: Lord, Zèga and Peasant in the Last Quarter of the 19th century................86*

*3.2. The Land Charters of the Churches of Amanu'el, Ledäta
and Däbrä Gälila*...*118*

Notes..126

**Chapter Four: Property and Modes of Property Transfer:
Individual Right and the Commercialization of Land**..................**130**

4.1 Property and the Making of Property Documents.......................*130*
4.2 Modes and Factors of Property Transaction............................*134*
    4.2.1 Sale and Redeemability of Land....................................*134*
    *4.2.2 Inheritance Related Bequeathal Involving Adoption and
    Will*..*150*
4.3 Land Concentration and the Reverse Process of Disintegration....*165*
Notes...174

**Chapter Five: Explaining Ethiopia's Economic Stagnation:
Land Tenure and the Problem of Underdevelopment**................178

Notes...199

Chapter Six: Conclusion...202

Bibliography..205

KEY TO THE TRANSLITERATION SYSTEM

Symbols: The following simple symbols are used in the text for the transliteration of Ethiopian words in none linguistic articles to produce the correct sound. This transliteration system is adapted from the Department of History at Addis Ababa University.

Vowels	Symbols	Example
1st order (Geez)	ä	zäfänä
2nd order (Ka'eb)	u	hulu
3rd order (Sales)	I	hid
4th order (Rabe)	a	rarra
5th order (Hames)	è	bèt
6th order (Sades)	e	eger
7th order (Sabe)	o	hod

Consonants	Symbols	Example
š	ሸሽ	šäšä
q	ቆብ	qob
chä	ቸበቾበ	chäbächäbä
ñ	ኞኞ	ñoñño
ž	ገዥ	gäž
y	ይታይ	yetaye
j	ጀበርና	jäbärna
ṭ	ጣጣ	ṭaṭa
çhä	ጬበጠ	çhäbäṭä
ş	ጸጸት	şäşät
mwa	ሏሚ	lamwa

ACKNOWLEDGMENTS

I have received much assistance from individuals and institutions when writing this dissertation. I would like to express my special gratitude to my Department and Faculty. The Department of History freed me from teaching obligations so that I could have enough time for writing. I have also used the computer services of the Department freely. I gladly acknowledge all this and other assistance given to me by the Department. My thesis advisor, Professor Merid, has helped me a lot with his substantive comments. He was eager to see me finish on time and constantly encouraged the finalization of the work. I would like to express my gratitude to Prof. Merid for he generously helped improve an argument which is critical of his viewpoint. Though I disagree with him I am indebted to him greatly.

The second person who has contributed directly and indirectly towards this work is Dr. Tekalign. His suggestions of many pertinent readings, including his doctoral dissertation were of great help to me. I have had many enlightening discussions about my thesis and future research with him. I gladly acknowledge the assistance I have received from him. I would also like to express my deep gratitude to Professor Bahru and *Ato* Shiferaw. The topic of the thesis itself was conceived in an incidental talk I had with Prof. Bahru. It was he who recommended the publication of this dissertation. He followed the progress of my research and has been a source of inspiration for me. Prof. Bahru together with *Ato* Shiferaw arranged for me to conduct library research in Rome and Naples. Professor Triulzi, the coordinator of the scholarship program of the Istituto Italiano per l'Africa et l'Oriente (IsAIO), arranged a scholarship grant to me. He did every thing to make my research in Rome and Naples rewarding and enjoyable. I have also received much willing help from Antonella Marteluce and other members of the IsAIO. Maria Catterina arranged my travel and training in Italian language at the University of Perugia. The time that I spent in Italy is among the best and the most fruitful in my life. I am grateful for the assistance I have received from all those who helped me to make my research rewarding and pleasant.

I am also deeply indebted to friends Abebaw Ayalew, Dr. Ayele Tarekegn and Kindeneh Endeg. Kindeneh has given me many substantive comments. Abebaw and Ayele consistently encouraged me to finalize my work. I have also received moral and material encouragement from my sister Emebet Zewdu. Ambaye Assefa, my uncle, and Gebeyaw Hunegnaw arranged for me to reproduce some useful manuscripts in Märṭulä-Maryam and Däbrä-Marqos. *Abuna* Zäkaryas and *Re'esä-Re'usan* Häylä-Maryam allowed me to go through the entire manuscript collections of the churches of Däbrä-Marqos and Märṭulä-Maryam, respectively. Both kindly allowed me to photocopy highly important documents and manuscripts. The IES chief librarian, *Ato* Solomon Desalegn, has given me his cooperation. Students Abere Mengistie, Dereje Mengistie, Muluqen Ambaye and Yohannis Assefa helped me to put into writing the interviews and documents that I recorded on cassettes during the process of my field work. Yirgalem Mahiteme kindly prepared me the maps and I have acknowledged his assistance. Last but not least my friend Demeke Tsehaye has taught me patience and cooperated me a lot during the process of writing this dissertation.

PREFACE

Considering the number of individuals actively involved and the scholarly works on the field Ethiopian history could claim to have been securely established in academic institutions. However, Ethiopian history still suffers from some serious lacunae, one of which is in the realm of social history. The most serious lacunae in Ethiopian historiography is the neglect of the ordinary citizen as subject of study. A shift of emphasis in scholarly concern to social history to dispel the old fixation on political and economic history remains a challenging task. This study is intended as a modest contribution to the social history of Ethiopia by making the peasantry and the landless and highly impoverished class of people called *zèga* a focus of study in Eastern Gojjam. The peasantry is a subject of great interest for us since it was the peasantry that carried the whole burden of the social order through the fruits of its labor.

A range of historical methods were used for the purpose of reconstructing the historical knowledge about the dynamics of the socio-economic relationships between lord and peasant and *zèga* in Eastern Gojjam in the period covered here. The first method involved extensive library research so as to gather information from published and unpublished primary and secondary documentary sources. Conducting library work on the theme of the thesis helped me frame the project. It also enabled me to have sufficient background knowledge about the subject of my study.

Two scholarly works that enlightened me greatly deserve special mention. Professor Crummey's recent book entitled *Land and Society* spanning many centuries and scanning many regions is one of them. The second highly illuminative and brilliantly original work is Dr. Tekalign's doctoral dissertation on the political economy of the modern Ethiopian state as it existed in the twentieth century. He gave me his dissertation and other pertinent readings directly relevant to my study area. Dr. Tekalign's doctoral dissertation does not directly fall within the time frame of my dissertation. However, like Prof. Crummey, he has given a very detailed and masterful interpretation of the land tenure system of the imperial era, especially of southern Ethiopia. The publication of Crummey's *Land and Society* came as a pleasant surprise to me. This work was pertinent to the kind of work I was intending to do. Though he was unaware of the existence of the institution of *zègenät,* which is one of the central themes of my study, this thesis has benefited very immensely from his work. Many of my previous uncertainties on what Tekalign calls the "state's reversionary right" to land have been cleared up thanks to Tekalign's work.

The Department of History, my second home, together with the IsAIO, offered me a unique opportunity to conduct research in Rome and Naples. My research in Rome and Naples proved very rewarding and amongst the best time in my life. The IsAIO library in Rome was the right place to make pertinent readings on the themes of my study. It is an excellent library with large number of collections not only on Ethiopia but also on other African countries. The University of Naples has also some of the best missionary and travel books and accounts on Ethiopia, including the study area, Eastern Gojjam. I also religiously consulted every journal I could find specially the journals, *History in Africa: A Journal of Methods* and the *Rassegna Studi Etiopici,* in Naples. Early issues of both journals could be found in AAU, but the recent volumes of these journals are impossible to find. Special emphasis was given to journals and materials which are not available or hardly accessible or both in, either the Kennedy library of the AAU or the Institute of Ethiopian Studies.

The archival canters of the Italian Ministry of Foreign Affairs and the Italian Geographical Society in Rome have also rewarded the researcher immensely though the material gathered is not integrated into this study. No archival material in the Ministry goes deeper in time than the second half of the nineteenth century. Gojjam captured the attention of many Italians to the effect that large amount of documents were generated on the region by them. King Täklä-Häymanot enjoyed friendship with the Italians and corresponded with them. I was given permission to reproduce all his letters to his Italian friends and other documents preserved in the archive of the Ministry and the Italian Geographical Society. However, I was not able to complete my research in the archive of the Italian Geographical Society for shortage of time. Nor was I able to visit the Vatican Library because of the tense international situation at the time when I was conducting research in Rome.

The library research in Italy was followed by an extensive and supplementary reading and research in the library of the Institute of Ethiopian Studies. The massive and dazzling collection of microfilmed documents deposited in the microfilm section of the IES library is of special importance for the study. No research on Gojjam could claim to be complete which does not consult the microfilm material deposited in the IES. Much of the documents in the microfilm section of the library are collected from various European libraries and archives especially from Britain, France and Italy. However, some of the highly pertinent documents like the <u>Carte d'Abbadie 18 and 19</u> have unfortunately eluded my efforts to get access to them. The IES has lost them.

Many other source materials from monasteries and churches in Ethiopia were microfilmed or photographed and added to the IES collection. Most of the photographing job from the study area was done by Daniel Ayana in cooperation with Crummey and Shumet Sishagne. His photographing activities provided the researcher a useful service .The fine job Daniel did involved photographing property documents which exist as marginal notes in manuscripts belonging to monasteries and churches in the study area. He has photographed massive new sources and documents pertinent to the study of social relations and intergenerational property transfers among the rank of landowners.

The fact that index is not prepared for the property documents meant that it was necessary to go through the entire length of the photographed or microfilm materials. Thus I worked my way through these materials in the IES. Useful documents were traced in this way and copied. The temporal and spatial coverage of the property documents is not uniform. There is very little documentation for the period between 18oo and 1874 in the microfilm or photographic collection on Eastern Gojjam. In other words there is an unfortunate congestion of property documents in late eighteenth century and the last quarter of the next century. This work has relied for the facts and interpretation essentially on these property documents microfilmed and photographed from Gojjam churches and monasteries and deposited at the IES. I can confidently and proudly say that I have scrutinized all the pertinent microfilm materials at the IES. My dissertation derives its originality from the use of these unexplored sources.

Of the rewarding sources for this study Täklä-Iyäsus provides a very useful data on the relationship between lord and peasant. He was familiar with the wide range of literature available in Gojjam. His well known work on the history of Gojjam contains eyewitness or at least contemporary accounts for the period considered since he wrote it by referring to living witnesses to events. The second work of Täklä-Iyäsus, which records the genealogy of the people of Gojjam is a singular document to the study of the social history of Eastern Gojjam. The customary socio-economic and political practices of the Gafat people, which he compiled and appended in this manuscript, contains many strands of custom with regard to land tenure and the relationship between *zègas* and their landlords and the society.

Travel literature forms another form of source material for this study. However, travel literature tended to focus on the nobility and other social elites with whom travelers had frequent contact. They provided and wrote a wealth of information only on villages and the peasantry found along trade routes and the immediate vicinity of towns and administrative centers. The focus of writing of travelers is largely on dramatic movements such as on military campaigns by lords into the countryside that involved peasants. They provide insights into peasant obligation to travelers. However, the normal peasant life remained unreported.

Updating and supplementing library research with intensive and extensive field study in Eastern Gojjam was necessary. Studying oral narratives could reconstruct the historical experience beyond described in documents for the period and region under study. Thus library research was followed by extended information gathering in the study area by interviewing elders and working on local records in churches and monasteries. The field study yielded the discovery of bulky property documents and manuscripts. I found two of such unique manuscripts that contain many precious documents in Märṭulä-Maryam and Moṭa. The one in Märṭulä- Maryam was reproduced and the other in Moṭa copied by the researcher. Moreover, the researcher has reproduced a manuscript that contains many land grant documents of the last quarter of the nineteenth century found at Däbrä-Marqos church. I was bale to use these sources together with oral data collected through interviews by the researcher for writing the dissertation. Combining oral data and documentary evidences served the study well in the absence of rich documentary record. To put it differently, combining oral and documentary sources made possible to provide a rich texture of historical detail.

ABSTRACT

The land tenure system constituted a useful social element for analyzing the socio-economic relationship between peasants and *zègas* and lords. The history of peasants and a highly impoverished and subordinate social class called *zèga* is discussed in terms of their relationship with other classes in the social system. This study has focused on introducing the institution of *zègenät* and delineating its implication on class and the land tenure system. *Zègenät* provides a penetrating insight into the nature of the rural society of Eastern Gojjam.

Apart from introducing *zègenät* into historical discourse on Ethiopia, this study has sought to review the literature on the agrarian history of the country. The institution has immense importance to offer judgment on the nature of the Ethiopian polity in the past and to determine whether or not private property existed. The study challenges the long prevailing notion that says *gult* was not property right to land. Contrary to previous assumptions, land including *rest* land, could be mortgaged, sold and willed. Any work which denies any material base in land for the Ethiopian ruling class is sustained by very flimsy evidence. The study has fundamentally departed from these orthodoxies. *Gult* did not simply represent the exploitative tributary relationship between lord and peasant which is most often assumed to be. Private and communal property rights in land did exist side-by-side for a considerable time in historic Ethiopia.

The agrarian order of rural Eastern Gojjam was closely akin to the social formation called feudal in Marxist terminology. The ruling elites were in a stronger position to turn away permanently considerable land from peasants to the control of corporate institutions and powerful individuals as *gult* land. This study has also narrated the mechanism of property transfer. The ways and means by which land and rights to land were transferred took many forms. Lords holding land on behalf of churches exercised ownership rights including free disposal by sale. This land transferred into the hands of social elites was usually worked by the labor of the *zèga*, though there was considerable number of peasants working their own land. If the problem of Ethiopia's economic stagnation in the past is liked to be made comprehensible, *zègenät*, which flowered in the second half of the 18th century, must be given a privileged position and historical past in the agrarian studies of the country. So far the recent agrarian history of the country has been studied in the context of the emergence of the modern Ethiopian state and in the framework of the political change in the country. However, this has so far proved an impediment to a clear formulation of how the state operated socio-economically.

The study contends that the property system was not an impediment to the economic growth of the country historically. Moreover, there is a body of empirical support to argue that the most efficient and effective method of achieving rural agrarian capitalism and introducing agro-industry is through encouraging private owners. The country has to open up for rural agrarian capitalism and it can not achieve development and food security by just multiplying the number of peasants and allowing unimpeded fragmentation. Private agrarian enterprises are naturally bound to be efficient unlike state and public controlled ones because the operation of the former is relatively free from bureaucracy. In other words the performance and efficacy of private enterprises is determined by the market place which bespeak that they would be subject to automatic control.

CHAPTER ONE

INTRODUCTION

1.1 The Geographical Setting

The name "Gojjam" has denoted different geographic units at different times. Based on historical processes a distinction is made between "Gojjam proper" and Gojjam in historical writing. In the medieval period Gojjam referred to the area virtually enclosed by the Blue Nile River, the broad geographical sweep extending from Lake Ṭana in the north to the great eastern and southeastern bends of the same river. The Blue Nile encircles the region, winding around it so as to form a river peninsula. From the 17th through to the 20th century, however, the name Gojjam came to refer to the much more restricted geographical area within the Blue Nile bend inhabited by the Amhara people.[1] This province consisted largely of the districts around contemporary Bichäna, Moṭa and Däbrä-Marqos. In short, Eastern Gojjam which will be studied in this thesis is virtually equivalent to the province sometimes described as "Gojjam proper."[2]

Eastern Gojjam has strongly marked geographical features which have deeply influenced its history. It is a region with very clear natural boundaries, made up of rivers and mountains. The Çhoqè mountain range located at the centre of the region of Gojjam divides it into two major watersheds. The summit of the range delimits the western and west central boundaries of Eastern Gojjam from the provinces of Agäw-Meder and Damot. The mountain range has also been an important linguistic frontier. The area west of the mountains was, and still is, inhabited by the Agäw people whereas the eastern section is thoroughly Amhara.[3] The Çhoqè Mountain constitutes the core of the whole region of Gojjam. Mount Berhän, which rises to 4154m, forms the highest summit of the Çhoqè mountain chain. There are also, among these mountain chains, some peaks ascending to an elevation of about 4145m.[4] These lofty mountain peaks form magnificent scenery overlooking all the rest of the land in the region.

The Çhoqè mountain massifs give rise to numerous rivers and streams flowing in almost every direction: north, south, east and northeast. Of special historical and geographical importance is the Blue Nile, locally called Abay. Its deep and broad gorge has helped to define and articulate the boundary of the region. It originates at Mount Gešä. At first the river flows northwards and enters Lake Ṭana. Leaving Ṭana it runs east and southeast, thereby forming a deep gorge and a definitive boundary that separates Eastern Gojjam from Gondär, Wällo, Shäwa and Wälläga, almost literally encircling the borders of Gojjam in every direction except in the west.[5]

The river Abaya, one of the headwater tributaries of the Blue Nile, constitutes the northwestern boundary of Eastern Gojjam. The river rises in the northeastern section of the Çhoqè range. It flows northeastwards to separate Eastern Gojjam from what was known as Mèçha, a small district to the south and southeast of Lake Ṭana. In its lower course, Abaya forms a deep and wide valley. It joins the Blue Nile at the latter's northeastern course. The Godèb is another river rising from the southern ridges of the Çhoqè mountain range. It separates Eastern Gojjam from Damot. Its course is towards the south of the mountains and it joins the Blue Nile River at the latter's southwestern course.[6]

The diverse geographical conditions of the region have had significance for the proliferation of its agrarian regimes. These varying agro-climatic conditions together with historical processes were also decisive in shaping the settlement patterns, mode of life and the socio-cultural patterns of the rural population of Eastern Gojjam. Evidence from recent aero-photographic studies of the agrarian landscape of Eastern Gojjam, including the Çhoqè mountain massifs, reveals that the pattern of field strips and population distribution evolved in the distant past, perhaps going back to ancient times. On the basis of the interpretation of the aero-photographic data, Marcaccini, who studied the features of the agrarian landscape of Eastern Gojjam, concluded that the system of field management in the Çhoqè area and the patterns of field strips in the region are suggestive of an old system of land management. The agrarian landscape was determined by the system of land use, which had developed in ancient times and persisted right down to the 20th century.[7]

According to Marcaccini topography does not always seem to be a particularly influential factor for determining the type of rural settlement. One reason that he advances is the fact that different shades of field patterns and settlement types ranging from entirely nucleated villages to very sparse settlements could be observed within uniform morphological conditions. He rightly concluded that the marked differences in the agrarian landscape of the same morphological conditions resulted from the social regime of land use and historical events.[8]

Marcaccini's argument is confirmed by oral traditions and documentary evidence. The property system that evolved over a long period of time in the past had a strong bearing on the overall agrarian landscape. Although its accuracy for the early period is doubtful, we have an older account of the colonization of Eastern Gojjam by individual settlers going four hundred years back. The oral history referring to this process of colonization and peopling of Eastern Gojjam is recorded in the genealogical book of Täklä-Iyäsus (hereafter Täklè for brevity), compiled in the last decade of nineteenth century. Täklè writes that the land in Eastern Gojjam was divided on the basis of ambilineal devolution of the generation of the early ancestors of the people, according to the operation of the *rest* system of land tenure.[9]

Based on his interpretation of the aero-photographical data of Eastern Gojjam taken in 1957/8, Marcaccini delineated three morphologically distinct agrarian regions which neatly fit into the three traditional divisions of agro-climatic zones: *dägga*, *wäyna-dägga* and *qolla*. However, the upper parts of the mountains of Çhoqè and Goncha are specifically *wurçhi* or frost zones, the coldest agro-climatic zone in Eastern Gojjam. This division is mainly influenced by rainfall and microclimate and other factors like variations in topography.[10]

By far the widest and most densely populated agro-climatic zone, which also hosts many of the noted churches in Eastern Gojjam, is the *wäyna-dägga*. In view of its historical importance this agrarian region merits lengthy discussion. The *wäyna-dägga* agrarian region is found within the elevation range of 1500-2300 meters. It is a wide zone between the limited areas of the *dägga* and *qolla* agro-climatic zones. The greater portion of Eastern Gojjam constitutes extensive plain that extend into the mountains and bear more the character of *dägga* type of climate than *wäyna-dägga*.[11] Here the topography is generally of wide plains with many isolated peaks here and there breaking the monotony of the tableland. This part of Eastern Gojjam, precisely or firmly located by Marcaccini as lying between "the basaltic traps and lower volcanic flows of Choke", was and still is predominantly characterized by its "nucleated settlement patterns and the division of the land into strip fields."[12] It has a history of successive Amhara occupation going back at least to the fourteenth and fifteenth centuries which saw the immigration of many Amhara colonizers into Eastern Gojjam. Marcaccini concluded that "[t]he strip cultivation, the traces of division into areas of use, the agrarian structure organized into rural units, are probably related to an ancient form of occupation of the land (*restegna*), with commun [nal] practices."[13] Uniformly shaped fields were the notable features of this agrarian region and the highlands ranging from 2400 meters through to 2600-2700 meters and in some points reaching 2800 meters. An infinite mosaic or motley variety of field strip cultures can be observed from the aero-photographic data, some long, others square, straight, etc.[14]

The *wäyna-dägga* region of Eastern Gojjam receives abundant rainfall for a good part of the year. Except in rare periods of drought, it receives reliable and sufficient rain between June and September to sustain enough pasturage for a good part of the year. Autumn and spring rainfalls were very important in Eastern Gojjam in the 19th century. In fact a good part of the study area receives rainfall for an additional month earlier or after the normal rainy season (*kerämt*). Plowden, a 19th century traveler to Eastern Gojjam, writes that "[t]he tropical rains, in most provinces [of Ethiopia], continue for three months or thereabouts-that is July, August, and September-but in some, particularly Go[j]jam, [they go] for nearly a month more, before or after that period."[15] Then, it seems the rains began to fall one month before they did in other parts and continued for one more month after they had stopped elsewhere. This description of the rainfall patterns of the region by Plowden might be taken in terms of climate than weather. This is because no serious and frequent rainfall anomalies or drought conditions triggered by shortage of rains have ever been recorded in recent centuries for Eastern Gojjam.

The other two agrarian regions, *dägga* and *qolla*, are located above and below the first one, respectively. The *dägga* agrarian region of Eastern Gojjam lies between the elevation ranges of 2300 to 2700 meters up to 3300 to 3500 meters. At some places the highest limit of agricultural settlement of this agrarian region reaches 3700 meters. The Çhoqè mountains and the Goncha massifs have a distinctly *dägga* type of climate. The high altitude of these mountain areas militated against the cultivation of some crops like *tèff*. Barley is reported as having been produced abundantly in this agro-climatic region in the 19th century. The region had also pasture for the grazing of sheep and other animals.[16] As a whole this agro-climatic zone is noted for its suitability for the production of barely. Täklè, writing in the last decade of the nineteenth century, notes that depending on the fertility of the soil, cultivators grew barley even at the top of the mountains of Arat-Mäkäraker, the southwestern section of the

Çhoqè massifs. However, he remarked that the area around Arat-Mäkäraker is so mountainous and precipitous that it was depleted of nutrients by the leaching effects of the rains. According to Täklè a third part of this area was barren, almost completely devoid of soil; it represented a very severe case of erosion. Cultivation was possible in the *dägga* areas only where the soil was not washed away.[17] Since the soil could not allow continuous cultivation fallowing was practiced. After two or more years of cultivation the land would be left to rest and enable it recuperate its fertility. Population in the *dägga* agrarian region is sparser. The population and cultivation rapidly diminishes as one ascends the mountains towards their summit.[18] Conversely settlement becomes denser as one descends the massifs and is confined to the edge of the mountains. It represents one of the coldest agro-climatic regimes in Eastern Gojjam.[19] As a whole the severity of the climate towards the upper reaches of the mountains militated against the production of varieties of crops and dense agricultural settlement. Accounts before or after the nineteenth century repeatedly describe the landscape as being essentially similar to the situation in the period we are studying.

The third important agrarian region is the *qolla*. This zone lies within the elevation range of 500 to 1500 meters. It roughly coincides with the valleys of the Çhe'e, the Abaya and the Blue Nile, stretching all along the side of the meandering course of the latter river. The lowest parts of the *wäyna-dägga* region have also *qolla* type of climate. Rains before or after the main rainy season is a less marked feature of this agrarian region. Cotton, sorghum and millet were chiefly produced in this agro-climatic region. Generally it is hot, dry and sparsely populated. As in the case of the mountain districts geographic conditions have determined the nature of the economic activities and the types of settlement in the lowlands too. As was always the case, Marcaccini points out that the agrarian landscape of the valley might also have been shaped by historical events.[20]

1.2 Rest, Gult and the Institution of Zègenät

A marked feature of Ethiopian historiography in recent years is the growing attention to the study and analysis of the agrarian structure of society. Thanks to the recent research by scholars such as Crummey, Tekalign and others, our knowledge of the nature of the privileges and rights of elites with regard to land and the tangled web of the social and economic organization regarding land and agricultural production have been clarified and refined.[21] Tekalign also provides tantalizing additional details about the characteristics of *zègenät*, a very curious social and agrarian institution which was very prevalent in Eastern Gojjam. I shall have occasion to deal with Tekalign's study in later pages. The most extensively argued and debated subject among scholars of whether feudalism existed in Ethiopia is also one aspect of the growing emphasis that the social context is receiving in historical investigation. The historiographical debate centers on whether the pre-1974 historical experience of Ethiopia should be described as feudal and whether it was closely similar or a deviant from European feudalism.[22]

Obviously, the notion of property, especially landed property, has primacy in the debate on feudalism. The ways in which productive resources were owned and surplus was appropriated are very important in the discussion of the inter-class relationships between lord and peasant. The major social groups in Eastern Gojjam with which I am concerned here are lords and *zègas* and peasants, with special emphasis on the latter. However, the dividing line between social categories is very hard to draw as in many other places and societies in Ethiopia.[23] Though it does not describe the full context of the state-peasant relationship the most common element in the definition of the peasant is "a rural cultivator", distinct from other rural social groups who do not have to work the soil for their living. However, within this broad category of "peasant" there has been a great deal of stratification. This will be discussed in the next chapter in some detail.

Too much research on rural Ethiopia has been conducted and/or stuck in the *rest* and *gult* syndrome. What my reading of the agrarian relations of rural Eastern Gojjam certainly suggests, however, is that there was a new material structure which does not fit into the patterns of the conventional type of *rest* and *gult* production and property relations and whose full story waits to be told. So far scholars have tried to use *rest* and *gult* as important analytical units to penetrate systematically and characterize the forms of agrarian institutions and societies in Ethiopia in the past. The forms of material structure in historic Ethiopia glossed by such words as '*gult*' and *rest* when looked at very closely were very complex and differentiated. In the 17th century Eastern Gojjam a new tenure seems to have emerged as a direct corollary of the fluidity of local conditions created by unsettled conditions since the sixteenth century. This new form of tenure was, to use the language of my sources, *zèga* or *zègenät*. It could roughly be translated as "tenancy." Also in the 18th and 19th centuries documentary sources we find lower level socio-economic relationship in Eastern Gojjam embodied in this form of tenure or institution. However, tenancy cannot fully describe the reality of this form of tenure. Upon examining and interpreting the sources referring to the *zèga* I have arrived at a tentative conclusion that practices resembling an incipient serfdom or an institution containing the germs of serfdom were prevalent in the region. The first appearance of this kind of tenure can not be dated earlier than the 17th century. Its establishment actually appears to have taken place in the second half of the 18th century, when sources referring to *zèga* in the form of charters and manuals for church officials crop up.[24] Its establishment in the 18th century, marks the central theme of chapter two, discussed and developed further in the subsequent chapter. The category of *zèga* and the institution of *zègenät* existed concurrently with *gult* grants to churches and individuals. Therefore, a brief discussion of the literature on *gult* and *rest* and the implication of the institution of *zègenät* to our understanding of the nature of landed property right is necessary, as given below.

The nature of the rights and privileges of social elites with regard to land and the extent to which we can talk of "landlords" is also a point of animated debate among scholars of Ethiopia. The works of scholars like Crummey, Hoben, Merid, Shiferaw and Tekalign provide a good basis for a discussion of the main issues involved in this debate.[25] The question, of course, is whether "lord" refers simply to officials and administrators or to *landlords with a strong stake in the land or people owning land*. The existence of landlords or elites owning land needs to be determined from a close analysis of the forms of property rights in the past, property rights that are intertwined with the complex institution of tenure called *rest*. In the past, however, the basis of the argument that there was no class of landlords in historic Ethiopia was the analysis of tributary rights on land, called *gult*. Thus the debate on whether or not the Ethiopian past can be characterized as feudal basically rests on how scholars understand the institutions of *rest* and *gult*.

The natures of *rest* and *gult* rights are fully encompassed by the definition that Hoben gives to the terms in his widely read book. Hoben writes that *gult* rights entail "fief-holding rights" whereas *rest* right confers "land-use rights." He adds that "[i]n its most general sense, *rist* refers to the right a person has to a share of the land first held by any of his or her ancestors in any line of descent."[26] According to Hoben, *rest* refers to the theoretically inalienable and inheritable land right of peasants. The peasant had the right to claim *rest* land through both the paternal and maternal lines. The individual *rest* holder could have only a usufructuary title because the ultimate title to land lays in the "descent corporation" or the lineage. This evokes the view that under such system of land tenure no right of alienation by individuals could be possible since the unit of land holding is the lineage. Hoben writes that the descent groups provide the framework within which individual rights could exist. This implies that the *rest* system of land-holding has a communal character because of the undifferentiated complex of rights. What all this means is that many individuals could have concurrent and miscellaneous rights over the same piece of land.[27]

For Hoben, *gult* confers material advantages to and forms the basis of political power for the elite. It also plays a useful role in the administration of land and the people occupying it. The bundle of rights which the state transfers to the *balägult* could include adjudication, governorship, and the right to collect tribute. Taddesse Tamrat also shares essentially the same view with Hoben as regards the role of *gult* in the administration of the country and adds that it was equally significant in the system of military mobilization. The *balägult* simply enjoyed the right to tribute in the form of part of the annual produce from the land. However, they could not claim tribute as owners. Hoben writes that both *rest* and *gult* right extended over the same land and they complemented each other as such: "It is of fundamental importance to remember that *rist* and *gwilt* are not different types of land but distinct and complementary types of land rights."[28] Thus the exact scope of the right of the *balägult* and the *restäñña* is somewhat blurred or is overlapping. These assertions by Hoben regarding the nature of rights of *rest* and *gult* have almost attained the status of the basic principles and have become "established" points of departure for analyses of class relationship and the land tenure system. Some differences of detail notwithstanding, this view is shared by a number of scholars, including Donald Crummey.

Crummey argues that in regions where the *rest* system predominated, *gult* was the tribute right exercised by the non-farming elite, and that the *balägult*, in his capacity as pure tax and tribute collector, had absolutely nothing to do with the production process and with the land. He asserts, like Hoben, that the *restäñña* had mastery over the means of production and enjoyed absolute autonomy of production.[29]

However, in his study of the situation in Shäwa, Tekalign explicitly notes the existence of a form of lordship called *mälkäññenät*. He distinguished three varieties of tenure in *mälkäññenät*, all of them entailing rights pertaining to a landlord and as good as manorial rights, with varying degrees of interference from the state. One form of *mälkäññenät* was held to the almost complete exclusion of the state in the relationship between the *mälkäñña* and the people and the land under his control. He described this form of *mälkäññenät* as one which "...entitled the holder to full manorial rights, including private and permanent ownership of all unoccupied land in the lordship, exercise [of] full administrative and judicial authority, and the retention of all tributes and legal fees from the landowners under his authority..."[30] What is important from the point of view of this study is that Tekalign writes of the *mälkäñña* as "lords" rather than simply as "officials."

Without abandoning the view that *gult* was essentially a tribute right Crummey further argues that the tribute right had acquired a character of property, being transferred by sale or otherwise without necessarily involving the state. In other words, the individuals at the receiving end of the buying and selling process could accumulate tribute rights over large amounts of property. Tribute rights were thus exchanged, negotiated, fought over, etc. The selling and buying of tribute rights over land (i.e. *gult*) provides additional evidence to the argument that *gult* was a form of property. He concludes that the insistence by scholars that *gult* was given and taken away only by the kings was incorrect, and that the *gult* holders exercised the right of transfer without necessarily obtaining the permission or sanction of the kings.[31]

Crummey and Tekalign are among the major exponents of the thesis that peasants in the *rest* system had absolute control over the process of production including the right to cultivate and plant as they wished, the only limitations imposed upon them being meeting the tribute and tax demands of the *bälägult* and the king and providing service obligation associated with their land.[32] Dealing with this point Crummey writes: " ...I will use *gult* in a generic sense to refer to all rights by groups or individuals to collect tribute..."[33] However, the important point in his analysis for my purpose is his argument that the perpetuation of tributary rights gives *gult* a property character. He does argue also that the essence of *gult* rights conceived as tribute rights was not limited in the generic notion of surplus extractive relationships since the power of the *gultänña* extended over *specific rural lands*.[34]

Another claim of Crummey on the subject of *gult* and *rest* is that neither refers to exclusive and absolute property rights in land. He argues that most often the land tenure system formed a combination and interlocking of the rights of the king, the *balägult*, the "descent corporation" and the individual peasant household. One form of tenure, he says, was contingent on the other. His definition of *gult* and *rest* and the dialectics of the relationship between the two forms of tenure are identical to those of Hoben. He writes that "[g]*ult* was used as a term to describe the tributary system in general. Often, it functioned as a distinct form of property right on the same lands on which *rest* rights existed. In that case, neither property right would be absolute but each would be limited by the existence of the other."[35]

Both Crummey and Tekalign concur that the *restäñña* could lose his ancestral land. Both argue that in uprooting the cultivators the state needed to have sufficient grounds to warrant the expropriation of the land by the outright exercise of what Tekalign calls the state's "reversionary right." This could happen for two important reasons. One ground, which could warrant the exercise of the "reversionary right" of the state or the eviction of settled occupiers, is sufficient misconduct such as criminal or political offences, collectively or individually. The second cause of forfeiture of title to *rest* land according to Crummey and Tekalign is the default of payment of tribute and tax.[36] However, as will be made abundantly clear in the pages below and subsequent chapters the *restäñña* lost their land during peace time and without committing any crime against the state.

Defining and delimiting the meanings and scope of *gult* and *rest* rights, Merid writes that *gult* "has never been a form of land tenure"; it was, he says, only "a system of defraying remuneration for services out of taxes and tributes which could have been collected in kind. *Gult* rights only conferred partial usufruct rights."[37] He goes on to state that even *rest* right did not allow "absolute ownership rights on the individual. It has done so on the lineage or descent group only."[38] According to Merid, though the individual members of the descent group enjoyed perpetuity of tenure they could not have an absolute interest in an allotted portion of the descent property in land. The justification for the inalienability of *rest* land, according to Merid, was the desire to preserve it for the needs of the present and unborn individuals in the line of descent; in his own words *rest* could not be alienated "because it belonged to the living and the yet unborn."[39] One could, of course, give out his or her land on terms of tenancy. Merid adds a few other points to his description of the *rest* system: one is that membership in a *rest* owning group could be obtained or acquired only through birth. The second is that there was no big private or individual ownership of land because of the workings of the *rest* system of land. Because of the *rest* system big holdings of landed property soon melted away. The third point is that the most important and overriding interest of the village community and the lineage was to achieve solidarity. He writes in this connection that "[t]hroughout history community solidarity and the *rest* system have been reinforcing and preserving each other. Individualism would have no place in the society."[40] The *rest* system also created conditions for excessive litigation and invariably acrimonious relationships among members of the descent groups.

For Merid *gult* was in all senses alien to the system of land holding. It was not a proprietary right in land. He boldly states that "[t]he Ethiopian ruling classes, having no real property that needed protection, did not have laws that set them clearly apart from their subjects."[41] The right of the *restäñña* over the land is not infringed upon because of *gult* since the state could not confer upon the elite any property title thereon. Instead, *gult* holders were merely being allowed to collect and use tribute or taxes for varying lengths of time. Taddesse also argues that the *bälägult* was not equivalent to a landlord since his right did not extend to the soil. The ownership of the land still remained firmly in the hands of the peasants. They were simply officials and administrators.[42]

The general descriptions of the principles of land tenure summarized above, though based on some undeniable facts, are subject to qualification. The application of the customary law of land was tempered by many local contingencies. The empirical evidence on the subject from the study area will suggest a view that contradicts some of the principles that are often stated as applying to all parts of historic Ethiopia.

At this point it will be apposite to mention the work of a scholar who represents a dissenting opinion on some of the issues from the established scholarship. Shiferaw Bekele, in a work that surveys the literature on land tenure, has convincingly showed the inadequacy of existing interpretations of the principle of land holding. In this illuminating and original piece, he calls for a questioning of the existing interpretations by the established scholarship of the institutions of *gult* and *rest* "in its entirety."⁴³ I concur with Shiferaw as regards the question of the nature of *rest* and *gult* right. For Shiferaw *gult* implies more than merely administrative control over land. He argues that scholars have all too often confused *gult* holders as simply administrators by claiming that *gult* entails a right over tribute. In actual fact, when it was granting *gult* the state was transferring land to the full ownership to the grantee. It thus involves a proprietary right in land. He points out that although there are differences in certain peculiar details from place to place, there was a large measure of commonality in the basic principles and concepts pertaining to land ownership in Ethiopia. This was so particularly from the Gondärine period through early twentieth century Ethiopia. Shiferaw concludes that "...in the Gonderine era, what was granted was the land rather than tributes only."⁴⁴ Unlike many scholars, he argues that the land so given by way of *gult* did not remain the property of the original cultivators or *restäñña*. There was no concurrent right of a miscellaneous character over land since it was individually or privately owned and the right of the *bälägult* and the *restäñña* were very clearly differentiated.

    I will describe shortly the essential principles of land holding in the region under study based on original sources. Before that, however, let me make some general comments about the system in this region. First and foremost, there existed an institution, called *zègenät* that was concurrent with *gult*. This institution is more mysterious because its emergence is extremely difficult to date or trace with confidence and precision. Yet, for the period and area covered by this study, the description of *gult* and *rest* and the rights they entailed would be incomplete without a discussion of this institution. This is a point I will come back to in later pages. Secondly, the material on the exercise of *rest* rights suggests some modifications to the description of the institution contained in the general studies I have referred to above. These modifications, I believe, are historically very significant. Unlike the assertions made by many scholars, the *restäñña's* right was not merely usufructuary. The *restäñña* that my documents portray could scarcely be distinguished from a freeholder *on his portion* of what can be referred to as the lineage land. That is, individual members of the same lineage group did not usually exercise concurrent rights over the specific piece of land and had clearly recognized rights with respect to land. Individuals, in other words, *did* exercise rights of ownership. In a number of cases total strangers (non-relatives) acquired land from people with whom they had no blood relationship at all. This happened through various mechanisms like debt, adoption-related inheritance, etc. *Rest* land was always attachable to debt. It could thus be mortgaged, including to outsiders. Aliens could, therefore, acquire interests and rights over land that they did not have at first. Access to land was not wholly governed by the traditional canon of descent. Although members of the descent group might put some limitations on the exercise of individual rights, *rest* owners nonetheless exercised rights of ownership that gave them considerable freedom to do pretty much what they liked with their portions. In Chapter 4 I will discuss the extent and limitations of individual rights over land in connection with the modes of acquiring or relinquishing property.[45]

The other area in which the material from my area of study suggests new perspectives is in the area of taxation and its relationship to agricultural production. A variety of conditions related to taxes and tribute, including unpaid labor, limited the freedom of peasants in agricultural production. Undoubtedly agricultural production was to a greater extent determined by local realities or the nature of the soil. However, evidence from charters in nineteenth century Eastern Gojjam indicate that peasants had to produce certain types of cereals or convert what they produced into products that were acceptable to the state or the *bälägult* as part of taxation.[46] Thus, the decision about what to plant was not only or always governed by the nature of the land itself but also to some extent by the needs and expectations of the ruling class.

There is also considerable evidence from local documents on unpaid and forced labor. The state and the *gult* holders for various activities and purposes employed the labor power of the rural farming population. Both the amount and the exact nature of the labor service are stipulated in very precise terms. The peasant not only paid tribute but also had to spend extra days working on the *hudad*, the field directly owned and managed by the lords, for the latter's personal benefit. As indicated in the land charters, peasants were required to cultivate, weed and harvest crops on the *hudad* lands of their lords.[47] All this will be made abundantly clear in chapter three. Peasant labor was also employed for the building and repairing of churches and the houses of lords.[48] The diversion of the labor power of the peasant almost certainly affected the process of production, since labor was among the key elements in the process of production.

Sources that I use in this study are chiefly land grant charters and land documents that have come down to us from the period under study. Land charters were commonly made out to corporate institutions and individuals in the Gondärine period and subsequently. We come across many pertinent examples of it in practically the whole of Eastern Gojjam in the eighteenth century and afterwards as will be seen in successive chapters.[49] Even prior to the Gondärine period; the drawing up of land charters was a common practice.

However, although big churches and monasteries were built prior to the 16th century, no land grant documents dating to those times have been found for the region under study in church institutions. This was mainly due to the destruction of documents, along with churches and monasteries, by the forces of Ahmed ibn Ibrahim in the 16th century. However, in terms of form and structure, these ancient land grant charters might have been similar to those of other areas in the country. Huntingford has published land grant documents for northern Ethiopia. He delineated some six clauses which the charters commonly contained. These are a) invocation b) the name of the grantor as well as the grantee c) the purpose for which the grant was made d) sanction against trespass of the grant e) list of officials at the time when the grant was made and f) immunity clause. *Gult* grant was made both for individuals as well as institutions mostly in perpetuity and as hereditary.[50]

The charters of the 18th and 19th centuries from the area under study share a number of common elements with those described by Huntingford. However, they also have some distinctive characteristics. Particularly notable is the detail to which they go with regard to the rights of the grantees, the obligations of the peasantry, the administrative and judicial rights of individual grantees holding land from the church, the obligation of the grantees towards the church, etc. Besides, as I have alluded to above, charters made in the 18th century and afterwards speak about a distinct class of landless people called *zèga* and a form of tenure called *rim*.

The earliest and the most important of the charters from Eastern Gojjam for the period under study is the land charter made out in 1767 for the church of Moṭa Giyorgis. It was made by Wälätä-Isra'el (daughter of Empress Mentewab, wife of Emperor Bäkkafa (r.1721-1730). The scope of the rights of the *bälägult* is defined in this document with unusual clarity. This land document is drawn very carefully and precisely in such a way that it does not create loopholes for differing interpretations and meanings regarding the rights of the lords with regard to land. For instance, the charters virtually exclude the peasants from interfering with the exercise of rights by the grantee on the portion of land that he/she had been given. We find the right of the grantees being the same as those of the *restäñña* over the *rim* land in respect of user and occupation and any disposal including alienation.[51]

As indicated above, one of the most important forms of tenure that we find in the land charters is *rim* land. The distinction between *rim* and *gult* is obscure. Sometimes, grantors drawing charters use both terms interchangeably. There seems to be a consensus among scholars that in the northern provinces, including the one under investigation, *rim* was basically a church tenure and the land was obtained by turning the *rest* holdings of peasants to those of social elites on behalf of the church. The peasants lost a considerable part of their land to churches by this form of tenure and some were made tenants on lands which had been their own originally.[52] *Rim* land given in perpetuity was free from many restrictions unlike a conventional *rest* land over which many concurrent miscellaneous rights could exist. The *rim* holder had the right to retain and transmit their holdings to their offspring and the only right that the Church had over such lands was reversion. It was not a right over the land of another. A *rim* holder could sell part or all of it; the only limitation imposed being to meet his obligation meticulously. Once land was granted to an individual or an institution (like the Church) the state did not interfere further. The only rights that remain are "reversionary rights", exercised when and if the grantee defaulted on his obligation.

The generic name for individuals associated with the church and holding land from it was *däbtära*. The category included ordinary people as well as prominent noblemen and women. When land charters were made out to institutions the division of the land between the *däbtära* and the *balärest* was carried out on two-third, one-third basis. Two-thirds of the land was transferred to the *däbtära* and the *balärest* retained the remainder of the land. It would be stipulated on the grant charter that the *däbtära* would have a right to possess and cultivate the two-thirds of the land formerly owned by the *balärest*. It was thus not just a right on the revenue from the land of the *balärest* that the *däbtära* were given; it was explicitly ownership of the land that was transferred to them. The *däbtära* could either cultivate his share of the land by himself/herself or settle his own people called *zèga* and collect rent.⁵³ The rights of the *däbtära* were not limited to a specific period of effective occupation; nor were they restricted in respect of succession and therefore transfer. The charter allowed full rights to the *däbtära* to dispose of their share, including alienation by sale. Subject to performing all their obligations they enjoyed definite security of tenure.⁵⁴

The *balärest*, besides surrendering two-thirds of their land to the *däbtära*, were still liable to provide labor services to the church. The charter further confirmed and reinforced the rights of ownership by laying down certain conditions concerning encroachments (through dispossession or other means). If the *däbtära* encroached on the *balärest* land he would be, like the *balärest*, liable to provide labor services to the church. On the *balärest* lands, appointments to the office of *çheqa-shum*, the lowest position in the administrative hierarchy, would be made from among the *balärest* peasantry. However, the *çheqa* was forbidden to collect taxes on the *däbtära* lands or even to enter the land of the latter in any official capacity.⁵⁵

I must point out here that treason, or failure to meet the tax demands of the state, were not the only grounds for expropriation of the peasantry. Rulers were in a strong position to take over or reallocate lands of the *restäñña* under all kinds of pretexts and there were probably many unjustifiable ejections of the *balärest*. The property rights of the *balärest* peasantry were thus very precarious and could be easily violated. Peasants could lose their *rest* rights in land in peaceful times, not necessarily in war. They could be made to surrender a good part of their lands to the lords even without having committed individual or collective crimes against the state. The establishment of big churches was generally accompanied with major land redistributions that led to near total expropriation of the peasantry in areas around the new churches.⁵⁶

The charter of Wälätä-Isra'el seems to have served as model for many similar charters and land grant documents to churches and monasteries. Virtually all of the pertinent of the 18th and 19th century land charters as well as those pertaining to churches of recent foundation imitated the land charter of Moṭa Giyorgis church.⁵⁷ Despite some differences, the principle of two-thirds for the *däbtära* and one-third for the *restäñña* prevailed. The structure of the Moṭa Giyorgis charter was copied in subsequent charters almost verbatim. Charters multiplied in the 19th century. The principle of division of the land of the *balärest* on the one-third and two-thirds basis was ostensibly taken as "normal" by the peasantry. Though we can not rule out the possibility that land grant documents and charters were open for contestation and disputation there is no record, oral or written, on the basis of which we can talk about resistance. Thus, it seems that the one-third/two-thirds principle was taken as normative practice both in the written documents and in the mentality of the public at large.

It would be helpful to cite a typical example of land grant charters that I will work with in this thesis in order to set the general framework in which the economic and social positions of lords and peasants evolved in Eastern Gojjam. This charter pertains to a grant of land to the church of Däbrä-Marqos by *Nigus* (King) Täklä-Häymanot of Gojjam (1881-1901). The pertinent sections that I quote below suggest the pattern established by Wälätä-Isra'el for the Moṭa Giyorgis church:[58]

> ...ለደብረ ማርቆስ በገባው በቅፈታ ደብተራውን ሲሰሩ ሁለት እጅ ለደብተራ ሲሶ መሬት ለባለርስት ይሁን ብለዋል።። በሁለት እጁም በቤታውም ያሰፈረውን ዜጋ ደብተራ ይዳኛ እንጅ አለቃ ሊቀጠበብት አይድረስበት ከደም ኡ ከይናፋአ ከሌባ ረዳኘትሪበቀር።። ይህንንም አፍርሶ ባለርስቱ ደብተራውን ቢቀማው ደብተራውም ባለርስቱን ቢቀማው ሹማምንቱም ደብተራውንም ባለርስቱንም ቢቀሙ ግይዱ በየራሱ »»ሳው ወቄት ይሁን።። በሲሶውም ከቤተክርስትያን ስራ አከአመት ባል መዋያ በቀርአከማህባር ቤት ስራ በቀር ሌላ እዳ ላይነቻው ነው።። ሊቀ ጠበቡትንም ከባል ዕሪም በቀር ሌላ ላይሸመው ነው።። ጮቅነቱንም ከዚያው ያጨስ ይሸም።።

...In the lands given for the support of Däbrä-Marqos when he (Täklä-Häymanaot) established the däbtära he said the däbtära shall have two-thirds and the balärest one-third of the land. The däbtära shall have authority over the zèga whom they settled both on their two-thirds [share of] land and on their residential sites. ... The aläqa or the liqäṭäbäbt [of the Church] shall not interfere [with his rights] except in cases involving homicide, adultery and theft. Any transgression of this on the part of the balärest, the

> *däbtära*, or the officials, and such transgression leading to the takeover of the properties of one party by the other, shall be punished by a fine of fifty ounces of gold. On the sisso [lands of the balärest] there shall be no obligations except work [in the erection or repairing] of the church [building]; payment of the holiday dues and work on Mahibär bèt. The position of liqäṭäbäbt shall be occupied by none other than persons who have rim. The çheqa shall be appointed from among the resident [balärest].

The following observation can be made from the quotation above. The *gult* that was granted was in the form of ownership right rather than a mere right over the tribute. It is explicit in the charter that the *däbtära* would not have any tributary relationship with the *balärest*. Both were awarded clearly recognized rights and obligations over separate pieces of land. Administrative powers were also clearly defined in ways that would not confuse the areas of competence of the *däbtära* and of the church officials. The *restäñña* retained one-third of his land and two-thirds of the land was surrendered to the *däbtära*. The *däbtära* were entitled not to the product of the soil but to the soil directly. The *balärest* were expressly forbidden to lay claim of *rest* on the land so alienated from them. The implication is that *däbtäras* could cultivate their lands, if they could do so, by themselves and those who needed additional labor could settle zèga of his or her own choice. This indicates that the rights of individual *däbtära* are not only specific but also exclusive. Though there might have been a disparity in prescribed documentary norms and reality the state had arrogated to the *däbtära rest* rights over two-thirds of the land formerly exercised by the *balärest* through direct expropriation. Whatever rights still remained of the latter's status as a descendant of the first occupant would now be limited to a third of the land.

What all of this indicates is that the *balärest* could easily be disinherited. Moreover the land granted to the *däbtära* was not granted on a temporary basis. It does connote permanent ownership rights since it allows the individual *däbtäras* to settle their own "subjects" over both their respective rural lands and homestead sites.[59]

The *däbtäras* established over the two-thirds of the land could discharge the responsibilities and obligations attached to their tenure by putting together money to pay for the clergy or to hire someone to provide the services to the Church on their behalf. Their tenure could not be disturbed unless they ceased to perform service to the church. Their property right over two-thirds of the land was apparently given in perpetuity and was transferable to heirs. Therefore the right of the *däbtära* over the land is in the nature of ownership though we could not say it was an absolute property. They (the *däbtäras*) were granted exclusive ownership of the land as a separate and individual title. They could also give or sell part of their land to others by means of a deed of conveyance in which they represented themselves as owners. It should be mentioned, incidentally, that the king had instituted an office for the sole purpose of recording land transactions involving the *däbtäras* and others.[60]

To sum up, the *däbtäras'* right is proprietary. Not only did they enjoy unrestricted rights of use but also full powers of disposal. There is a strong safeguard against dispossession in the charter since it provides for the punishment of other parties that might try a forceful expropriation of the *däbtära*. If any of the parties attempted to expropriate wrongfully (the land of the *däbtära* or the *balärest*) or committed any attempt of forceful ejection of one another's land, each was liable to a fine of 50 ounces of gold.

1.3. Delimiting and defining the meaning and the socio-economic scope of the term zéga or the institution of zégenät in Eastern Gojjam

The charters like the one quoted above did not usually limit themselves to recording the names and the obligations of the *däbtära* and the location and size of land allocated to the latter. They also defined the relations between the lord and his subjects, referred to as *zègas*. The document quoted above employed the category of *zèga* side by side with the *restäññas* and social elites referred to as *däbtäras*. The *zègas*, it appears, were very similar to serfs although not exactly serfs. The social distance between the *zèga* on the one hand and the *balärest* and the *däbtära* on the other appears to have been wide and significant. The fact that the *zègas* were left under the complete jurisdiction of the *däbtäras* and that they were settled from elsewhere over the two-thirds of the *däbtära* land and residential sites are indicative of the wide social distance separating the three (*zèga*, *däbtära* and *balärest*) and the big difference in the status of the three interacting groups. Thus the *zègas* constituted a single category of humble and near personal dependants who were bound to the lord in some measure and to his land in particular. The power of the lord over the *zèga* was pervasive and strong. Unlike the *balärest* (also called *baläsisso*) who were immune from interference on their *sisso* land and also enjoyed the right to be tried in the court of the *aläqa* and the *liqäṭäbäbt*, the *zègas*, however, were almost completely subject to the jurisdiction of their individual lords. The charter did not allow the *zègas* to have recourse to a third party in relation to the *däbtäras* in all civil cases. Only criminal cases involving the *zègas* were reserved for hearing by courts above those of the *däbtära*.[61]

What the *zègas* depended on for their sustenance is difficult to say with certainty. Obligations of social and economic nature that the *zèga* owed the lord were not defined in the charter. In the arrangement made by the *däbtäras* and the *zègas* custom may not have required any written agreement between them or it was left entirely to the discretion of the lord. Presumably, there were certain rules that customarily determined the limits of the obligation of the *zèga* to his lord. It is possible to conceive that the *zèga* was remunerated for his service in either of the following two ways. Either he would be given a plot of land that he would cultivate for himself or he would take a share of the harvest on the land of the *däbtära*. Whether or not the *zègas* settled on the *bota* (homestead site) of the lord appears to have made a difference. *Zègas* who lived on the *bota* of the lord in Däbrä-Marqos and cultivated small plots to sustain themselves were closer to a farmhand, particularly so if the lord lived on the farm.[62] *Zègas* who did not live on the *bota* of the lord or who made arrangements of crop sharing with the lord were closer to a tenant. Nonetheless there were additional obligations and conditions that do not allow us to reduce the definition of the *zègas* to either farm hands or tenants. For the purpose of appreciating the nature of the institution of *zègenät* we need to refer to other sources containing information about the *zègas*.

As I have alluded to above, charters made out in the 18th century and afterwards most often speak about a distinct class of landless people called *zègas*. In these land grant documents we find categories or groups specifically described as *zègas* side by side with the *balärest* and social elites most often referred to by either of the following two generic terms of *däbtära* or *mäkwanent*. Informants unanimously and widely acknowledge it as an important institution in the region.[63] The institution of *zègenät* was such an important and universal phenomenon in the region that princes and princesses granting charters found it necessary to devote space to it in the charters. Almost all of the 18th and 19th centuries land charters involve clauses that define the general context within which the *zègas* and the *däbtäras* might work out their relationships.[64] Many tantalizing additional details about this institution are also found in the manual or administrative handbook compiled for the great monastery of Däbrä-Wärq and other two churches as well as in the works of Täklè.[65] It is striking that these various facts and the information contained in these sources, most of them mutually independent and separated both by time and space, are in perfect accord with each other in characterizing the institution. These sources exhibit a telling consistency in defining and delimiting the meaning and the socio-economic scope of the term *zèga*.

But before going on to discuss the various sources that give us information about this institution as it existed in Eastern Gojjam it might be useful to distinguish it from social arrangements or social units in other regions to which the same term applied. As far as I am aware this institution does not appear in specialized studies except that of Tekalign's work on the district of Bächo in Shäwa. He also mentions it briefly and as a sideline story in his discussion of land measurement and distribution towards the close of the nineteenth century. The *zègas* here appear side by side with *gäbbars* in land measurement documents.[66] The Shäwan use of the term appears to conform to the same concept of dependence as used in Eastern Gojjam. However, before discussing the Shäwan use of the term a more convenient starting point or basis of analysis of the term *zèga* or *zègenät* is oral poetry and dictionary sources.

It is interesting to note from the beginning that oral poetry and dictionary sources as well as land charters and other sources used for this study are almost identical in defining and delimiting the socio-economic scope and the meaning of *zèga*. First let us start with the dictionary meaning of the term. In its current official use the English equivalent of the term *zèga* or its noun *zègenät* is citizen or citizenship.[67] However, its current meaning has *fundamentally departed* from the old usage of the term. It is important to note here the fact that the Amharic dictionary published in 1970 defined the term in its old usage, as will be stated a little later, thereby showing that the term was in everyday use by the public till recently in its former usage or meaning. The change of meaning most probably occurred following the 1974 change of government. However, the transition or the change in value of the term *zèga* or *zègenät* probably started prior to the 1974 revolution.

The direct dictionary meaning of the term *zèga* in the Amharic and Ge'ez dictionaries connotes or translates to mean a subject and highly impoverished person. The definition could also translate to mean a subordinate person under the overlordship or socio-economic domination of someone. Moreover, both the Ge'ez and Amharic dictionaries and oral poetry pin down the term *zèga* in exactly the same way. For example the direct dictionary meaning of the term *zèga* in the Ge'ez dictionary of Kidanä-Wäld Kiflè is that of a subject people. Both Kidanä-Wäld and Dästa Täklä-Wäld (the author of the 1970 Amharic dictionary) defines becoming a *zèga* or "መዜገን ሮቂ ናመገዛት አ መዋረድን -which translates to mean- being humbled or lowered and subjected." [68] To elucidate the meaning of the term *zèga* Dästa cites a saying which runs that "እግር ዜጋ ነው- which literally means [One's] leg is *zèga*." This shows the harshness of the daily toil to which the *zègas* were subjected. It does also connote subjugation or subordination for the group it denotes. The term *zègenät* is also defined as "ተገዥነት-which literally means subjugation." According to informants the term *zèga* was used to refer to a highly impoverished person with the lowest level of social status. The humble position of the *zèga* is testified by two important sayings. The first one runs as follows, "ወድቆ ይነሲል በእጅኦ ዜግቶ ይከብራል በልጅ" - which literally means "one who falls down rises with the help of one's hands, one who becomes *zèga* (lit. poor) can become wealthy [only] with the help of ones children." The second interesting saying runs as "ንጉሥ በዘውዱ ዜጋ ባመዱ እንዲታወቅ- which literally means A king is recognized by his crown where as a *zèga* is known by his poverty."[69] Moreover, in Gurage language the term *zèga* which is still in everyday use, is applied to denote a person who has nothing he could call his own. In the different dialects of the Gurage language including Siltè the terms "???Ò" and "ዜግነት" are defined as *"poor person"* and *"poverty"*, respectively. The Tigriñña dictionary of Yohännes Gäbrä-Egziabhèr published in 1956/57 defined the term *zèga* as "ተገዥ"which means "subject" thereby conforming to the same concept of dependence as in the Amharic and Gurage languages.[70] The linguist Leslau has showed the striking similarity of concept and meaning of the term *zèga* in both the Amharic and Gurage languages. He took the term *zèga* to mean *serf* in the Amharic language. Moreover, the semantic analysis of the term *zèga* by Tekalign in the modern Amharic dictionary connotes or translates to mean a "subject people" or "colonized people."[71]

In explaining the Christological debate within the Ethiopian church Alämayähu Mogäs states the position of the followers of the *Qebat* sect on the nature of Jesus Christ as "በተዋህዶ ዜገአ ደክየ ከስጋ ሲዋሕድ የባሪ ክብሩን አጣ ኦ ለቀቀ ሲቀባ ግን ወደጥንት ክብሩ ተመለሰቷ" which literally means: "At the moment of incarnation (union of the human and divine nature) the Word become *zèga, poor and He, therefore, is disgraced and lowered Himself. He lost His divine nature because of the Union. However, because of the Unction He was restored to His eternal glory*" (emphasis added).[72] In other words he defined the process of the union of the human and divine natures as a process of becoming *zèga* which involved a conspicuous demotion in the status and glory of divinity. Further evidence to the humble status of *zèga* comes from an article which calls for the administrative independence of the Ethiopian Orthodox church from the Coptic church of Egypt. This article is printed in a periodical called *Berhänena Sälam*, an Amharic weekly news-paper published in the early decades of the 20th century. The author of this particular article wrote of the need to liberate the Ethiopian church from the administrative control of the Egyptian church in a somewhat aggrieved tone as follows: "የግብፅን ሰው ብትሾሙ የኢትዮጵያ ቤተክርስትያን ለግብጽ ቤተክርስትያን ዜጋ ተወራጅ ሁና ስዘላለም ትኖራለች፡፡ የኢትዮጵያ ሰው ግን ሊቀጳጳስነት ብትሾሙ በነጻ መንግሥቴው ላይ የኢትዮጵያ ቤተክርስትያን ነጻ ሁና ትኖራለች፡፡ግን የኢትዮጵያ የጀግኖች ድምጽ እንደዚሕ የሚል አንድ ነው ነጻዋ ኢትዮጵያ ከጸዋ ቤተክርስትያን ጋር ብቻዋን."[73] This can be translated as -if you continue appointing an Egyptian bishop the Ethiopian church would remain a subordinate and *zèga* of the Egyptian church forever. However, if you appoint an Ethiopian for the position of patriarch, the independent Ethiopian state will have a free church. The interest of valiant Ethiopians is a free Ethiopia with a free church." The author characterized the relationship of the two churches as essentially a colonial one. This is very close to the meaning given in the Ge'ez and Amharic dictionaries. It is also exactly in the above sense that texts used for this study generally characterize the *zèga*. Both in socio-economic and political as well as class terms *zèga,* therefore, referred to an extremely poor and subordinate person with the lowest level of material condition and social status. *Zèga* thus carried with it some degree of lack of *social* rights and privileges for the group that it denotes.

Tekalign found out that despite the difference in nomenclature there was uniformity in essentials of the rights and obligations of the *zègas* and the *gäbbars* in the period and the region he studied. But what is important from the point of view of this study is that Tekalign argues that despite the similarity in the obligations between *zègas* and *gäbbars* the former carries a certain difference of social status and distinction from the latter. This arose from the application of the term to a specific group of people despite, that is, the similarity of the group with the *gäbbars* in terms of their obligations as landowners. In the various numerous layers in which the scribe classifies tenure during land measurement and allocation the two terms *zèga* and *gäbbar* are used in completely different contexts though the nature of his sources has not enabled Tekalign to be very explicit in identifying the conditions leading to the distinction between tenure in *zègenät* and *gäbbar*. Tekalign has clearly identified one important circumstance leading to the use of the term *zèga* in the land documents he analyzed. He writes that the term *zèga* was used to refer to the native population whose occupation of the land predated the arrival of the Shäwan overlords in the Bächo area in Shäwa but lost their land subsequent to the imposition of Shäwan rule. However, there are reasons to believe that the distinction between *zèga* and *gäbbar* is neither cultural nor legal. *Zèga* was applied to describe the tenure conditions of those individuals (analogous to subjects) who were brought under the control of the Shäwan state and forced to enter into new terms of socio-economic relationship of dependency with the state or new lords. Moreover, the term *zèga* was not only applied to the indigenous people but also to non-natives to Bächo, that is, to individuals who settled in the Bächo area from elsewhere and entered into the same form of socio-economic relationships like the former (people of Bächo) with the lord. This means that in terms of ethnic origin the *zèga* might have come from Amhara, Gurage and the Oromo who were the dominant inhabitants of the land around Bächo. This is a further confirmation to the fact that the distinction between *zèga* and *gäbbar* was not a legal and cultural one. With the virtual expropriation of their land the status of the indigenous people was transformed and they became *zèga*. The state sold land (which had once been their own) to them, in disregard of their right of former occupancy which they might otherwise have possessed in virtue of their being native, on terms of payment of rent or tribute by the latter to their new overlords.[74]

The term *zèga* was, therefore, applied to describe both the indigenous people whose status had been transformed and strangers who had become *zèga* of a lord following the imposition of Shäwan rule to distinguish the terms of their socio-economic relationship with the lord from other forms of tenure. Many of the people around Bächo who were indigenous to the area became subjects on lands which were once their own. Tekalign's study also shows that the term *zèga* was used in another more diffuse sense to refer to people, including strangers, who had come under the lordship of a certain person. The lord, referred to as *mälkäñña* (lord), might have lured the *zèga* to their lordships by selling to them parcels of land for the continuous tenure of which the latter might be required to pay rent or tribute, as the case might be. On the occasion of land redistribution the *mälkäñña* served as a trustee on behalf of the *zèga* in determining the amount of land to be reserved for the *zèga*, both stranger or native.[75]

Though tenure in *zègenät* in Shäwa presents a very feeble echo in certain respects (to be discussed below) to that of Eastern Gojjam there are some common denominators of this institution in both regions. From Tekalign's study, it can be concluded that though there are peculiarities of details there are some similarities of concept in the tenure of *zègenät* in both Shäwa and Eastern Gojjam. The principles, in other words, are basically similar in both regions. First both in Shäwa and Eastern Gojjam the *zègas* seem to have been constituted at times of chaos or shortly afterwards. Thus the explanation for the emergence of the institution of *zègenät* has to be sought in chaos and virtual or near virtual expropriation of the natives. However, in both Shäwa and Eastern Gojjam the right of the previous occupiers of the land was recognized in some measure. In the case of Shäwa they were allowed to resume their occupation through sale by the state of a portion of their former land, in the case of Eastern Gojjam the tenure conditions of the *zègas* varied from time to time. The *zègas* in the 17th century were allowed to retain one-third of their former holdings[76] while those in the 18th and 19th centuries are depicted as completely landless. Broadly speaking the other element of similarity between Shäwa and the study area (probably more so in the latter) is that the *zègas* might have lived under the lord of the area to almost full exclusion of state interference in the relationship between the two.[77]

However, despite a certain degree of similarity there are many important differences in the essentials of the institution of *zègenät* in Shäwa and Eastern Gojjam. First, as it will be made abundantly clear in subsequent chapters, the term *zègas* in Eastern Gojjam, unlike in Shäwa, refers to a distinct class of people under the complete subjugation of their lord and very close to serfs particularly in late eighteenth and nineteenth centuries. However, in dealing with this point for Shäwa Tekalign says that "...despite its apparent connotations of a socially subordinate group, no direct inference can be made from the term itself to argue that *zèga* denoted a particular community of people..."[78] Secondly, in Eastern Gojjam, unlike in Shäwa, the *zèga* class had no legal personality. They did not have full rights even over their dwelling places and valuable moveable property. Unlike in Shäwa the *zègas* in Eastern Gojjam could not hold land in their own right, although that right, as pointed out above, was recognized prior to the eighteenth century.[79] They could have parcels of land for their private cultivation and sustenance only if the lord was willing to give them. Moreover the tenure in *zègenät* seems to have had longer duration in the study area than in Shäwa. There are many other important differences between the tenure in the *zègenät* in the two regions. However, space would not suffice to discuss all of them here. It is apparent, however, that the peculiar features of the institution of *zègenät* in Eastern Gojjam justify investigating it as a fundamental element in local social structure. The failure of this institution to appear in the literature of other regions is either because of its marginal incidence or to lack of research and attention to it by scholars. There is no doubt, however, that further research is necessary before *zègenät* is stated as a pan-Ethiopian institution with local variations or an institution significant only in Eastern Gojjam and some parts of Shäwa.

For Eastern Gojjam, the institution of *zègenät* sheds great light on the nature of social classes and the agrarian and property relationships between lords and farmers. When we scrutinize the sources on the institution of *zègenät* a few dominant features stand out from the various descriptions and references. It was a form of near servility which kept the individuals to which the term *zèga* was applied immobilized even though it is not very clear whether they were tied to the lord or to the soil.[80] That he might have been tied both to the lord and to the land should not be ruled out, even though this might not enable us to make a direct comparison between the *zèga* and the European serf.

In some cases land charters converted many villages into lordships, with the peasantry on the land converted to *zèga*. When this happened the peasantry on the land was sometimes given the option of either continuing to live on the land as *zègas* or of leaving. In other words, if the old inhabitants refused to be treated as *zègas* the land charters empowered the landlords to evict the old peasants and settle new ones.[81] With the granting of the charter to the lord, the opportunity also arises for the lord to define the obligation of the *zègas* to himself. This means that the *zègas* could be subjected to more or less onerous terms pertaining to the disposal of labor and their produce. The *zègas* would therefore be deprived of some of the rights that come with a full and absolute control over the means of production. Like the terms of engagement as *zègas*, the terms of separation could also be more or less onerous. The latter could include loss of control over his dwelling or important movable property. The lord could take everything from a departing *zèga*, including items like his bed, his stone mill (grindstone), his pestle and mortar and *gan* (very large jar). In fact, these household objects seem to have constituted a standard list of items that would be forfeited by the *zèga* when and if separation was permitted. It is from these varying terms of "separation" or "severance" that one infers the degree of immobilization of the *zègas*, not from a legal stipulation that they were immobilized. Such a legal stipulation did not, in fact, exist. While we can say that the *zègas* theoretically enjoyed freedom of mobility, this theoretical right would be as good as non-existent if mobility involved loss of virtually everything, land or other property.[82]

In many specific cases that I have studied, the *zègas* were subjected to very onerous terms. In fact, one can say that they were no better than serfs. The lord employed the labor power of the *zègas* on land that had become his. Thus the dependence of the *zègas* on the lord was structured in the production process. In the manual for the officials of the three monasteries of Däbrä-Wärq, Gethsemane and Mäqdäsa-Maryam (the location of the last mentioned is unknown to me), the *zègas* are listed lower down in the social scale along with people whose livelihoods derived from doing menial jobs. The rule required masters and lords residing in the town and monastery of Däbrä-Wärq or absentees who owned land in the town to register and notify the church officials of the number and names of their children, servants and *zègas*.[83] This is indicative of the humble status of the *zègas*.

Because of its importance for understanding the patterns of production and in order to better locate the position of a class in the overall system of production it would be necessary to show the development of the institution of *zègenät* in the specific context of lands or areas covered in my sources. Clearly this institution has gone through various stages of evolution and the later practice crystallized out of the early precedents in the 17th century. In other words princes and princesses granting land in the 18th and 19th centuries employed the category of *zèga* because a foundation had been laid for it earlier although sources prior to the second half of the eighteenth century are on the whole unclear or silent on the subject. However, pedantic presentation of the pre-eighteenth century antecedents of this institution is out of the scope of this study and consciously deferred by the researcher for another time for the extremely fragmentary nature of the sources could not cohere together or refused to allow a rich texture of historical detail when pieced together. Precise delineation of the characteristics of this institution could be made only from the study of 18th and 19th century documents. However, this does not mean that methodologically this study is not a diachronic analysis. The purpose of this section of my study is limited to introducing this institution and to figuring out its general characteristics from the available evidence. Moreover establishing its roots firmly needs further research. I would also like to emphasize that this institution and the sources are not synchronic since its development over a space of a hundred and fifty years could be treated based on primary sources. Thus the movements leading to the emergence of this institution would be attempted in brief from the limited sources we have. Let us begin with a very general outline of its features and early precedents out of which the later practice developed.

The first explicit mention of the term *zèga* is to be found in documents dealing with the rebellion of the senior military regiments called *Querban* and *Mizan* against Emperor Zä-Dengel in the early 17th century. The condition that led to the revolt was the famous decree of *"meder gäbbar wäsäbe härä"* which Crummey has translated as "Man is Free and Land is Tributary." This situation is expressed by contemporary document recording the events as follows "ወበውእቱ 1ዓመት ተጸብዖም ሐራሁ ስሐጼ ዘድንግል እለ ይብልዎሙ ቁርባን ወሚዛን ወእራስ ዘሥላሴ በምክንያት አዋጅ ዘአንገረ ውእቱ እንዝ ይብል ሰብእ ሐራ ወገባር ምድር ፡ እስመ አመጸ ኩሉ ዜጋሆሙ ወቀተልዎ በኩናት በማእከለ ደምብያ ዘውእቱ ባርጫ-which means [t]he soldiers called *Querban* and *Mizan* and Ras Zä-Sellasè revolted against Emperor Zä-Dengel because of the decree he issued that says "Man is free and land is tributary." Their (the soldiers') *zègas* [had] rebelled [in consequence]. [Therefore] they killed him [the king] with a sword at Barçha, in the middle of Dämbya."[84]

Here the term *zègas* is undoubtedly a reference to peasants cultivating the lands that the soldiers believed to be theirs. For the peasantry the decree freed them from obligations to the soldiery and they rose in support of it. For the soldiery it threatened to take away their social and material privileges and they drove them to a rebellion that led to the killing of the king. With the killing of the king the decree was prevented from implementation. Crummey has explained these events in terms of class struggle. He has provided an excellent analysis of the events surrounding the decree. Though he is unaware of the existence of the institution of *zègenät* or the importance of the term *zèga* and its far-reaching implication, Crummey considers those peasants who stood against soldiers as serfs. He writes that the decree sought to abolish serfdom.[85] Be that as it may; the mention of the term *zèga* in the 17th century testifies that the institution already existed prior to the 18th century.

Täklè also employed the category of *zèga* in recording sixteenth, more frequently seventeenth century events. In short he traces the origins of the institution of *zègenät* to the 17th century.[86] This dating accords with the time during which the royal court and its entourage had a temporary presence in the area of present-day Eastern Gojjam and the Lake Ṭana region. It is this royal presence that seems to have created the situations that led to the emergence of *zègenät*. The monarchy had a number of political and social problems to attend to and correct in the region. Some of these problems dated from the sixteenth century and the early decades of the seventeenth century. Beginning from these early times, Eastern Gojjam had become to all intents and purposes a refuge for a variety of people fleeing the Oromo, who had moved into many parts of what is today southern and central Ethiopia. One of the most important movements of population into Eastern Gojjam induced by the expansion of the Oromo was that of the Gafat.[87]

There were already significant communities of Gafat in the region whose background and conditions of settlement in the region is not very clear. It is not also clear what specific readjustments had to be made to accommodate this new wave of Gafat who fled their homelands under the pressure of the Oromo. It is not clear if the Gafat moved into the region as conquerors or as refugees seeking shelter. Their impact on the distribution of land as conquerors would obviously have been different from their impact as disorganized refugees. But the Gafat were not the only group whose increasing presence in the region was complicating the ethnic, social and economic picture in the region.

The Oromo also pushed into the region on the heels of the Gafat. Although the coming of the Oromo might have had military dimensions, it is also possible also that significant numbers were settled in the region as followers and supporters of Christian princes like Susenyos who had had extended periods of adventure among the Oromo.[88] It is important to keep in mind, however, that as this ethnic and social picture was getting complicated through migratory waves that brought the Gafat and the Oromo into the region, there were pre-existing communities that were struggling to maintain control over resources and as far as possible to regain control from these later-coming groups. Equally significantly, there were military elements (collectively referred to as *çhäwa*) whose presence in the region is related to the attempts by the monarchy to re-establish control or limit further incursions by the Oromo. Some of these *çhäwa* might have been recruited from local populations but many must have been brought in from other Christian territories.

It is also important to keep in mind that these waves of migration and subsequent struggles over land were taking place within a relatively short period of time, so that one can refer to the decades between the late 16th and mid 17th centuries as a half-century of chaos and disturbance. Some of our documents give brief but significant indications of how land had become dear and expensive during this period. For instance, a general of Emperor Fasilädäs by the name of Asgader (whom we will meet later in relation to his role in the reworking of the tenure system) is said to have built a church at Zewa, around the upper course of the river Muga, and endowed it with land that he purchased for fifty ounces of gold. This is a fine testament to the fact that land was becoming a commodity and more scarce than ever before. Incidentally, the church was burned down and remained in ruins till the early eighteenth century when a certain *Däjjazmach* Amonyos rebuilt it.[89] It is also interesting that, as further indication of the scarcity of land in the region, the land that was formerly the endowment of this Church was later distributed among seven notables, referred to in our sources as *"mäsafen[ts]"*(noblemen and princes).[90] It was thus not only individuals but also churches, not only the Gafat and the Oromo but also the *çhäwa*, not only ordinary people but also members of the elite who lost and gained lands during these unsettled times. It was thus to bring order to the complications brought about by these chaotic conditions that the arrangements of the mid-17th were undertaken.

Täklè credits *Ras* Asgader, the governor of Eastern Gojjam under Fasilädäs, for the settlement of the confusion through a new redistribution of land. Asgader apparently had a personal stake in the reorganization, for he also settled his own followers, one thousand strong cavalry and another one thousand strong infantry.[91] The *Ras* established many local ties by creating *gult* lands for himself throughout the region.[92] It is difficult to work out the principles that governed this redistribution of land. We know that in some places, as in the districts of Ennäbsè and Ennäsè, previous or "ancient" owners of the land were recognized as *arogè täsäri*, (former grantees) and allowed to retain control over all or part of their holdings. Though the scarcity of the sources inhibits us from making categorical statement it is very likely that the *arogè täsäri* might have been on the land from before the sixteenth century.[93] However, a recognition of their tenure rights did not mean that they were totally untouched in this reorganization of tenure under Asgader. They might have been removed from certain pieces of land to be resettled on some others.

The most significant development in this reorganization of tenure, however, was the reduction of a considerable number of the peasantry to the status of *zègas*, associated with the loss of rights of ownership on land. The one common denominator of all *zègas* was that they were not recognized as full owners of land. In terms of social origin, they could have come from any of the communities that inhabited the region at the time, Gafat, Oromo or Amhara. There were places in the region in which even the pre-sixteenth century owners lost control over land. Täklè notes, for instance, that some 367 people of Gafat origin in Bibuññ, located to the southwest of the town of Moṭa, were expropriated and made "*gäbbars*" and their descendants remained in that status right down to the nineteenth century. His information suggests that the lands were actually transferred to the crown, from which it was subsequently passed to "the eight royalty" (*simintu zufan*).[94] This eight royalty, according to tradition, referred to the eight children of *Ras* Be'elä-Christos who was a cousin of Susenyos and an important official of his court.[95] "*Y äzufan-agär*" consisting of lands of this kind, as well as "*Yäwäyezäro-agär*" (referring to lands passed on to female members of royalty) were found in many parts of Eastern Gojjam and Damot.[96] The grant involved the right of use and it was heritable. Almost all of them apparently date from this redistribution of tenure in the second half of the seventeenth century and some of them date from early times. The female descendants of medieval emperors (like Lebnä-Dengel) owned these lands and their descendants retained it till the nineteenth century.

Thus the central element in the redistribution of land under Asgader was that many of the former peasants, indigenous to the area, become subjects on lands which were once their own. Not all of the peasantry was completely dispossessed however. Some, according to Täklè, were allowed to retain a third of their former land and live under the jurisdiction of their lords. Täklè notes that the amount of land dispossessed from the local population was two-thirds of the land and they were allowed to retain only one-third of their former land. This shows that the principle of land division between the *däbtära* and the peasantry carried out on the basis of two-thirds for the former and one-third for the latter which is frequently attested in the 18th and 19th centuries land charters might have also evolved in the 17th century. It is also indicative of how this principle of land division was a deeply embedded in the local tradition among the people of the area of study. The *zègas* who were completely dispossessed might have been descendants of the relatively recent settlers in the region, particularly descendants of the Gafat. Thus a hereditary taint was attached to the *zèga* class. This, at least, is what we can tentatively gather from Täklè's account.

As I have pointed out above, the status of *zèga* involved not only losing land or retaining only a portion of it, but also accepting the new terms of a relationship with the new lord. Even *zègas* who retained a third of their former holdings were subject to new terms of relationship with the lord, and their tenure was made conditional. It appears that a large number of the Gafat who refused to continue to live in the region as *zègas* left the area and moved into the neighboring regions like Gondär and Wällo.[97]

From the foregoing it is apparent that the creation of the new institution of *zègenät* owed itself to two concomitant phenomena. One was the scarcity of land, creating pressure on particular plots of the available land and making eviction necessary to create room for new settlers. The other was the fluidity of local conditions as a result of the unsettled conditions since the sixteenth century. This later phenomenon created the overall conditions under which the reorganizations and the evictions were justified. Our sources suggest that land tenure in Eastern Gojjam attained a greater degree of stability after the reorganizations under Asgader. Whatever readjustments were made afterwards were minor and insignificant. That is why a detailed study of this major reorganization is necessary. In the following chapters I attempt to do this and to delineate the social contours that the resultant tenure system created.

NOTES

[1] Merid WoldeAregay,"Political Geography of Ethiopia at the Beginning of the Sixteenth Century" in *Accadamia Nazionale Dei Lincei IV Congresso Internazionale Di studi Etiopici,* vol.1 (Rome, 1974), p.621.

[2] An excellent and extensive description of the geography of Eastern Gojjam in its state in the nineteenth century including its boundaries is provided by Charles Beke, "Abyssinia-Being a Continuation of Routes in that Country" in *Royal Geographical Society* ,vol.14 (London, 1844), Pp.1-46.

[3] James Bruce, *Travels to Discover the Source of the Nile* vol. III (Edinburgh: Edinburgh University Press, 1964), Pp.256-258, 591-653.

[4] Ibid, The Ethiopian Mapping Agency, *National Atlas of Ethiopia,* 1981,the scale of the map is 1:4,000,000,p.11, Paolo Marcaccini, "Osservazioni Aerophotographiche sul Paessaggio Agrario nella Regione del Ciocche(Goggiam,Etiopia)" in *Rivista Geographica Italiana* vol.xxxv (Firenze:LaNuova Italia,1978),p.239.

[5] Bruce, *Travels*, vol. III.Pp.633-653.

[6] Beke, "Abyssinia-Being a Continuation of Routes", pp.3 and 46.

[7] Marcaccini, "Osservazioni Aerophotographiche sul Paessaggio Agrario", p.261.

[8] Ibid, p.242.

[9] See notes 19, 24-36 below.

[10] Marcaccini, "Osservazioni Aerophotographiche sul Paessaggio Agrario", pp.238-261.

[11] Ibid, pp.240-251.

[12] Ibid, p.261.

[13] Ibid.

[14] Ibid, pp.241-251.

[15] W.C.Plowden, *Travels in Abyssinia and the Galla Country* (London: Longmans, Green, and Co., 1868), p.28.

[16] Marcaccini, "Osservazioni Aerophotographiche sul Paessaggio Agrario", pp.251 and 254, According to the classification of the Ethiopian Mapping Agency the highlands with the elevation range of 2300 up to 3300m have *dägga* type of climate. But according to Marcaccini's study, in Eastern Gojjam the *dägga* agrarian region is far extended ranging between 2700to 3500m.

¹⁷ Täklä-Iyäsus, "The Genealogy of the People of Gojjam", MS. folio one recto. The final unpublished version of this MS. can be found in the National Library, registered there as MS.527.Unlike the draft copy the final version has not much geographical notes. The draft copy was discovered last year in private hands at the town of Däbrä-Marqos. I have a draft copy of the genealogy and discussion referring to Täklä-Iyäsus's work is based on this copy unless and otherwise stated. Hereafter the draft copy with me would be referred simply as Täklä-Iyäsus followed by folio number.

¹⁸ Marcaccini, "Osservazioni Aerophotographiche sul Paessaggio Agrario", p.251.

¹⁹ Beke, "Abyssinia-Being a Continuation of Routes", p.29.

²⁰ Marcaccini, "Osservazioni Aerophotographiche sul Paessaggio Agrario", pp.256-258 and 261.

²¹ D. Crummey, *Land and Society in the Christian Kingdom of Ethiopia: From the Thirteenth to the Twentieth Century* (Urbana and Chicago: University of Illinois Press, 2000), pp.8-12, Tekalign Wolde-Mariam, "A City and its Hinterlands: The Political Economy of Land Tenure, Agriculture and Food Supply for Addis Ababa, Ethiopia, 1887-1974"(PH.D.Dissertation, Boston University, 1995), pp.51-62.

²² J.M.Cohen, "Ethiopia a Survey on the Existence of a Feudal Peasantry" in *Journal of Modern African Studies, 12*(1974), pp.665-72, D. Crummey, "Abyssinian Feudalism", in *Past and Present,* 89 (1980), pp.115-38, Ege, S. *Class, State, and Power in Africa. A Case Study of the Kingdom of Shawa (Ethiopia) about 1840 (*Wiesbaden: Harrassowitz, Verlag,1996), pp. 6-8, F. Gamst, "Peasantries and Elites without Urbanism," in *Comparative Studies in Society and History,12*(1970),pp.372-92,A.Hoben,*Land Tenure Among the Amhara of Ethiopia: The Dynamics of Cognatic Descent*(Chicago/London:1973),p.1 note no.1.

²³ Donham, D., " Old Abyssinia and the New Ethiopian Empire: Themes in Social History" in D.Donham, and Wendy James(eds.),*The Southern Marches of Imperial Ethiopia: Essays in History and Social Anthropology*(Cambridge: Cambridge University Press,1986),pp.3-48.The most important work on the nature of class, and class relation in Amhara society belongs the sociological book of D.Levine,*Wax and Gold: Tradition and Innovation in Ethiopian Culture*(London/Chicago: University of Chicago,1965).

²⁴ Täklä-Iyäsus, "The Genealogy of the People of Gojjam", folio8v-9r, Mäzgäb, MS. Däbrä-Marqos. I am singularly successful to have reproduced this manuscript which is a *gult* registry found in the town of Däbrä-Marqos. It contains many land charters which King Täklä-Häymanot (r.1881-1901) of Gojjam gave to many churches. Copy of this manuscript is also microfilmed by the UNESCO and deposited in the IES and registered as IES,MS.No.1397/98.Folios5r through to folio 62r of the MS. is almost entirely devoted for recording *gult* grants of many churches including the abbreviated *gult* grant of Wälätä-Isra'el to Moṭa Giyorgis. Other land charters dating from the eighteenth century included Mäzgäb, MS. Moṭa Giyorgis. This contains, the longest list of *gult* land register, hosts of small and big grants to individuals and institutions and land transactions since the second half of the eighteenth century down to the twentieth century. The researcher has copied considerable part of it. The charter of Wälätä-Isra'el which served as a model is copied and deposited in many places. The document is found and catalogued in Daniel Ayana," A catalogue of land tenure related micro film from Gojjam churches and monasteries," Gebrä-Häwaryat, MS. Yägwära Qwesqwam, Catalogued as 89,XVI.23-25.This document is also incorporated in Wäna-Mäzgäb, MS. Däbrä-Eliyas, cataloged by Daniel as 89,XVIII.9-31.

²⁵ Crummey, *Land and Society*, pp.8-12, Hoben, *Land Tenure Among the Amhara of Ethiopia*, pp.1-15, Tekalign, "A City and its Hinterlands", pp.50-61,see also Merid Wolde-Aregay, "Land tenure and agricultural productivity, 1500-1850" in *Proceedings of the third Annual Seminar of the Department of History* (Addis Ababa, 1986),Shiferaw Bekele, "The Evolution of Land Tenure in the Imperial Era" in Shiferaw Bekele(ed.), An Economic History of Modern Ethiopia 1941-74(Dakar :Codesria,1995).For the best discussion on the semantic analysis of the terminologies related to land titles, taxation, names of lands, functions etc. in the recent period see J. Mantel-Niecko, *The Role of Land Tenure in the System of Ethiopian Imperial Government in Modern Times*(Warsaw:1980).Richard Pankhurst has also a monograph for the earlier period, *State and Land in Ethiopian History Monographs in Land Tenure*,vol.3(Addis Ababa: Addis Ababa University Press,1966).

²⁶ Hoben, *Land Tenure among the Amhara of Ethiopia*, p.13.

²⁷ Ibid, pp.12-15.

²⁸ Ibid, p.5.

[29] Crummey, *Land and Society*, p.2, Hoben, *Land Tenure Among the Amhara of Ethiopia*
[30] Tekalign, "A City and its Hinterlands", p.50.
[31] Crummey, *Land and Society*, p.9.
[32] Ibid, p.12, Tekalign, "A City and its Hinterlands", p.50.
[33] Crummey, *Land and Society*, p.11.
[34] Ibid, p.9.
[35] Ibid, p.12.
[36] Tekalign, "A City and its Hinterlands", p.51-55, Crummey, *Land and Society*, p.11.
[37] Merid, "Land Tenure and Agricultural Productivity", p.118.
[38] Ibid, p.119.
[39] Ibid.
[40] Ibid.
[41] Ibid, p.122.
[42] Taddesse Tamrat, *Church and State in Ethiopia,1270-1527*(Oxford:Clarendon Press,1972). p.101.
[43] Shiferaw, "The Evolution of Land Tenure in the Imperial Era," p.99.
[44] Ibid, p.96.
[45] See chapter four. Evidence shows that *rest* land could be sold to non-relatives and birth was not the only means of acquiring or establishing right to *rest* land. Individuals were able to exercise acts of ownership over their rest land. This is made abundantly clear in the discussion on property and modes of property transfer and the commercialization of land at some length in chapter four.
[46] Mäzgäb, MS., Däbrä-Marqos, folio 8v, folio 10v etc.
[47] Ibid.
[48] Ibid, folio 10v.
[49] See note no.24 above.
[50] G.W.B.Huntingford,*The Land Charters of Northern Ethiopia: Studies in Ethiopian Land Tenure*,vol.1(Addis Ababa: Institute of Ethiopian Studies and Faculty of Law,1965),pp.4-8.
[51] See notes no.56 and 60 below and note number 23 above.
[52] D.Crummey, "The Term *rim* in Ethiopian Land Documents of the 18th and 19th Centuries" in Alessandro Bausi, Gianni Dore and Irma Taddia(eds), *Anthropological and Historical Documents on "rim" in Ethiopia and Eritrea* (Torino:2001),pp.65-81,see also in this same volume

Joseph Tubiana, "The Nature and Function of the Ethiopian *rim:* a Short Note",pp.59-63.

⁵³ Daniel Ayana, "A Catalogue of Land Tenure Related Microfilm from Gojjam Churches and Monasteries," Gebrä-Häwaryat, MS. Yägwara Qwesqwam, Catalogued as 89,XVI.23-25.This document is also incorporated in Wäna-Mäzgäb, MS. Däbrä-Eliyas, cataloged by Daniel as 89,XVIII.9-31.

⁵⁴ Ibid.
⁵⁵ Ibid.
⁵⁶ Ibid.
⁵⁷ Mäzgäb, MS.Däbrä-Marqos, folio10r and folio39r, Donald Crummey, Daniel Ayana and Shumet Sishagne, "A Gonderine Land Grant in Gojjam: The Case of Qaranyo MadhaneAlam" in Bahru Zewde, R.Pankhurst and Taddese Beyene (eds.),*Proceedings of the Eleventh International Conference of the Ethiopian Studies* ,vol.1(Addis Ababa,1994),pp.103-16.

⁵⁸ Mäzgäb, MS.Däbrä-Marqos, folio 10r.
⁵⁹ Ibid.
⁶⁰ Ibid, folio 15r
⁶¹ Ibid, folio10r
⁶² Ibid.
⁶³Informants, *Märigèta* Libanos, *Mägabi* Ayähu Estäzya interviewed (at Martula-Maryam) on 16/7/02, *Ato* Aychelè Täräfä, interviewed (at Martula-Maryam) on 1/8/02, *Ato* Negatè and *Ato* Härägä Wäyen Käbädä, interviewed (at Mota) on 25/02/08.

⁶⁴ Daniel Ayana, "A Catalogue of Land Tenure Related Microfilm from Gojjam Churches and Monasteries", Arba'etu Wängèl, MS. Bichäna Giyorgis, catalogued as 89,II, 3-8.Space would not be enough to list dawn all charters containing clauses regulating the relationship between *zèga* and *däbtära* besides the charters cited above.

⁶⁵ Daniel,"A Catalogue of Land Tenure Related Microfilm from Gojjam Churches and Monasteries", Tarikä-Nägäst Zä-Ityopya, MS. Däbrä-Wärq, catalogued as II.11-33;III.3-18.The title Daniel gave to this manuscript is a misnomer. The content does not suggest the title. This is a codification of the usages and rules of the monasteries of Däbrä-Wärq and Gethsemane. The third monastery is difficult to identify. Internal evidence shows that the need for further codification of the custom and usages of the two monasteries arose from the dispute between them. The judgment

of King Täklä-Hämanot settling the dispute between them is also found in the Mäzgäb, MS.Däbrä-Marqos, and folio18v.

[66] Tekalign, "A City and its Hinterlands", p.112.

[67] Yältyopya Qwanqwawoch Ṭenatena Meremere Ma'ekäle-Ethiopian Languages Research and Study Centre, *Amareñña Mäzgäbä Qalat (Amharic Dictionary)* (Addis Ababa: Artistic Printing Press, 1993 E.C), p.445

[68] Kidanä-Wäld Kiflè, *Sewasäw Wäges Wämäzgäb Qalat Häddis Nebabu Bägeez Fechew Bamaragna (A Book of Grammer and Verb,and a New Dictionary.Geez Entries with Amharic Definitions (*Addis Ababa:Artistic Printing Press,19489-E.C.),pp.412 and 418. See also Dasta Takla-Wold, Ya Amarenna Mazgaba Qalat (Addis Ababa: Artisitic Printing Press, 1962 E.C.), p. 479.

[69] Informants, *Mägabi* Säyefä-Sellasè Yohännes interviewed (in Addis Ababa) on 17/11/02, Mazgaba Se'el, IES MS No.7, folio 85 recto.

[70] Wolf Leslau, *Etymological Dictionary of Gurage (Ethiopic)* vol.III (Wiesbaden: Otto Harrassowitz, 1979), pp.703 and 718, Yohännes Gäbrä-Egziabher, *Mäzgäbä Qalat Tigereñña Amhareñña (Ethiopian Dictionary Tigrigna Amharic*(Asmara: Artgraphic Eritrea, 1948-49),p.667

[71] Tekalign, "A City and its Hinterlands", p.112.

[72] Alämayähu Mogäs, *And Eräñña, And Mänga*_(Commercial Printing Press, 1989 E.C), p.26.

[73] "Selä Abun Nägär Kä A'emero Gazzeṭa Yätägäläbäṭä" *Berhänena Sälam* No.10, March10, 1927, p.78

[74] Tekalign, "A City and its Hinterlands", p.113.

[75] Ibid, pp.113-115.

[76] Ibid.

[77] Ibid.

[78] Ibid, p.113.

[79] Täklä-Iyäsus, "The Genealogy of the People of Gojjam", folio11r.

[80] Girma, "Ancient Customary law of the Gafat", pp.70 and 72.

[81] Mäzgäb, MS.Däbrä-Marqos, folio 15r.

[82] Ibid, folio10r, Daniel,Tarikä-Nägäst Zä-Ityopya, MS. Däbrä-Wärq, catalogued as II.11-33;III.3-18,*Idem,*Gebrä-Häwaryat, MS. Yägwära Qwesqwam,Catalogued as 89,XVI.23-25.

[83] Daniel, Tarikä-Nägäst Zä-Ityopya, MS. Däbrä-Wärq, catalogued as II.11-33; III.3-18.

[84] Jules Perruchon, "Notes pour l'Histoire d'Éthiopie: Règnes de Ya'qob et Za- Dengel (1597-1607)," Revue Sémitique 4(1896), pp.359-360.
[85] Crummey, *Land and Society*, pp.65-66.
[86] Täklä-Iyäsus, "The Genealogy of the People of Gojjam", folio11r.
[87] Bairu (ed. and trans.), *AsmeGiyorgis and his Work...*, Pp.199 and 245.
[88] Ibid, pp.163, 239. Susenyos was usually accompanied by the Oromo in his expedition and raids against Eastern Gojjam. The southern parts of the present region of Eastern Gojjam especially the area around the modern town of Däjän was the veritable ground of raid for him and the Oromo. Moreover, it was his ceaseless raids against the Gafat that made the latter to cross into Eastern Gojjam from Shäwa in large numbers, in the sixteenth and seventeenth centuries (see Ibid, pp. 197-201).
[89] Daniel, "A Catalogue of Land Tenure Related Microfilm from Gojjam Churches and Monasteries," Gädlä-Giyorgis, MS. Dima Giyorgis catalogued as 89.XIV.8-9.
[90] Ibid.
[91] Täklä-Iyäsus, "The Genealogy of the People of Gojjam", folio9v.
[92] Informant: *Märigèta* Libanos.
[93] Informants: *Ato* Negatè, *Ato* Yerdaw Kassa, interviewed (in Ennabse) on 9/7/02 and *Ato* Dässè Färädä, interviewed (in Ennabse) on 30/07/02.
[94] Täklä-Iyäsus, "The Genealogy of the People of Gojjam", folio11r. It is the only instance where Täklè referred to those dispossessed of their lands during the seventeenth century in Bibuññ by princes and lords as *gäbbar*.
[95] Informant, *Ato* Härägä-Wäyen, *Märigèta* Libanos.
[96] Fantahun Birhane, Gojjam, 1800-1855 (BA thesis in history, Department of History (HSIU), 1973), appendix No. I.
[97] Täklä-Iyäsus, "The Genealogy of the People of Gojjam", folio 11r.

CHAPTER TWO

GULT LORDS, ZÈGA AND THE BALÄ-REST: THE STRUCTURE OF THE SOCIETY IN EASTERN GOJJAM, C.1767-1874.

2.1 The Property System and the Institution of *Zègenät:* Main Features and Characteristics.

The chaos and insecurity of life in the 17th century, as we have seen in the previous chapter, probably led to the emergence of the institution of *zègenät*. Likewise in the period known as the *Zämänä Mäsafent* (which lasted c. 1769-1853), or shortly before, some departure from the pre-existing mode of access to land seems to have started. The 18th century, especially its second half, witnessed unprecedented disturbances and the ascendancy of regional lords. The power of the monarchy had collapsed almost completely and provincial lords had become virtually independent. My information on Eastern Gojjam for the 18th and 19th centuries shows that at the local level the *Zämänä Mäsafent* brought about significant changes. To begin with, the regional ruling houses were able to make increasingly direct intervention in the tenure systems, so much so that in some places they embarked on a thorough redistribution of property. Secondly, the new terms of access to land favoured the lords over the peasantry because the obligations of the latter were increased considerably or at least the documentary records show the attempt.[1] These changes represented a marked departure from conditions in the days of monarchical power. The monarchy before its collapse in the 1770s appears to have curtailed the capacities of local rulers to intervene in local property and tributary relations.

Meanwhile, in Eastern Gojjam a regional dynasty had established itself in the second half of the 18th century. The significance of the *Zämänä Mäsafent* was that, therefore, it afforded this local dynasty an opportunity to redistribute property and through that to strengthen its position. By far the best evidence supporting the disappearance of state interference in the relationship between lord and peasant in the study area is the fact that the local dynasty went about distributing as well as defining the forms of tenure with little regard for or reference to the imperial centre. These redistribution and redefinitions were made in almost complete disregard of extant charters that invoked the names of the ineffectual kings at Gondär (the imperial capital). What all of this entailed was the erosion and in some cases the revocation of the rights of the peasantry over *rest* lands.[2]

Gult grants thrived during this turbulent period. Some big churches were founded and many old churches were endowed.[3] Most of the pertinent documents regarding land date from this period. Local rulers also became big landlords in their own right. Their enhanced political status vis-à-vis the monarchy was thus accompanied by their growing interest in agriculture on lands gained through eviction. For instance, *Ras* Häylu I (r.c.1770 -1794) who was the ruler of the whole region of Gojjam, including the area of study, had concentrated large estates in his hands during this period. He apparently put to work gangs of *zègas* with as many as five hundred pairs of oxen. According to information collected by Täklè, Häylu acquired his land through outright eviction of the *restäñña* as well as local notables. This suggests, without doubt, an increasing arbitrariness with regard to *rest* land on the part of local rulers.[4]

Täkle, our source for this information, indicates that the *zègas* whom Häylu transferred from elsewhere and resettled as labourers on his large personal estates were of landless Muslims. The economic and cultural segregation of Muslims, which prohibited them from owning land in Christian dominated places made landless agricultural labourers readily available to big landlords to cultivate their lands acquired through outright expropriation of the *restañña*. Häylu reportedly stationed soldiers on the lands that he took over by outright expropriation to supervise and make sure that the *zègas* who worked the estates were effectively supervised. The extensive interventions of Häylu in local land matters, particularly his revocation of the property rights of local notables, apparently created considerable and rather permanent tension between him and other elite types. Häylu's land policy earned him the enmity of the elite so much that, at least on one occasion, the latter are said to have organized an abortive conspiracy to kill him.[5]

The 18th and 19th centuries are also notable for a rise in exchanges involving land. Given the fact that the buying and selling of land in the context of the *rest* system was generally an exception rather than the rule, the substantial frequency of land sales during this period constituted a veritable revolution. Our sources for Eastern Gojjam show that it is roughly from about the middle of the eighteenth century that men from all walks of life started to engage in buying and selling land, both urban and rural.[6] Trade in land of such intensity had no known precedent in Ethiopian history.

The charters from Eastern Gojjam also contain clauses allowing grantees the right to dispose of *rim* lands and town lands by sale, indicating that the land tenure system legalized private and exclusive ownership of land. One such charter, allowing the *däbtära* free disposal of land, was given to the church of Moṭa Giyorgis as we shall see below. The actual disposal of land chiefly took the form of outright sale and other forms that were generically referred to as *wurs*. The latter sometimes meant voluntary transfer, very close to a gift or bequeathal. Sometimes, however, it meant transfers involving the exchange of money plus other kinds of obligations by the beneficiary of *wurs* to the benefactor. Due to these relatively strong rights to dispose of land, both rural and town properties were bought and sold quite frequently from about the mid-eighteenth down to the twentieth century. As envisaged in the charter for the church of Moṭa Giyorgis, there developed a more vigorous and extensive trade in land in Moṭa more than anywhere else in the region.[7]

There is also a strikingly high incidence during this period of a system by which prominent lay personalities, women as well as men, undertook to perform specialized services for the church as "priests, deacons or *däbtära*." Apparently, the undertaking was that these persons would "buy" or in other ways provide other persons who would give these services to the churches. Persons holding land in the domain of the Church were generically referred to as *däbtära*. The direct meaning of the term *däbtära* is choir-man and/or scribe, but the word was used to refer to people holding land from the church in return for the specific service rendered. The term *däbtära* referred to broad social entities and a very strange mixture of people ranging from the king to a very humble choir-man.

In general, there was during this period a considerable transfer of land from the peasantry to lords and to institutions like the Church. Likewise there was a striking coincidence between fresh redistributions of land and markets in land. There was also a system of carrying out obligations to the Church by proxy.[8]

The most important land grant in the period was made in the eighteenth century by Wälätä-Isra'el to Moṭa Giyorgis church and to five small monasteries found in the district of Ennäsè. A total of 350 *däbtäras* were established over 1000 *gašas* of land. The list of the specific fields and villages distributed to the *däbtäras* is recorded in the MS. called Mäzgäb (Registry) in the church treasury.[9] This is probably the longest list of *gult* land register to exist as far as the researcher is aware. The MS. is not however bound together but made of loose leaves. Nor is it catalogued and registered by the Ministry of Culture. Copies of the document detailing the relationship between the *zèga* and the *däbtära* and the *restañña* and the *däbtära* that Wälätä-Isra'el set down are found in the manuscript collections of the monastery of Märṭulä-Maryam, the churches of Däbrä-Eliyas, Däbrä-Marqos and Yägwära Qwseqwam, all found far apart from each other.[10]

The events leading to the recording of the charter in the last three churches are interesting by themselves. King Täklä-Häymanot made grants to the churches of Däbrä-Marqos and Däbrä-Eliyas on the basis of the precedent set by Wälätä-Isra'el. In fact, he ordered Wälätä-Isra'el's charter to be copied and deposited in the *gult* registry of the two churches. However, the document was also found as an insertion in a manuscript found at the Yägwära Qwseqwam church, located in the district of Libän, in the south-western part of eastern Gojjam. It was copied from Däbrä-Eliyas, in connection with an attempt to settle a dispute between peasants and the clergymen attached to the church. Details about what rights of the church were under contest by the peasantry can not be given or known from the historical record. The original grant to Yägwära was made by *Däjjazmach* Wälta, one of the senior officials of *Ras* Häylu in the eighteenth century. Like many *gult* charters in the region, Wälta drew up his land grant to Yägwära on the model of Wälätä-Isra'el's, i.e. on the basis of the formula of one-third to the *bäläre̱st* and two-thirds to the *däbtära*. However, the document appears to have been destroyed, which reason necessitated its copying by the orders of *Ras* Häylu II, the son and successor of Täklä-Häymanot. The latter needed the copy in order to settle the dispute that arose between the church and the peasants in the early twentieth century.[11]

Because of their importance for the themes and theses of this work and the articulation of the system or rights and obligations linking and/or separating the *däbtäras* and the *restäññas*, it would be helpful to present two somewhat lengthy quotes from the charters of East Gojjam. The first was a charter made by Wälätä-Isra'el and the second was a grant charter made to Däbrä-Eliyas on the model of the former given by Täklä-Häymanot:[12]

የዳሪው ጨዋ ተከተማው ጨዋ ጋር መጺጠር የለውም፤፤ እዳ ቢመጣ ማህበር መክሮ እንደጎኑ ይጥልበታል እንጅ አለቃ ሊቀጠበብት አይጥልበትም፤፤ በከተማውም በገጠሩም ለአለቃም ለሊቀጠበብትም እራት ቀለብ የለውም ኡ ቤት መስራት አአጥር ማጠር የለበትም በባላገሩ፤፤ ደብተራውም ዜጋውን ይዳኛል፤፤ ደም ቢፈሥ ኡ ፈርሥ ቢፈርሥ ኡ በይናፉ ኡ በሌብነት ቢገኝ አለቃ ሊቀጠበብት ነው ዳኛ፤፤ ደብተራና ደብተራ በቦታ በሪም ቢጣላ ዳኝነት የለበትም፤፤ አለቃውም ሊቀጠበብቱም ረደብተራ በተሰራብት አገር ሪአምስትያ እንስተውበታል፤፤ ያለቃውና የሊቀጠበብት ብላቶን ጌቶች ለራሳቸው ይድናሉ እንጅ ተወራጁ አይድንም፤፤ያጋፋሪውም እንዲሁ ነው፤፤ የሊቀአበውም ከጨዋው በጢስ ቁናና እሀል ኡ ሲሶው አበሉ ከከተማው ውስጥ ነው እንጅ ከእዳሪው የለውም፤፤ የጭቃውም ስራ እንዲህ ነው፤፤ ረየጭቃሪ መጋፈሪያ ለሰው ወርቅሬ የሚከፍልበትሪ መሬት አለው በጋሻ 1 ጨው፤፤ በከተማው ውስጥ ገብቶ ጭቃ አይመራም አይሰራም በሲሶው ነው እንጅ፤፤ በሁለት እጅ በደብተራው መሬት እዳ እንግዳ የለበትም፤፤ ደብተራውም በሬ ቢያገኝ አርሶ በሬ ቢያጣ አስጠምዶ ይበልዋል፤፤ ባለርስቱ እዳውን ከፍሉ ይበልዋል እንጅ ደብተራ ከገጠሩ ርስቶ ነው ብሉ ከሲሶው ምድር ከባላ እዳም ይከፍላል ቤተክርስትያንም ያሰሪል፤፤ የመስዋቱን የጣኑን የመብራቱን ሀገር ገበዙ ነው ዳኛ፤፤ ደም ቢፈስ ፈርስ ቢፈርስ ግን አለቃ ሊቀጠበብት ነው ዳኛው፤፤ የገበዙን ተወራጂ ማህበሩ ቻይነተኛው ገበዝ ጋር መክረው ቦታ ያለው ቤተክርስትያን አገልጋይ ተመርጦ ነው እሚሾም፤፤ የሹመት እሪም አለው፤፤ ለዚሀም ተወራጅ ሹም አለው፤፤ ቦታ እሪም ገዝቶ ከሚአፅፍ ለገበዙ ተወራጅ 2 ጨው ኡ 0 በግ አለው፤፤ በአለቃና በሊቀጠበብትም ምሳ አለባቸው፤፤ 6ምሳ በአለቃውአ0ምሳ በሊቀጠበብቱ አለባቸው፤፤ ምሳ ግን ሲያበሉ5ፍሪዳ የልደት0 5ፍሪዳ የፋሲክ አላቸው፤፤ ፍሪዳውም የሚወጣ ከሲሶው ነው፤፤ ከምሳውም ሺማግሌው ተመርጦ በጭቃው ይበላል፤፤

የፍሪዳውም ወርቅ 16ጨው ነው፡፡ በግም ዐበበግ አላቸው፡፡ በቱ የሚወጣ ከጭቆች ነውአፍሪዳው የሚወጣ ከባለሲሶው ነው፡፡ የዐሩሩ ሹማምትም አበላቸው ከአፍርንጇ ሽንኩርትኦ ብላቸውም ሁለት ሆኖ ይከፈላል፡፡ አንዱን እጅ አለቃው ይወስዳል፡፡ አንዱ እጅም መጦ ለሁለት ይሆናል፡፡ አንዱን እጅ ሊቀጠበቱ ይወስዳል አንዱን እጅ አምጦተው 3ክፍል ያደርጉታል፡፡ አንዱን ገበዝና ርእሰ ደብርአንዱን ቀኝጌታና ግራጌታ ይወስዳታል፡፡ አንዱን ክፍል ሁለቱ መጨኖቸና እሞች ይቻፈሉታል፡፡ መሪና ቀስም ተስቸር ሲበሉ ሀጋቸው መሪው በላይ ቀስ በታች ግምባር ነው፡፡ ሁለት እጅ ለመሪ ሲሶ ለቀስ ነው አቀባለቸው፡፡ ፍታትም በየተቀበረበት ይፈታል፡፡ የደብሩም ገጠር አይሀድ የገጠሩም ደብር አይምጣ፡፡ የደብር ስርአት አልቸልም ያለሰው ከደብር ቀብር አስበ መቃብር ስጦች ይሄዳል፡፡ የቀኝጌታ የግራጌታ የመጨኔ 5ትያ 11 ጋሽ አላቸው፡፡ አለቃ ሊቀጠበብት ቢሆን ማህበሩን ከላበላ ከበታች ነው የሚቆም፡፡ ያበላ እነደሆን ይከብራል፡፡ ውድሞውንም ከገጠር ያለው ባለሲሶው ይሰርዋል፡፡ እሚያሰራው ጭቃው ነው፡፡ ቤተክርስትያን ሲከደን ግን የከተማው ጨዋ ሳር ያግዛል፡፡ በሲሶው ግን ወቀፉን ኦገመዱን ሳሩን አምጦቶ ይከድናል፡፡ የደብተራው ዜጋ ኖር ሲሄድ ጋን ኦ አልጋ ኦ ወፍጮ ኦ ሙቀጫ ስጦቶ ይሄዳል፡፡ ቤት አፍሶ አይሄድም፡፡ የደብተራ ምሽት ገበያ ብትውል አትቀረጥም፡፡ ዜጋም ቤቱን እሳት ቢፈጀው በተሰራ ቤትም ገብቶ ያቢፈርስ ሲሄድ ሰርቶ ይሄዳል፡፡ በመስዋት መሬት እዳ እንግዳ የለበትም፡፡

The peasants in the town shall not be liable jointly with those in the countryside [for the payment of occasional levies]. If occasional levies are to be imposed the community of the church shall determine what should be the amount [he peasants in the town] shall pay and not the aläqa and the liqäṭäbäbt. Both the town and the surrounding countryside do not owe the obligation to provide stipend and meals to the aläqa and the liqäṭäbäbt. The bälagär are free of the obligation of building houses and putting up fences [for the aläqa and the liqäṭäbäbt]. The däbtära would preside in judgment over the zèga. If they (the zèga) are implicated in cases involving murder, adultery, theft and the killing of animals the cases will be seen by the aläqa and the liqäṭäbäbt. And when the däbtära quarrel with one another over rim land and town plots there is no judgment fee. [This is because] all over the regions in which the däbtära are established both the aläqa and the liqäṭäbäbt would already have taken a fifth of the land for themselves. The blatèngètoch of the aläqa and of the liqäṭäbäbt are immune from any obligation but this exemption does not apply to their subordinates. The same is true with the agafari. The stipend of the liqä'abaw is one qunna from the peasants from each house and a third of his stipend shall be paid to him from the town. The duties of the çheqa are as follows; he has a mägaräfya (unit of land measurement) from lands paying [tribute?] in gold. He has one rock-salt from each gaša. The çheqa is not to enter and interfere in the administration of the town except in the sisso land. On the two-third of the däbtära land there shall be no dues and obligation. If the däbtära owned oxen they shall cultivate their lands [by themselves]; short of this, they shall rent [out their lands to others] and exploit their land. The balärest holding their sisso land shall meet his obligation and exploit his land, however, if the däbtära encroach into the sisso land laying claim of rest right he shall have obligation to pay tribute and build a church. The gäbäz will act as a judge in the land given to support Mass, incense and mäberat. The judges in cases involving the killing of a stolen animal and death will be the aläqa and the liqäṭäbäbt. The subordinate of the gäbäz shall be elected by the community in consultation with the principal gäbäz from among those holding urban sites and serving the church. The office has rim [land] attached to it. The subordinate of the [gäbäz] shall have two rock-salts and three sheep

deducted [for his stipend] from the revenue collected from registration fee paid by those purchasing urban sites and rim land. The aläqa and the liqäṭäbäbt have to provide meals. The aläqa has to provide seven meals and the liqäṭäbäbt ten meals. They shall receive three beef cattle for Christmas and five beef cattle for Easter. The beef cattle shall be contributed from the sisso land. The shimagellè invited by the çheqa shall partake of the meals. The price of the beef cattle is sixteen rock-salts. They shall also receive ten sheep. The sheep are to be contributed by the çheqa; the beef cattle shall be contributed from the baläsisso. The stipend of the eight officials from färänji (European) onions is as follows: the stipend will be divided in two portions, one-half belongs to the aläqa. The other half will be divided into two portions. Half of it goes to the liqäṭäbäbt. The remainder would be divided into three portions. One portion belongs to the gäbäz and the re'esädäber, one portion belongs to the qaññgèta and geragèta and one portion would be divided among the two mäçhänoch and emoch. The rule for the märi and qès partaking täzkar meal [is as follows]; the märi shall take the upper and the qès lower front seats. The märi shall receive two-thirds and the qès one third [?]. Burial prayers should be performed wherever one is buried. The däber shall not go to the gäṭär and the gäṭär shall not come to the däber. If one can not afford the charge of the däber he pays for the asäbä-mäqaber (burial fee) and departs. The geragèta, mäçhänè and qäññgèta will have one gaša each. Even the aläqa and the liqäṭäbäbet if they do not provide meals for the community they take lower seats. If one provides a meal he shall be honoured. The enclosure shall be built by the baläsisso in the countryside. The çheqa will supervise its construction. The peasants residing in the town shall contribute thatching grass. The baläisso shall bring wäqäf (building material), thatching grass and rope and cover the roof. If the zèga of the däbtära departs he shall offer a gan, a millstone, mortar and bed. He cannot depart demolishing his dwelling. If a wife of a däbtära goes to market she shall not pay market fee. If the house of the zèga is destroyed by fire or if the house in which he dwells is demolished he shall build another before departing. The land given to support the Mass is immune from taxation...

ይህንም ረለደብረ ኤልያስሪ ሲሰሩ በሞጣ ስርዓት ሁለት እጅ መሬት ለደብተራ ሲኦ ለባለርስት ይሁን ብለዋልረንጉስ ተክለሀይማኖትሪ፤፤ ድማህ ገነቱ ይህን አፍርሶ የደብተራውን ቢቀማውአየባለርስቴንም ቢቀማውአያንዱንም ደብተራ አንዱ ቢቀማው ኦርስተኛ ውንም ደብተራው ቢቀማውአደብተራውንም ርስተኛው ቢቀማውአግይዱ በየራሱ፡፡፡ ወቀት ይሁን ብለዋል፤፤ በዚህም ጻጻሥ ኤጲስ ቆጶስ እጨጌ ኦቆሞሰኦ ቄስ ገዝቦታል፤፤ የዳኝነቱም ቢሆን ደብተራው በደብተራውአባለሲሶው በባለሲሶው አላቃው በአላቃው ስራት ጸንቶ ሊኖር ነው፤፤ በሞጣ ስራት፤፤

When he [Täklä-Häymanot] established this (däbtära of the church of Däbrä-Eliyas) he declared that the däbtära should have two-thirds and the restäñña one-third of the land according to the establishment of Moṭa. If the Demah-Gänät in violation of this, seeks to dispossess the däbtära or the balärest; or if the däbtära attempts to dispossess another däbtära, or if the däbtära and the restäñña seek to dispossess one another the fine on each party shall be fifty ounces of gold. This has been sanctioned as inviolable by the Bishop, the episcopos [ates], the eçhagè, the qomos and the qès. As regards judicial matters the däbtära shall abide by the rules pertaining to their group; the baläsisso shall abide by the rules pertaining to their group. The aläqa shall, likewise, abide by the rules provided for their group. These are the terms of the Moṭa system.

The first problem that should be addressed is the precise nature of the right of the *däbtäras* over the land. A detailed and careful analysis of the charter above suggests that it would be inaccurate to describe the right of the *däbtäras* as a right over tribute only. The charter defines both the scope and the specifics of the rights and obligations of the *däbtäras* and the *restäññas*. Probably the most explicit and definitive statement in the grant is the stipulation that "If the *däbtära* owned oxen they shall cultivate their lands [by themselves]; short of this, they shall rent [out their lands to others] and exploit their land." There is also another equally definite and bold statement in the charter that pronounces that "On the two-thirds of the *däbtära* land there shall be no dues and obligations."[13] The scribe of the charter of Wälätä-Isra'el (the first long entry) is unequivocal on this point, unlike the scribes of many other charters who did not trouble themselves much to define the specific rights of the *däbtäras* over their *rim* land in plain terms. It is apparent from the first stipulation that the *restäñña* and the *däbtära* had no concurrent rights over the two-thirds of the land, which was given to the latter. The *balärest* was entitled to only one-third of his *rest* land the two-thirds already effectively granted to others and that those others should keep and cultivate the remaining two-thirds. Control by the *restäññas* over the two-thirds of the land is fully forfeited. As the charter makes it exceedingly clear the right of the *däbtäras* was firmly rooted in the soil.[14] *Rim* land was therefore first and foremost a right to the land not a right to the tribute. It referred to lands over which the subject of the *däbtäras*, known as *zègas*, would be stationed. In fact, if *gult* is understood to mean tribute extraction, that term may not be fully descriptive of the rights of the *däbtäras* over their lands.

The charter deprived the *restäññas* of *rest* rights on the two-thirds of their lands, which now came to be occupied by the subjects or *zègas* of the grantees. The provision that the officials of the church had no right to interfere in the holdings of the *däbtäras* or over two-thirds of the land so long as they did not violate the conditions set out in the charter is indicative of the fact that grants were made to them in perpetuity. Any attempt on the part of the *restäññas* to hinder full property rights by the *däbtära* was made punishable by a fine of fifty ounces, which was considerable. Presumably the injunction and the associated heavy fine imposed on possible *restäñña* trespassers is meant to affirm the reality of the surrender of their land. Nobody would dare to challenge the rights of the *däbtäras* and risk a liability of fifty ounces of gold![15] Once granted, two-thirds of the land thus remained under the effective occupation or control of the *däbtäras*.

The grantor, Wälätä-Isra'el, left only one-third of the land in the hands of the *restäññas*. This right of the *restäññas* is acknowledged by the charter in the injunction that the *däbtäras* should not encroach over this one-third of the land. It is interesting to recall the provision in the charter quoted above that even the rights of the *restäññas* over the remaining one-third seems very precarious. Although the fine of fifty ounces of gold can be found in the abridged charter of Wälätä-Isra'el set down in the many manuscripts in Mota and other churches [16] the injunction is lacking in the long and extended charter copied and deposited in the churches of Yägwära Qwesqwam and Däbrä-Eliyas from which the charter above is taken. Thus the injunction of fine and the strict restriction against violations of the grant might have been a latter addition by King Täklä-Häymanot. Although the charter provides some safeguard for the right of the *restäññas* over the one-third of the land, still the holding of the *restäññas* seems to be precarious. For example the consequences for *däbtäras* who violate the terms of the grant were not that serious. No fine was to be imposed for such an act but the *däbtära* would simply render himself/herself liable to additional services and obligation due to the church. Moreover, the surrender of two-thirds of the land did not end the obligation of the *restäññas*. Labour dues or the obligation to render customary payments like contribution of an ox for festive occasions was demanded.

The right of the *däbtäras* on the land is of the nature of ownership in perpetuity, free from interference. The only condition was rendering service to the church. Moreover there is one indication of the exclusive and almost absolute nature of the right. The *däbtäras* held their *rim* lands individually. This can easily be deduced from the provision of the grant for contingencies in connection with quarrel or encroachments on any other's holding. Besides rural lands the *däbtäras* were settled in the towns and they acquired rights to live therein in perpetuity, only subject to good behaviour and fulfilling their obligation towards the church. One useful indication of the permanent nature of the right of the *däbtäras* over the town sites is that no town sites were re-granted subsequent to the settlement of the first batch of the *däbtäras* concurrent with the establishment of the church. Moreover the charter asserted the right to sell *rim* land and *bota* by the *däbtäras* and it did occur as envisaged by the charter as indicated above.[17] The extended charter does not for example require the *däbtäras* to get the approval of or the permission of church officials to sell their *rim* land or *bota* and to erect buildings over their urban sites.[18] The *däbtäras* would build permanent structure over their *bota* like houses or plant permanent trees which could render revocation difficult if not impossible and unless sufficient conditions warranting such an action existed. Thus the *däbtäras*' right over *rim* and *bota* is in the nature of private ownership though one can not dare to say that their right was in the nature of an absolute freehold. They had the right to transmit their holdings to their offspring. *Bota* and *rim* land could be forfeited if, and only if, the holder died heirless or defaulted on his obligations to meet the demands of the church. Thus we can not say that the holdings of the *däbtäras* were temporary and precarious.

Undoubtedly, there is considerable lack of clarity on the meanings of *gult* and the dialectics between *gult* and the complex combination of group and individual rights that we know by the term *rest*. What the documents that I have presented above show, however, is that *gult* was in Eastern Gojjam a right to property acquired by the elite in the eighteenth century distributions. It will be inaccurate to describe the right of the *däbtäras* over the two-thirds of the land as a right to tribute.

There are other important points that stand out from the charters above that deserve attention and elaboration. One is the juridical right of the *däbtära* over his *zèga*. Nowhere is the institution of *zègenät* describes with such clarity as in the document quoted above. This is the earliest charter, as early as 1767. Its provisions for the *däbtäras* are very complete and it depicts the *zègas* in somewhat harsh terms, imposing some limitations and conditions on their mobility. The charter implies the existence of an intricate web of rights and duties in the relationships between the *zègas* and the *däbtäras*. The relationship is an unequal one; the *däbtära* is clearly of higher standing, both in material and social terms, than the *zèga*. The following observations can be made from the quotation above. Wälätä-Isra'el gave a special and privileged status to all the *däbtäras* connected with the church, giving specialized services in various capacities, freeing them all from obligations and tribute, like market fees and court fees and other advantages of exemptions from many other obligations due to the church. Many fortunes were amassed by the *däbtäras* and people associated with the church. They enjoyed immunity from any intervention by the local *çheqa* for any reason whatsoever. The *çheqa* were forbidden to levy any tax on the two-thirds of the land of the *däbtäras* in the countryside and in the town and even to enter the latter. The *aläqa* and the *liqäṭäbäbt*, and the *çheqa* under them, had administrative authority, including rights to levy taxes, only on the *sisso* land*s*. Two-thirds of the land was settled by the *zègas* of the *däbtäras*.[19] Over these lands, property was the most important point of inter-class interaction. The dyadic economic and social relationships which church tenure in *rim* entails is therefore essentially the relation between the *zègas* and the lords in contradistinction to what is often stated to be between the *däbtäras* and the *restäññas*.

The *däbtäras* were immune from interference by government officials in their relationship with their *zègas*. The implication of this right is too obvious to call for extensive elaboration. Though pragmatist consideration might have tempered what might otherwise have been a very harsh exploitation of the *zègas*; and with due allowance to the fact that the relationship between documentary norms and realty should be left an open question, it would not be difficult to conceive that the *däbtäras* could demand of their *zègas* whatever obligation they wanted since the latter did not have their obligations defined and placed in the charter. It is possible to presume that they would be made to pay at the will of the lords, given the fact that the lords' rights were absolute or comprehensive and that the latter had the right to dictate the terms of their relationship with the *zègas*. This would undoubtedly mean that the obligations could be not only onerous but also irregular. This is ,therefore, evocative of the possibility that it was not only that the terms of tenure of the *zèga* were very precarious but it was also that his labour was not his own. Though not in strict property terms, in fact, it might be said that in some respects that *zèga* was only a little better than a slave. Legally, also the *däbtäras* were given some rights over the person and behaviour of the *zèga*. As mention has already been made, the granting of *rim* land was always accompanied by a delegation of juridical power to the individual *däbtära* over the *zèga*.[20] It is apparent that the judicial rights exercised by the *däbtäras* were comprehensive and total, the only exceptions being cases involving crimes such as theft, adultery and murder. The granting of rights to the *däbtäras* to try all civil cases involving the *zègas* would enable the former to have a high degree of discretion in the matter of disposing of the labour of the *zègas* since they were made judges and landlords at one and the same time.[21]

The specific labour services, economic obligations and social relationships of the *däbtäras* with the *zègas* might have been regulated by custom. However, as mention has already been made it is not hard to see that the *zègas* perhaps lived under a very harsh subjection since the charter is concerned only with punishments to be meted out by the lord and the church officials (in criminal cases) without any provisions for the *zègas* to appeal if the lord mistreated them or denied them their right of mobility or if the lord broke his part of the contract. Equally important, however, is that the *zègas* could not leave the estate of the lord without meeting what we might call "terms of severance" or "separation." These included, for instance, the rebuilding of dwellings that might be needed by incoming *zègas* (the charter mentions for example that a *zèga* whose dwellings had been consumed by fire could not just leave without re-erecting the structures). In another source dealing with the subject of the mobility of the *zègas* they were required to pay money to get the permission for departure and there was a ban upon leaving without payment, except by the permission of the lord. The *däbtäras* exacted either a sum of money or more frequently the best elements of the movable property of the *zègas*: his large jar (*gan*), his pestle and mortar, his bed and his stone mill. The *zèga* was given freedom to leave the land if he agreed to leave these objects.[22]

It is impossible, however, to make a complete analysis of the nature of the socio-economic relationships between the *zèga* and the *däbtära*. Hence the need for considering more cases in the pages that follow. Further evidence about the humble status of *zègas* comes from a charter drawn up in the second half of the nineteenth century. This charter is incorporated in a *gult* register found at Däbrä-Marqos. Unlike the eighteenth century land grant this is a secular land grant. However, the evidence contained in this charter (though it involved people and places not covered by the study) from different periods reflects striking similarities with the evidence in church land grants and provide additional details on the legal relationship between the *zèga* and his lord.[23]

Considerable villages in Kutai, northern Wälläga, specifically in a place called Lèmat beyond the Blue Nile were transferred to *Däjjazmach* Wärqènäh (Wärqè for short), an official and son-in-law of King Täklä-Häymanot. The reason for the expropriation of the land is clearly stated in the grant document to Wärqè. The native population in Lèmat were dispossessed of their land apparently for reasons of collective crime committed against the army of Täklä-Häymanot's general, Wärqè. The revolt was apparently a resistance movement waged against the imposition of the Gojjamè rule over northern Wälläga in the second half of the 19th century when Gojjam expanded though briefly into that region. Wärqè's soldiers were killed by the Lèmat Oromo and the latter's land was transferred as a blood price to Wärqè. The native people forfeited their right over the land and Wärqè could now evict them. This situation is expressed in the following words, "የሌማት ጋላ የደጃዝማች ወርቄን ሰራዊት ክርስቲያኑን ፈጂቶ ርስቱን የደም መሬት ሆኖ አሳልፏል። ልኑር ቢል ለደጃዝማች ወርቄ ዜጋ ሆኖ ሊኖር ነው።" This literally means that "The Lèmat Galla (Oromo), having destroyed the Christian army of *Däjjazmach* Wärqè, their *rest* has been transferred as blood price. If they choose to live, they shall become the *zèga* of *Däjjach* Wärqè."[24] And on folio 38verso column two, we have the following similar charter for *Däjjach* Wärqè reaffirming the earlier grant with some additions to provisions on the right of toll tax and market fee over many areas:

ንጉስ ተክለ ሀይማኖት ለራስ ወርቄ ከሊሙ ድዴን ፤ከይባንቱ የደብል ምኣን፤ ከጊዳ ኪረሙን፤ ከአሞሩ እነወንድን ፤ ከሆሮ ዱልቻንና ገንጂን ገራዶን ፤ ሉቅማ የበሩንና የገብያዉን ሲሶ፤ ከኩታይ ሌማትን የደም መሬት አድርገዉ ምስለኔ የማይገባዉ ገዢ የማያዝዘዉ ጉልት ይሁንለት ብለዉ ስጥተዋል። በዚሀም አዋጂ ተነግሮበታል። ግይዱም ይህንን አፍርሶ ለገባ » ወቄት ነዉ።

King Täklä-Häymanot granted to Ras Wärqè one-third of the market fees and proceeds from the toll gates of Didi in Limmu, of Yädäbälmo'a in Yebantu, of Kiramu in Gida, of Enäwänd in Amoru, of Dulcha, Gänji, Gärado and Luqema in Horro. [He also] granted to him the lands of] Lèmat as gult in Kutai as blood price, [with total] immunity from the interferences of the meslanè or of governors. A proclamation has been issued to this effect. The fine for the transgression of this is fifty ounces of gold.

The revolt was considered as an act of treason and crime against the regional ruler which resulted in the virtual eviction of peasants from their *rest* land. The above charter undoubtedly created very large populations of *zèga* since the decision to evict the population by the king seems to show that Wärqè was given power to evict summarily not only the rebels who did the actual fighting but also those who supported or took side with the rebels against his army. This is because the document referred to the dispossessed *balärest* in collectivity i.e. it employed a plural noun and hence it was apparently carried out without distinction between those persons who were involved in the offences and whole communities. The revolt justified the virtual expropriation of the former occupants of the land by the king by virtue of his right of reversion. Unlike the *balärest*, the right of occupancy of the *zègas* was not recognized at all.[25]

Wärqè could have carried out the act of expropriation following his empowerment to impose summary eviction. As has been discussed above, the status of *zèga* involved not only losing land or retaining only a portion of it, but also accepting new terms of socio-economic and legal-administrative relationships with the new lord. Following the granting of the charter, therefore, the native people would be subjected to new terms of relationship with the lord, and their tenure was made conditional. A reference to the wish of the people themselves is made. They were faced with very difficult choices. They could either live under their new lord Wärqè as his *zègas* or leave their former land and settle elsewhere. Though some of the former occupants of the land might have refused to allow themselves to be treated as *zègas* we can assume that most of them would have been much less inclined to depart since it is a very hard decision to make to leave the very soil where one was born and had lived long. Many might have chosen to live under Wärqè in their new status than to depart. Moreover, Wärqè could have been willing to retain them on favourable terms of agreement than to take the trouble of looking for other *zègas* to settle on his estate. In all cases, however, the status of those who accepted the lordship of Wärqè would be completely transformed, becoming his subjects. In disregard of their former free status they were considered henceforth as being *zègas* and their land instantly became the estate of Wärqè.[26]

The recognition of the right to depart in itself also shows the confidence of the lord that he could find other people to become his *zèga* by being settled on the new land he had thus acquired, which in turn testifies to the existence of many landless people. The charter does not provide direct evidence to support this hypothesis but it seems a logical and warranted inference. Wärqè apparently evicted them soon after he had received from Täklä-Häymanot an official affirmation of forfeiture of the right of the indigenous people. In the original charter there is a clause inserted safeguarding the freedom of choice for the former occupants of the soil but in the second which reconfirms the provision made for Wärqè by the first charter the clause is omitted. The explanation for this could only be that either the former occupants had agreed to live under Wärqè as his *zègas* or that the latter had already settled other *zègas* from elsewhere, which rendered the insertion of the clause unnecessary. The allowance of the exercise of the right to depart or not given to the native people whose land was being transferred as a blood price can be considered as an echo of the provision of freedom of mobility to the *zèga* contained in the sources discussed above. The second charter was given to Wärqè after he was promoted to the status of *Ras* and many privileges such as the right to collect a third of the toll tax and market fees from many places were awarded to him.[27]

The legal and administrative powers of Wärqè and the obligations he could impose on his subjects are not defined in the charter. But it seems that he had unqualified legal jurisdiction over his *zègas* to the complete exclusion of the government officials. Any attempt by any government official to transgress the provisions of the charter to Wärqè was made punishable by a payment of a fine of fifty ounces of gold. There is no provision in the charter for the *zèga* to be judged by anyone other than their new lord; nor is there any provision as to whom they could appeal to for protection against his actions.[28] A concomitant circumstance of the provision for the right of unqualified jurisdiction of Wärqè over his *zègas* was that he could exercise all kinds of seigniorial rights over his *zègas*. Sources suggest that bondage neither to the soil nor to the lord seems to be characteristic of the institution of *zègenät*. However, since the grant for *Ras* Wärqè was supposed to be permanent and immune from any interference by government officials the obligations of the *zègas* could be transmittable from generation to generation. In effect, therefore, the charter might imply the creation of hereditary classes of lord and *zèga*.

We are yet too far away from reaching anywhere nearer to the point of making a precise definition and delimitation of tenure in *zègenät*. Thus before rushing to doing that and to satisfy and clear up a little of the uncertainties of mind of a sceptical reader, certain representative sources remained to be discussed. One of the most fascinating manuscript sources used for this study which contains pertinent and definitive references about this institution is the administrative handbook or manual of the monasteries of Däbrä-Wärq and Gethsemane. Therefore, to understand the nature of the socio-economic relationships between the *zèga* and his lord we must supplement our information with a brief reference to the almost identical information to the rights of the *zèga* and the lord contained in the manual for the officials of the above monasteries and the genealogical book of Täklè.[29]

The manual is a normative attempt to regularize practice of the monasteries of Gethsemane and particularly of Däbrä-Wärq. What makes this manuscript so important is the amalgam of customs that it contains and its large volume. It is indeed an immense historical treasure. Although the scribe claims ancient origins for the two monasteries all that is recorded for the period after the sixteenth century is fairly accurate. There is clear evidence as to the conditions leading to the further codification of the customs and usages for the two monasteries. The need for codification arose from the quarrel amongst the monastic community over the distribution and administration of the revenue from the lands under the control of Däbrä-Wärq. The manuscript was compiled after the reconciliation of the community.[30] This took place most probably towards the close of the nineteenth century or the early twentieth century. The obligations and the rights of the various people connected with the monastery, ranging from those of the abbot to those assigned to do menial works like the digging and guarding of graves are defined with almost mathematical precision.[31]

In the many specific references that this source contains, the *zègas* are depicted as being subjected to very onerous terms of socio-economic relationship with their lords. The relationship of personal dependence that is of master and servant seems to have been very strong and common in certain areas. Both in the customary law of the Gafat and the manual for the officials of the above monasteries, the rules regulating the relationship between master and servant or lord and subject are a theme of the widest concern. It is stipulated in the manual that a master-less or a lord-less man who has been liberated subsequent to the death of his former master should not be allowed to reside or stay in the monastery of Däbrä-Wärq. He had to put himself in the service of a new master and failing this he was allowed either to be a monk, a soldier or to work on the land of the monastery as a tenant. The original intention of this provision was perhaps a concern for public order in the town of Däbrä-Wärq. The rule required lords, merchants and any one owning land in the town to register and notify the names of their children, *zègas* and servants occupying their respective land in the town. Failure to do so, or the commission of any crime by the servant or *zèga* of the lord, would result in the imposition of fines or the forfeiture of residential sites in the town of Däbrä-Wärq.[32] The obligation and the right of the *zèga* in the manual are stated in similar vein as in Täklè's (as we will see below). The following entry from the manual is evidence of this:[33]

...የባለርስት ዜጋ ልሂድ ባለ ጊዜ ገንዘቡን ማጀት በገረስ ደጅአፍ በመለስ የቤት እቃውን ሁሉ ይወስዳል ቤቱን ለባለርስት ያስቀራል የቀረው ገንዘብ ግን ለዜጋው ነው ሲኖርም የሚከፍለው የአመትባል ነጭ አሞሌ ቀይ በርበሬ አንድ በግ ያክፋይ 15 እንጀራ ድስት ወጥ ገንቦ ጠላ ይሰጣል በጢስ ፡፡

When a zèga belonging to a lord wishes to depart he shall take all the household utensils inside the house starting from the door-step and all that is contained within the majjät (a room in a house where most of the household objects are kept). The house shall belong to the lord. The rest of the property belongs to the zèga. While living [as a subject, the zèga] pays for feast days a white salt-bar, red-pepper, a sheep for akefay(?),15 enjjära, one dest wät, and one gänbo ṭälla.

..ማህበር ቄስ ደብተራ ብላቴንጌታ ከይናፉ ፣ ከሌባ ፣ ከደም ዳኝነት በቀር አይበላም፡፡ ...ማህበር ከሌባ ፣ ከደም ፣ ከይናፉ ዳኝነት በቀር ዜጋቸውን ዳንተው ቅድ ዳኝነት ደግሞ ከሹም እዳ እየተቀበለ ለዜጋው የሚያስታውቅ እዳ የማይነችው 11 ብርገብርዜ በየደጃቸው አላቸው፡፡ በዜጋቸውም መሽ አዳሪ ወታደር አይመራባቸውም፡፡

The community [of] priest, däbtära and blatèngèta should not pay court fees except for cases involving adultery, theft and homicide.... The community shall sit in judgment over their zègas except in cases of theft, adultery and homicide, and have a bärgäzè (errand man) whose sole obligation would be to notify them the judgment of the court of the officials and the dues the šums would demand from their zègas. Soldiers over taken by night should not be quartered over the zègas belonging to them (the däbtäras, priests, etc.).

በደብተራውም የሲሶ ፡ የተ4አንድ የሚያርስ ቢኖረው እዳ እንግዳ አይነከውም፤፤ መላክ ፡ መውጣት መውረድ ለደብተራ ነው፤፤ ከጨዋ ጋር አይገባበርም፤፤ እዳ እንግዳ፡ ቤተክርስትያን መስራት የለበትም፤፤ እሁድና የመቤታችን የማያገለግል ደብተራ ፡ በአለቃው ፈቃድ የማይላክ ፡ የማይወርድ ፡ የማይወጣ ደብተራ ከቦታው ተነቅሎ እንደ ጨዋ ይገብራል፤፤

If the däbtära has under him a cultivator on the basis of one-third or one-fourth he is immune from obligation and the hosting of official guests. The däbtäras' [responsibility] is to deliver messages, go up or down on the orders [of the church officials]. They would not share tributary obligations with the çhäwa (lay peasants). They should not have the obligation of building church, hosting guests and paying dues. A däbtära who does not provide services on the day of our Lady Mary and on Sundays, who does not obey, who does not ran errands on the orders of the aläqa would be evicted from his residential site and made to pay tribute like the çhäwa (peasants).

As one can easily observe the consistency of the manual and the charter of Wälätä-Isra'el in characterizing *zègenät* is indeed striking. One can also accept the reliability and the quality of the manual as a source with comfort. All this is suggestive of the existence of certain accepted general principles in tenure in *zègenät* and homogeneity in socio-economic practices throughout the region. The first entry illustrates the extent of the freedom of mobility and certain customary payments of food that a *zèga* had to pay while living under a lord. Unlike the charter of Mota Giyorgis church the demand upon the *zèga* for the permission of departure is not very harsh. In this case the *zèga* is allowed to take with him or possibly dispose of while departing all the important moveable properties except his dwelling. The manual allowed the *zègas* the right to take with them their precious movable properties in their dwelling. Our sources make a distinction between *zègas* and other forms of agricultural labourers. This suggests an interpretation that the *zègas* formed a separate category of people very distinct from slaves and other forms of agricultural labourers. They were dependent on a lord because they held their houses and their fields from him. This arises from the use of the term *zègas* to denote a separate community of people under landlords distinct from other categories of people. They are depicted as forming a class better than the slaves and domestics despite the fact that they did not own land and dwell on the estate of their masters. Again the freedom for departure testifies that the *zègas* did not appear to constitute a class of bondmen. They were free from any form of involuntary ad-fixture to the lord or even to his land. The condition that tied the *zègas* with their lords was the obligations arising from residence on the land of the lord. To put it differently, the *zègas* were near agricultural farmhands subject to the socio –economic as well as administrative and legal dominations of the lords from whom they held their tenements but they were regarded as free. The first entry gives some hint as to the nature of the obligation of the *zègas* other than labour service to their lords. On some festive occasions the *zègas* had to give their lords presents like sheep, salt-bars and food for the occasion.[34]

The second entry is mainly about the relationship between the *zèga* working over the land belonging to the people attached to the monastery. The term community as used in the text is to refer to all the clerical people connected to a *däber* or a monastery with the exception of the officials. It includes the *däbtäras* and the priests. Each plot or agricultural field of the individual members of the community were operated by a gang of *zèga* cultivators directly and individually controlled and free from the intervention of the officials of the church. As stated in the quotation above (first entry) the zègas working over the land of the clerical lords were immune from the obligation of hosting guests.[35]

There was some degree of control exercised by the local administrative body in the church's domain over the zégas pertaining to judicial matters. Thus the zègas were subject to an exploitative hierarchy. Church officials tried all court cases beyond the competence or right of individual lords. They could impose fines or occasional dues, which the zègas had to pay on the notice by the bärgäzè. According to informants bärgäzè was an errand man whose duty was to deliver the orders of the officials of the monastery to the individual lords. The officials of the church were entitled to impose dues according to their discretion to be collectively paid by the zègas on occasions of collective offence by them.[36]

However, every zèga was to a greater extent under the private jurisdiction of individual lords. Thus one important factor that gave the däbtäras a large measure of control over the zègas was the conferment of seigniorial rights like juridical rights over them. Like the charters of Wälätä-Isra'el and Täklä-Häymanot quoted above the manual gave the däbtäras many privileges including immunity from the payment of judgment fee except in criminal cases. Moreover, like the charters quoted above the manual authorizes individual lords to punish their respective zègas including the right to try all civil cases. Furthermore, soldiers were not allowed to stay in the house of the zègas or enter into their territory. Even, church officials could not cause any kind of obstruction in their juridical authority except in cases which were of criminal nature.[37] All these rights of the individual lord empowered him in effect with all the pervading manorial rights. The zègas were virtually at the beck and call of the lord. Generally they were almost reduced to a status of that of serfs. In other words their obligation bears a hallmark of servitude.

The third entry is concerned mainly with the rights and obligations of the individual däbtära. It would be implicit from the entry that the däbtäras enjoyed a very clear autonomy in his unit of production along with the people cultivating his land. He could rent his land to one or more zègas and enjoy the fruit of production, including the exercise of all kinds of seigniorial rights over his land and the people working his land. We can presume that very large number of zèga cultivators were deployed over the scattered fields controlled by an individual däbtära.[38] Direct inference can be made from the third entry that using the labour of zègas, who are here depicted as sharecroppers, was a widespread practice. Even in the individual holding of the *däbtära* which might otherwise have been managed by household labour the *däbtäras* would draft labour from outside of the household unit. It is stated that the people working the land of the *däbtäras* who were *zègas,* though the term *zèga* here (third entry) is not explicitly mentioned as cultivating the land of the *däbtäras,* could receive either *sisso* (one-third) or one-fourth of the produce. This would not seem to be an accidental note on the part of the scribe but a reflection of the common economic arrangement between landlords and *zègas* in the time. The *zègas* working over the *däbtäras* land were immune from the obligation of hosting guests. The *däbtäras* would naturally chose working his land through his *zègas* than assume direct and a not always easy responsibility for cultivation and mobilizing an agricultural force for the cultivation of his fields. Moreover the obligation and service he was required to give to the church, as a precondition of his ownership, was not difficult. However, if a *däbtära* refused services due from him there is an absolute right or power of reversion or eviction vested in the church officials over the *bota* occupied by the former. In the above entry treating the rights and the obligations of the *däbtäras* it is stated that if a *däbtära* holding church land fails to fulfil the conditions of his holding custom empowered the officials of the church to evict him from his residential site. But he would retain his farmland though he was liable to dues and obligations as a peasant under the monastery's administration.[39] This much can be teased out or observed from the quotation above. We now pass on to discussing another source which provides highly important information about the *zègas* or the institution of *zègenät.*

Täklè provides additional details on the nature of the socio-economic relationship between the *zèga* and his lord. We catch a glimpse of the modes of the socio-economic operation of the institution of *zègenät* in the customary law of the Gafat compiled by Täklè in the last decade of the nineteenth century and edited and translated by the scholar Girma Getahun. The customary law deals mainly with the relationship between the artisan *zègas* and their landlords or masters. This is, according to Girma, the result of the bias of the sources of information of Täklè since most of his informants appear to have been artisans themselves. With regard to tenure in *zègenät* and the mode of the socio-economic operation of the institution of *zègenät* Täklè was simply committing into writing (through interview and in all probability through observation) a practice that could come into his and his informants' notice. This practice undoubtedly evolved in the preceding centuries. Certain obligations of the farmer *zèga* are also similar to the artisan *zèga*. There were many artisans who were engaged in several kinds of craftsmanship in the region. Täklè enumerates many classes of artisans specializing in pottery, weaving, tanning, jewellers, etc. in Eastern Gojjam. Though there were artisans in the rural setting working independently and catering for the needs of the rural population many of them worked under the patronage of the courts of the regional lord. They catered to the needs of the great lords and the king. Those who worked for the royal court had also a distinct name, called *jan shällami*.[40] For the purpose of better exposition I have cited the following entries from the customary law appended in the final version of the genealogical study of Täklè. Girma translated *zèga* and *zègenät* as subject and tenant but I have opted to use the terms *zèga* and *zègenät* as in the original Amharic document to avoid confusion.[41]

> ሽማኔ ዜጋ ኾኖ ሲኖር ለባለቤታው በዓመት አንድ ጊዜ ጨርቅ ሰርቶ ያለብሳል፤፤ ከፋኝ ብሎ የተሰናበተ እንደኾነ ሁለት ጨውኣ አንድ ጋን ኣ ረእንድሪ ወፍጮኣ ሙቀጫ ና አንድ የቤት ጠገራ ስጥቶ ይጌዳል፡፡ በዘግነት ሲኖር ጉልማ ቢጎልም ለባለመሬቱ እርቦ ረስፈርሶ አይባልም፡፡ግን በሶስቱ ዓመት በዓላት አንድ አንድ ጨው ና ማጥሪያ ረጨርቆሪ ይሰጣል፡፡ጌታውም በሶስት ዓመት በዓላትረእርሱንሪከሚስቱ ና ከልጆቹ ጋር ጠርቶ ያበላቸዋል፡፡ ረሽማኔውሪ አማላጅ ጠልቶ ሳይሰናበት በሌሊት ጠፍቶ የሄደ እንደሆን በጌታው ረቤትሪ ደጃፍ ረወይምሪቱብን ረአጠገብሪ ሁለት ጨው ጥሎ ይሄዳል፡፡ ይህን ከላደረገ፣ ረተፈልጎ በተገኘ ጊዜሪ እሄደበት አገር በሽማግሌዎች ተፈርዶበት ዐሰር ጨው ይከፈል ይባላል፡፡ዜጋ ሰራተኛ ለጌታው ሚስት ሽማ፣ለጌታውም ሽማ ሲአሰብስ፣እርሱረእንደነርሱ?ሪ ክቡር ኾሆንጉ ብሎረአዲስ?ሪ ሽማ አይሰብስም፡፡ ሽማኔ ጨርቅ የሚሰራበት ዋጋረቁረጥ ነውሪ ሞ ክንድ ጋቢ በሁለት ጨው፣ ጃኖ ሽማ በሶስት ጨው ተቁና ጢፍ፣ አንድ ሱሪ በቁና ጢፍ፣ ሞ ክንድረድግሪበሶስት ቁና ጢፍ "<፡፡

> When a weaver lives as a *zèga*, he is supposed to make some fabric and cloth to the landlord of [and

64

his wife?] once a year. If he takes his leave on the grounds of being unhappy, he departs having offered two rock-salts, a gan, a mill stone, a mortar and an axe for domestic use. Whilst living in zègenät, if he was granted gwelemma (small plot of land), he may not be asked [to handover?] a quarter of the produce [in tribute]. However, on each of the three annual feasts he should give [to the landlord] one rock-salt and a piece of filtering cloth. The master [on his part], invites him with his wife and children and feed[s] them. If a weaver dislikes [to send an] intermediary [to his master], but absconds at night without bidding farewell, he leaves two rock- salts by the master's doorstep. If he fails to do that, he shall be made liable to pay ten rock-salts by the elders of the locality he moved [in] to. A weaver zèga, whenever he offers šämma to the master and his wife, he is not supposed to wear one [like them], considering himself [equally] respectable. A weaver charges [the following fixed] price for making fabric: two rock-salts for thirty cubit long gabi, three rock-salts and a qunnatef for jano šämma, one qunnatef for a pair of trousers, three qunnatef for thirty cubit long[degg].

ፋቂ ዜጋ ለጌታው ጀንዲአ መጠጊያአንቀልባና ምራንረበየአመት? ሪአንድ ጊዜ ይሰጣል፡፡ሚስቱ ረለጌታው ሚስትሪ ስፈት ትለጉማለችመንዴሬያ ትፈትላለች፡፡ሬታውሪ በሶስት ዓመት በዓላት ባረደ ቁጥር ረዜጋውንሪ ከሚስቱ ና ልጀቹ ረጋርሪ ጠርቶ ያበላቸዋል፡፡በነጋታው እቤቱ ገብቶ ያርዳል፡፡ለችገረው የሀገር ሰው ሁሉ የደም አፍሳሽረድርሻሪለርሱ ነው፡፡ጀንዲ ና ጭልጊ ለአለፉበትኦ ምራን ለፈተለበት ከዐውድማ ረየሚሰጠው?ሪዝግነቱ እንደ ረሌሎችሪ ሙያተኞች ነው፡፡

A tanner zèga gives to his master a leather bedspread, cushion, a baby-back-carrier and a piece of thong once [a year]. His wife may bind grass

> *baskets with leather [for the mistress]. She may also spin a low quality yarn [for the latter]. Every time [the master] kills [an animal] for the three annual feasts, he invites [the tanner], his wife and children and serve[s] them food .He may go back to his home and kill [an animal] on the following day. When he kills [animals] for all the local people in need [of his service], the butcher's due belongs to him. For tanning a leather bedspread, for making a skin bag of bull's hide, or for making plaited thongs his dues of grain from a threshing floor is like [those of] other artisans.*

The quotation above gives further confirmation to the fact that the term *zèga* was used to denote a distinct and socially subordinate community of people under the overlordship of a person. One of the central issues that the study would like to address from the above excerpts is the right of free movement of the *zègas*. As one of the above entries make it is apparent that the law generally forbade a *zèga* to abandon his landlord without the latter's consent. The first entry clearly bears this out having included the stipulation in the law, which demanded the *zèga* to send intermediaries to get the permission of the landlord to depart. A *zèga* departing permanently had to ask for and get granted the permission of the landlord. This is indeed the most oppressive form of lordship. The *zèga* was given full allowance for departing but was also immobilized in some measure. He was required to pay a "separation" fee or "severance" fee. The "separation" fee could be a deterrent or a bar for the freedom to depart. In this case he was required to pay two rock-salts and to leave behind his house and all the important properties therein as indicated above. The household objects listed to be left behind included those we met while discussing the land charter of Moṭa Giyorgis church. However, other than the house, large jar (*gan*), a mill stone, a mortar and pestle, "an axe for domestic use" and two-rock salts are demanded by the lord to be left behind by the *zèga*. Unlike the charter of Wälätä-Israel a bed is not listed among the household objects to be left behind by the *zèga* when departing. These minor differences notwithstanding the "separation" fee appear to have been standardized.[42]

It is possible that the landlord could refuse to give his *zèga* permission to depart. The fine for an unauthorized departure was very heavy. If the weaver *zèga* quitted without the knowledge of the landlord he would be compelled to pay eightfold the normal amount of the separation fee in salt bars in the new abode he moved to. The wife of the tanner *zèga* was subject to menial jobs in the house of the landlord as the second part of the document shows. There might have been a growing tendency to force all the members of the *zèga* class to the obligations of domestics, i.e. to do menial household jobs. Besides all this there was an exaction of many products the tanner *zèga* produced by his craft. The weaver *zèga* received a certain size of land, which was specially set aside for his maintenance. His primary duty was the payment of one rock-salt and a piece of cloth thrice a year on the occasion of the main Christian feasts.[43] Thus the artisan might lease his small plot of land given to him by his lord or could cultivate it on his own. We can also presume that artisans especially those working for big lords and the king had *gult* land given them though we do not have supportive evidence.

The landlord on his part invited his *zèga* together with his wife and children at more or less regular intervals, coinciding with principal Christian feast days. However, the obligation of the landlord, if it can be called so, towards his *zèga* was very light and appears more or less as occasional or voluntary in nature. The weaver *zèga* was not allowed to dress like his landlord, an indication of a strong sense of rank and status on the part of the lord. If this can be accepted as true for the farmer *zèga* too there was a certain stamp of inferiority and social stigma resting on most of the *zèga* class.[44] No provision is made in the customary law of what the *zèga* could do if his lord refused him departure against his will. There is a great deal of similarity in the language between the customary law and the charter of Wälätä-Israel and the administrative handbook of the monastery of Däbrä-Wärq in defining the obligation of the *zèga*, particularly at the time of his departure. To sum up, many of the customs of the Gafat people which Täklè committed into writing, though at a later date, provide a very fine complement to the information about the *zèga* contained in charters and church manuals and confirm the reality of the institution and its characteristics. It is possible to cite the evidence from many similar texts about the *zèga* but no purpose can be served by multiplying examples. Enough has been said about the institution and the evidence cited can hardly be doubted.

On the basis of the above discussion and on the basis of the available information we can figure out the following patterns and characteristics of the institution of zègenät with which we are now familiar. In all of the documents discussed above the word zèga was used primarily to describe or portray near un-free persons maintained essentially as farmhands on the estates of lords. In some of the documents they are depicted as sharecroppers and hence they were also similar to tenants. However, *zègenät bears more of the character of serfdom than tenancy.* In other words it is understandable primarily as a form of serfdom. Undoubtedly it was a class institution anchored on the agrarian base structure. Moreover, the depiction of the zègas in some of the documents shows that there was a certain stigma and stamp of inferiority resting on them. Of course informants claim that the term zèga was a very pejorative one and the most terrible insult that one could hurl against someone.[45] Thus both in the material and social senses the status of zèga class did represent a deeply impoverished and subordinated community of people. Their relationship with the lord had some personal character however weak their tie with the former. It was a special arrangement of economic and social dependence between lords and farmers and artisans, though farmers had higher status than artisans. However, it is apparent that the zègas were bound neither to the lord nor even to the soil. If the zègas wished to go away *or* abandon their land they could do so but they owed to their lords the obligation of the severance fees. When they left to make their fortune elsewhere on their own will there was nothing that forcefully bound them to the lord.

The charters and custom provided the lords with a subtle legal sanction to refuse their zègas permission to leave save upon payment of some commodities and meeting some obligations. In some instances the restraints to free mobility seem to be more severe than others. As a whole the severance fees fixed and the articles which the zègas had to pay and leave behind before they could depart were not perhaps heavy. This points to the fact that the zègas had an absolute discretion either to continue or severe their socio-economic relationships set by custom with their lords. The regional state or lord did not determine or regulate the obligations of the zègas towards their lords except setting some general framework under which the two could work out their socio-economic relationships in charters. Though they were not completely deprived of the right of appeal to courts above those of the zègas' lords, the latter had monopolized the right to determine all civil cases including economic and social relations. Only the criminal cases were preserved for the exclusive hearing of the courts beyond those of the individual lords.

Important issues like the possession or transmission of their properties, if they had any, were to a greater extent left to the discretion of the lord though there are some stipulations in some of the sources considered above safeguarding the rights of the *zègas* with regard to taking some moveable household objects. The *zègas* employed in agricultural production were subject to daily labour services and perhaps lived in a state of harsh exploitation or subjection. The exaction of the best articles of movable properties at the departure of the *zèga* and the obligation to meet any labour demand of the lord could represent some of the demands commonly made on the *zèga* class. Both the artisan and farmer *zègas*, especially the latter, had obligations characteristic of a servile status.[46]

Having figured out the dominant features of *zèga* it remains to ask the question how widespread the *zèga* class was? This is very difficult question to answer since our sources completely fail us on this point. The existence of *zègas* throughout Eastern Gojjam side by side with free peasants is not, however, hard to envisage. The institution of *zègenät* is a carry-over from the seventeenth century. It is attested to by an uninterrupted succession of texts referring explicitly or implicitly to it, particularly in the second half of the nineteenth century.[47]

However, for the early nineteenth century documents describing *zèga* are lacking. But after c.1874 we are overwhelmed by the multiplicity of charters and documents describing *zèga* directly or indirectly. Sometimes there is an explicit mention of the *zèga*. At other times the scribes simply mention the principle of land division and the model upon which the charter was drawn. Like the 18th century, the 19th century witnessed the foundation and the expansion of many big churches accompanied by extensive land redistribution according to the precedent laid down in the preceding century. Even we could not know how much land was held in *rest* around big religious institutions. Because of the great increase in the *rim* land held by persons in the 19th century, the *zègas* might have been as numerous as the *baläsisso* especially in certain districts like Gozamin where the church of Däbrä-Marqos is located. Thus one can picture a rural Eastern Gojjam settled and worked by a vast majority of independent *restäñña*, but side by side with them a not inconsiderable sprinkling of the *zègas*. The number of the *zègas* was perhaps large particularly in areas around churches and monasteries.

Undoubtedly the *zègas* formed an important element in the overall social structure of the rural population, particularly around areas where, as indicated above, the density of churches is thick.[48] In the 18th century there might have been a large number of *zèga* subjects, since we have evidence that *Ras* Häylu I alone had 500 ploughs operated by a gang of *zègas*.[49] They were not a negligible group. Given the existence of charters mentioning directly or indirectly the *zèga* class one would be tempted to make a tentative conclusion that just as all land would have been held as *rest* by the *restäññas* and landlords so every man operating the fields would have been either *zègas* or *restäññas* or both.

The condition leading up to the development of *zègenät* in the interest of the lord can be explained in terms of the almost virtual autonomy of the region of Eastern Gojjam from the imperial centres. From the second half of the 18th century through to the end of the following century Eastern Gojjam escaped monarchical intervention particularly in the relationship between lords and their *zègas*. Täklè traced, as we have seen in the previous chapter, the precedents and movements for the making of *zègenät* to that early northward displacement of the Gafat people. It is very difficult to date with precision and confidence when the body of law recorded by Täklè developed. *Only* a general date can be proposed. Täklè attributed the social and political practice of the Gafat to have been introduced by Gafat clan leaders called Mänbäro and Däbšin. Among the subjects dealt with in the socio-economic and political practices of the Gafat compiled by Täklè includes the regulation of the support that the parishioners had to give to the church, etc. Thus this socio-economic and political practice compiled by Täklè must have been developed only after Christianity had become the religion of the Gafat. Contemporary Portuguese sources speak about the existence of large numbers of pagan Gafats and other pagan peoples in the seventeenth century in Eastern Gojjam.[50] However, it is unlikely that many Gafats were still pagans by the seventeenth century. Tentatively I would suggest earlier than the eighteenth century for the development of the law. And the later practice of *zèga* undoubtedly developed from earlier precedents. Most of the *zèga* of the eighteenth century and afterwards might have been originally *restäññas* subsequently made *zègas*.

To have a complete picture of the socio-economic relationships between lords and the peasantry, the modes of operation of the administration of revenue as well as the sources of revenue and privilege of the former will be attempted below. Moreover, the social structure (created by the land tenure system and the institution of *zègenät*) of the rural population over which the lords had strong socio-economic and political control will be delineated.

2.2 Property, Surplus Appropriation and the Social Structure of the Society.

Most of the church lands as we have seen were owned by the *däbtäras* individually and exclusively. But usually churches and monasteries did not absolutely relinquish the lands, which were occupied by the *däbtäras* on their behalf (churches and monasteries). They (churches and monasteries) retained their right to revoke the land occupied by the *däbtära* or their subjects on the occasion of failure to provide service and to give it to others. Therefore churches and monasteries had ultimate corporate property right over the individual *däbtära* land and formed a class of what I would like to call them tentatively till a better term is found *"corporate landlords"* over the lands under the domain of church administration. We find corporate landlords just as exclusivist as an individual lord could have been with regard to the exercise of their property right. Though most land grant documents followed the model of the Moṭa Giyorgis charter pertaining to the principle of land division between the *däbtära* and *restäñña* there was great variety in the rights and privileges accorded to churches and monasteries vis-à-vis the peasantry. As a concomitant result of the varieties in the privilege accorded to corporate landlords and the people associated with them by charters, we come across a great variety of practices as regards to the form and method of collection of revenue and in the dues and obligations of the independent peasantry in the domain of the church. Charters also shed a great light on the structure of the society that prevailed in the period under study. The income generated from the peasantry under the domain of the corporate landlords was used for the remuneration of individuals performing specialized services for churches and monasteries or in order to defray the expenses incurred for the administration of the land and the people occupying the land under their domain.⁵¹

Other than the difference in peasant obligations towards the elite arising out of the variety in the privilege and right accorded to the latter by charters there were many other factors that contributed for such a difference in the nature and method of assessment of peasant dues. Plowden provides us a far more intimate account of the reasons for the difference in the nature and method of assessment among villages and between districts around the middle of the 19th century. One of the factors leading to the variation in the kind, method and amount of tax assessment, according to Plowden, who was a contemporary observer of such matters, was"…the traditional custom of each village." ⁵² However, it can be concluded that the peasants' obligations were in the form of cash (salt-bars and also Maria Theresa Thaler since the second half of the eighteenth century), payment in kind and labour services.⁵³

In all parts of the region peasants under the control of corporate landlords either tenurially or administratively, in addition to the payment of tribute or rent, were liable to corvée labour. In all the charters dating from the second half of the eighteenth century corvée labour, usually taking the form of labour service on the construction of churches, was uniformly made a charge upon the peasantry under the domain of churches. Peasants were required to build enclosure walls around churchyards, erect buildings and fences for church officials and repair the church in times of need, including providing construction materials for repairing as we have seen in the charter of Wälätä-Isra'el quoted above. However, it is stipulated in this same charter that "[b]oth the town and the surrounding countryside do not owe the obligation to provide stipend and meals to the *aläqa* and the *liqäṭäbäbt*." Moreover, unlike peasants in many other places, those under Moṭa Giyorgis were freed from the "… obligation of building houses and putting up fences [for the *aläqa* and the *liqäṭäbäbt*]."⁵⁴

In the lands controlled by the corporate landlords or institutions either tenurially or administratively the economic relationship between the former and the peasants was invariably based on either payment of a stipulated amount of tribute (or fixed cash) or sharecropping. Charters and manuals show that the payment of rent and tribute were usually fixed at a definite quantity of the produce of the harvest usually in *çhan* though we can not rule out to the existence of some other kinds of arrangement. One of the most important units of measurement of tax in grain that we find in official documents is *çhan*. According to Pankhurst a *çhan* was equal to 280 litres but it varied from place to place.[55] In the manual for the officials of the monastery of Däbrä-Wärq it is stated that the monastery rented out its untilled land under its ownership to tenants who settled on the land based on a sharecropping arrangement. According to this relationship the tenant would receive one-third of the produce and the rest went to the church. Two oxen and a cow would be provided by the monastery to help the tenant get started at the time of his settlement.[56] Whether the tenant was provided with the agricultural implements or not is not clear. Presumably, the tenant himself provided for the seed and all the necessary agricultural implements in addition to his labour. It seems also that weeding and other expenses of cultivation were the responsibility of the tenant. The method by which other churches and monasteries collected rent from tenants working on their land is unknown to us. However, it can be assumed that there were certain generally accepted norms as a whole though there must have been some differences in the amount demanded by monasteries from their tenants and the method of assessment.

The payment of tribute by the peasantry to churches was usually made partly in the currency of the time, the salt-bar and partly in kind. In certain villages, however, only a given quantity of wheat and other agricultural products was collected every year to meet the special needs of the church. Certain villages paid tribute in a certain number of loads of firewood (nine loads of firewood) for the monastery of Däbrä-Wärq and incense to be used by the churches during services. Special attention was given for villages donated for the support of Mass which paid tribute in wheat. In the large percentage of the land charters such villages were administered by the *gäbäz* and villagers were exempted from some onerous labour dues and taxes. For example the charter of Moṭa stipulated that the peasants occupying the land given for the support of Mass were free from hosting guests and other dues.[57]

In some places the levy was in honey, animals, *šäma* (cloth), etc.[58] In the case of one land grant charter (the charter of Yägwära Qwesqwam made out by *Däjjach* Wälta in the 1780s) the scale of the levy is adjusted according to the means and the capacity of the peasants to pay tribute per month and annum. According to this source the levy was fixed at three *ladan* (about three litres in content) of *tèff* per pair of plough oxen, one and half *ladan of tèff* per one plough ox and one *ladan* of *tèff* per digger or those without oxen and cultivate crops by digging with hoe, per annum. According to this same source villagers were required to pay 20 *qunna* of grain per month, one *faga* (container made of gourd) of honey as stipend of the *täqoṭari* or collector of the revenue, two rock-salts as *yädas* (marriage fee), nine rock-salts for *yämeserach* (the announcement of good news).[59] According to Pankhurst a *ladan* measures three to four litres of grain.[60]

Dues were also calculated per area of land under cultivation. In some areas ten rock-salts were levied per *gaša* per annum. Land rights entailed duties. Thus noblemen and women who received land on condition of providing the same services which *däbtäras* were expected to give to churches or monasteries were not exempted from providing service. They were obliged to provide service to the church and if services were not rendered they would either be fined or the land under their occupation would be completely forfeited. In one land grant, it is stipulated that if one defaulted to meet his obligation of church service for a single day he would be fined sixteen rock-salts. Noblemen and women who owned land on behalf of the church of Yägwära Qwesqwam were required to subscribe two rock-salts per *gaša* per annum, which were paid as wages to deacons and priests.[61] All in all the payment of fixed tribute in the form of kind or cash to churches and monasteries by peasants under the administration of churches and monasteries was the norm. Presumably the payment of fixed tribute was in the interest of the peasantry and perhaps motivated them to increase their agricultural production though the historical record fails to let us know the feeling of peasants on this count.

Basically corporate landlords derived their wealth from rent or tribute and also from their *hudad*. Yet it must be added that toll tax, levies on local trade, fees and fines from various sources such as burial, judgment, registration, appointment, etc., were the much sought after sources of revenue. The officials of big churches and monasteries occupied the same position as the secular lords in their relationship with the peasants. They were marked out apart from those under their socio-economic and political domination by their power and status. They were accorded various sorts of socio-economic and political authority to subject and exploit the peasantry. The church officials and people attached to the church, which included noblemen, and women, were given a specially privileged status. The privileges and exemption which the church people of Moṭa Giyorgis and Yäwish Mika'el (whose charter was made out by

Ras Märed, r.1796-1800) were given, can serve as illustrations of the general status this class of men enjoyed vis-à-vis the peasantry.

Besides the document cited in this chapter, Wälätä-Isra'el issued a series of charters in favour of the *däbtäras* for specific privileges and exemption from any obligations and taxes due from their properties. In one of the charters which she issued, for example, she gave the church of Moṭa the right to tax transactions pertaining to the buying or selling of oxen, mules, horses, donkeys and cows which was determined at the rate of one rock-salt from both transacting parties. The *däbtäras* on the other hand were immune from such a payment. Moreover, as the charter already quoted shows, they were freed from the payment of registration fee of their town sites and *rim* land transactions into the central registry. Unlike the peasantry they were also exempt from the obligations of repairing and building the church and putting up fences. They were exempt from the payment of legal fees too. Likewise, the wife of a *däbtära* would not pay market dues.[62]

Much of the church wealth was amassed by church officials specially the *aläqa* and the *liqäṭäbäbt* who held the highest administrative positions. It was a general practice to remunerate church officials both by granting land attached to their office for their direct benefit and deduction of a certain percentage of the revenue from the rent and tribute and taxes collected from the peasantry. The amount of one's share was determined and scaled corresponding to his position and rank in the church administration. In Moṭa, the *aläqa* and the *liqäṭäbäbt* took two-thirds and one-third from the total appointment fee, donation, market levy and judgment fee, respectively. Half of the total tax collected from market levies on such merchandise as onions, cotton, red pepper and *gèšo* (an herb used for preparing *ṭälla* local beer) was deducted for the *aläqa* before it was divided between the lesser officials, in varying quantities, corresponding to their various ranks. From the toll tax collected four rock-salts and two rock-salts were deducted every week for the *aläqa* and the *liqäṭäbäbt*, respectively. The tax collected on grain belonged to the remaining members of the church community. Market levy was not to be collected on other merchandise brought for sale to the market of Moṭa except the above ones. However, this did not apply to other areas. In certain market centres like the town of Däbrä-Wärq, it is stipulated in the manual for its officials that everything brought to the market for sale was taxable. The *aläqa* and the *liqäṭäbäbt* of Moṭa also received appointment fees both from the *çeqa* and from church officials. All but one important church office below the *aläqa* and the *liqäṭäbäbt* were granted with the payment of an appointment fee. Thus office was one of the lucrative sources of revenue. For example the *çheqa-shums* in Moṭa who were brought under the church's administrative hierarchy in the *sisso* land would pay four hundred rock-salts on the occasion of their appointments, all of which went to the *aläqa* and the *liqäṭäbäbt*.[63]

The rights and privileges of the officials of the church of Yäwish Mika'el are essentially similar to those of Moṭa. As regards the socio-economic and legal and administrative rights of the *däbtära* over the *zègas* there was no difference between the charters of the two churches. In other words the privileges and rights of the *däbtäras* were essentially the same in both churches. However, there are certain important differences. The division of the land between the peasants and the peasantry was based on half for the *däbtäras* and half for the *restäññas*. Unlike in Moṭa people in Yäwish and its environs were liable to provide daily for two consecutive weeks to the *aläqa* thirty pieces of *enjjära*, two jars of *ṭälla*, and two dishes of *wäṭ*, and to the *liqäṭäbäbt* fifteen pieces of *enjjära*, a jar of *ṭälla*, and one dish *wäṭ* on the occasion of the appointment of the two officials.[64]

Church officials derived income from sources other than their land. One of such useful sources of income of church officials and a drain on the economy of the peasant was from feasts on the occasion of *täzkar* (commemoration), weddings and major feasts. The importance of feasts or banquets in the economy of the church is very well known. The manner of the distribution of food and drink prepared for feasts has elicited instructions and clauses in virtually all of the land charters with some picturesque detail. Considerable space is spent in the administrative handbook for the monastery of Däbrä-Wärq on instructions regarding the seating arrangements and the manner in which the distribution of food and drink was to be carried out on festive occasions.

Considering the care and the attention given to the distribution of food and drink on the occasion of *täzkar* feasts in the charters and manuals it seems that the death of a person might have been as much a moment of deep sorrow for his kinsmen and friends as the greatest joy for the clergy. *Täzkar* played an important economic role in the economy of many churches. The manual contains instructions with picturesque detail concerning the administration of the revenue from prayer services made for the dead souls extending from the day on which the person died up to many years, according to the capacity of the relatives of the deceased. This in itself can make a remarkable subject of study. Although the church spelled out a different set of religious reasons for the need to observe *täzkar* it was undoubtedly related to social and economic issues. There were hosts of people who received much of their remuneration from *täzkar*, including the abbot. The dead man's properties that were in the category of personal effects had predefined destination. Moreover the skin, choice cuts and certain parts of the animal slaughtered for *täzkar* feasts and other festive occasions belonged to various officials of the church, all precisely defined in the manual. For example it is stipulated in the manual that from the ox and cow slaughtered on festive occasions in the lands under the administration of the church choice cuts or parts like the *däbit* (that part of the slaughtered animal around the gristle and the blade), *qäfät* (?) and *goden* (rib) were reserved for the *gäbäz*, *talaq and tanash* (rump), *melas* (tongue) and *sänbär* (?) were the right of the abbot, etc. The amount and diversity of the rations or menu is scaled according to the rank and status of the church dignitaries.[65] Thus the distribution of food and drink was carried out with almost mathematical precision. Pankhurst has also studied similar practices in the courts of big secular lords. According to Pankhurst favoured cuts were the preserve of persons of distinction. Different parts of the slaughtered animal were distributed to different individuals, as minutely regulated by custom.[66]

I have concentrated on the socio-economic relationships between lords and peasants specifically in lands under the domain of churches. This is because of the bias of sources. However, generally there was more or less similar relationship between lords and peasants in the secular estates too. We see that lords had immense power over the lands they ruled. The role of the local rulers in land matters especially as regards to the authority of allocating and reallocating land to new holders was very strong, and this happened during the last decades of *Zämänä Mäsafent*. There was extensive redistribution of land during this period. Fantahun, who wrote a pioneering work on the history of the region during the *Zämänä Mäsafent*, asserts that there were many lands given to officials and warriors in the form of *gult* in this period as reward for military services. But he writes that lords could not easily disturb the *rest* rights of the peasantry and therefore the right of the *gult* holders did not extend to the land.⁶⁷ However, this is not acceptable in light of the discussions above, based on massive new sources suggesting to the contrary.

In Eastern Gojjam and Damot there were many estates quite separate and distinct from lands held by officials usually called by the picturesque name of "*yäwäyzäro agär*" or "*yäzufan agär.*" The important mark of these lands is that they were absolute private property of and permanently attached to the female descendants of kings like Na'od (r.1494-1508), Lebnä-Dengel (1508-1540) and Susenyos (1607-1632). Beside their special administrative status with respect to the whole land, regional lords in Gojjam had absolute rights over certain lands and districts. For example during the *Zämänä Mäsafent Däjjazmach* Gošu had taken large part of Fitäbädeñň, a district in Damot as his personal estate.⁶⁸ Usually lords such as *Däjjazmach* Birru of Eastern Gojjam called for mobilizations of soldiers and even peasants and female inheritors with the threat of virtual expropriation for failure to responded to the call, for in such cases eviction was justifiable.⁶⁹

Due to the intervention of lords in land matters and the general control they enjoyed over land there was a continuous change in the fortune and status of peasants in their own lifetime. Indeed the agrarian population was in a throes of socio-economic change in the period under study. One important circumstance bringing such conditions was the periodic transfer of large areas of lands belonging to peasants to the non-farming ruling elite that usually accompanied the expansion and endowment of new and old churches and monasteries. Hoben's study demonstrates the flexibility of inheritance practice in the *rest* system of land tenure. His study shows the extent to which the customary law of land was qualified and access to *rest* land was controlled by a myriad of socio-economic and political factors. The *rest* system could offer a lasting hereditary right. However, the land use right could be lost to the ruling elite or to the king and the *balärest* could become a tenant in time. Thus there must have been a continuous change in the amount of land held by individual households, together with their social status within the peasants' own lifetime.⁷⁰

The society was characterized by a very strong and rigid hierarchical principle. Rank and status ethos and symbols were all-pervading and were jealously guarded. The clergy basically shared the same status motifs and we find the hierarchical sentiment most articulate in monastic rules and charters. The administration of big monasteries and churches demanded the establishment of an elaborate administrative hierarchy filled by hosts of officials ranged one above the other. There was a marked difference in the wealth and power between them clearly set down in charters and rules. We find the strong hierarchical sentiment vividly at work on formal occasions. On festive occasions one had a clearly identified seat to take. Every one took his/her respective seat, arrayed very carefully according to rank and status on formal occasions. Evidence contained in the administrative handbook of Däbrä-Wärq shows us that if one deliberately took a seat which is not his, this act would stir up a very deep feeling. It was considered a slight on the honour of the wronged. It is stated that the offender could be fined up to fifteen ounces of gold.[71]

Church officials had many retinues or following, including soldiers. In the monastery of Däbrä-Wärq officials had different number of servants and assistants, each according to his rank and status in the established hierarchy. For example the abbot and the lesser officials of the monastery of Däbrä-Wärq had hereditary servants with distinct names, called *gefu'an* (literally oppressed, exploited) who had obligations similar to serfs. The number of servants assigned to individual officials ranged from one to seventy-two. The manual ordered them to provide a prompt obedience to the officials. The monastery probably paid the servants. The clause inserted in the manual assigning servants to church officials concluded the provision with the sentence "ይህ መሆኑ ሹመት ክብር እንዳያጣ ነው-"which literally means "[t]his is done so that office will not lose its importance."[72]

The land tenure system created many social contours among members of the society. Conventionally the Ethiopian society in the past is regarded as falling into the broad tripartite division of peasantry, noble and clergy based on functional specialization.[73] This holds true for the study area too since it was a component part of Ethiopia. However, there was a great deal of internal differentiation among the three accepted categories and in the society in general. Based on the discussion presented in this chapter we can confidently talk of the existence of big and petty landlords with strong interest in land and labour. Lords, as used in this study were constituted by a range of people with many titles and different status including the social group of the clergy who occupy the same position as the secular lords in their relationship with the peasants.

That there was internal differentiation or stratification within the agrarian population of Eastern Gojjam could hardly be doubted. One obvious indicator of the existence of different strata among the peasantry is the fact that in the charter of Yägwära Qwesqwam the scale of the tribute demanded was adjusted according to the means of the peasant. In the case of this land charter peasants were divided into those who owned a pair of oxen, one ox and none-at all (diggers).[74] This is telling evidence to the fact that the broadly defined social category of peasantry is not fully descriptive of the reality of this stratification and division within the former if we consider the economic standing of the individual peasant. Members of the agrarian population were sharply divided from each other by their economic standing.

In contrast to *zègas* under the strict socio-economic domination of the landlords there were independent peasants cultivating their own land explicitly and interchangeably referred to in the sources as *balagär*, *çhäwa*, *balärest* and *baläsisso*. Moreover, there were, among the rural population, agricultural labourers. The practice of employing agricultural wage labourers and sharecroppers was common in the region.[75] However, these wage earners often referred to as *araš* (farmers) should not be confused with the *zègas* although they had basically the same kind of relations to the means of production. Unlike the *zègas* the *araš* lived besides the homes of their employers, usually under the eaves of the houses,[76] which afforded a more frequent contact between the two. Perhaps the number of the *zègas* was also quite larger than that of the *araš*.

The *zèga* class involves a classification problem of certain difficulty since it does not neatly fit into the character of peasants. Certainly there was much difference in status and rank between the *restäñña* and the *zèga* even when the latter were free from any personal and hereditary bond to the landlords. This difference arose from the different relationships each had with regard to the means of production, the land. The *zègas* and the institution of *zègenät* appear to have been the Ethiopian brand of serfs and serfdom, respectively. As mentioned in this chapter, indeed informants acknowledge that the word *zèga* had pejorative connotation.[77] Both in the material and social senses the *restäññas* had very high status compared to the *zègas* since they had landed property in their own right and which they worked on their own unlike the latter. The *zègas* are depicted as completely landless in the documents considered for this work although we can expect that they had some land given to them from their lords for their maintenance as the citation on the artisan *zègas* shows. However, even that was to the extent of receiving only small parcels of land. Therefore, in practice the *zègas* formed a single class below the socio-economic levels of the peasantry and found throughout Eastern Gojjam. Thus, the rural population of Gojjam can be divided in to two broad categories based on the nature of relation to the means of production namely the independent peasant proprietors and the *zègas* class largely put under the jurisdiction of individual lords on whose land they lived. This rural structure persisted until the end of the nineteenth century, although the number of *zègas* in the second half of the nineteenth century had apparently shot up and reached record heights. This could happen because of the construction of many new churches and the rebuilding of old churches which called for extensive redistribution of land throughout the length and breadth of the region as will be discussed in the next chapter.

Land charters made out in the last quarter of the 19th century continued to employ the category of *zèga* and contain important information about the institution of *zègenät* which closely echo the general practices discussed above in the preceding century, in the days of Wälätä-Isra'el. This is true particularly with regard to the rights of the landlords and the *zègas* and the *restäññas*. Of course we find many of the customs and practices of the preceding century still applying and maintained intact in the last quarter of the 19th century. What all this means is that tenure in *zègenät* is diachronic rather than a synchronic institution occasioned by some invisible causation which soon disappeared. Let us see the extent to which this can be supported by evidence from land charters and documents from the second half of the 19th century. To put it in a rhetorical question, to what extent were the principles and strands of custom contained in the charters of the second half of the nineteenth century copied or carried-over from the days of Wälätä-Isra'el? To what extent did Täklä-Häymanot follow the precedent of his illustrious forebears in formulating charters? The pages that follow are devoted for finding out the answer for these questions.

NOTES

[1] D. Arnauld, *Douze ans dans la Haute Ethiopie (Abyssinie)* Vol.I (Vatican City: Biblioteca Apostolica Vaticana, 1980), p.259, Plowden, 138. Täklä-Iyäsus, "Yä Gojjam Tarik", pp.48 and 51-55.

[2] The biggest land grant in this period was made by Wälätä-Israel and her grand son *Ras* Märed, Daniel, "A Catalogue of Land Tenure Related Microfilm from Gojjam Churches and Monasteries", Wängel. MS. Moṭa Giyorgis, 89. IX, 4-6, *Idem*, Fetha Nägäst, MS. Yäwish Mika'el, 89,XVI, 6-9, *Idem*, Dersanä-Mädehänè-Aläm, MS. Qäranyo Mädehänè-Aläm, 89, VIII, 11-18. Hereafter the charters and land documents microfilmed by Daniel's and deposited in the Institute of Ethiopian Studies would be referred as Daniel followed by the manuscript, place from where it was microfilmed and the catalogue number.

[3] Ibid, Täklä-Iyäsus, "Yä Gojjam Tarik", p.49.

[4] Täklä-Iyäsus, "Yä Gojjam Tarik", pp.48 and 50.

[5] Ibid.

[6] Crummey, *Land and Society in the Christian Kingdom of Ethiopia*, p.183.

[7] The biggest record of land transfer in the study area is found in Moṭa set down in the unbounded and un-inventoried Mäzgäb. This property manuscript contains an immense historical treasure. It contains a total of 500 folios. Though the quires are irregular and the folios are not the same size generally most of them measures 40 X 40cm.The second biggest property manuscript in the study area is the manuscript, called Däqiqä Näbeyat, MS.Märṭulä-Maryam, inventoried by the Ministry of Culture as G1-IV-16.There are 264 folios of which folios 193 to 264 are entirely used for recording property dealings. The researcher has reproduced it.

[8] D. Crummey and Shumet Sishagne "Land Tenure and the Social Accumulation of Wealth in the Eighteenth Century Ethiopia: Evidence from the Qweswqam Land Register", in International Journal of African Historical Studies, vol.24, no.2 (1991), pp.252-253.

[9] Daniel Ayana, Wängèl, MS.Moṭa Giyorgis, 89.IX, 4-6.The number of the *däbtära* established by Wälätä-Isra'el, according to informants, was 350, Informants: Ato Ayänäw Tezazu, interviewed (in Mota) on 20/08/02, and *Ato* Härägä-Wäyen.

[10] Mäzgäb, MS. Moṭa Giyorgis.

[11] Daniel, Gebrä-Häwaryat, MS.Yägwära Qwesqwam, 89,XVI, 23-25, *Idem*, Wanna-Mäzgäb, MS. Däbrä-Eliyas, 89, XVIII, 9-31,Däqiqä-Näbeyat, MS. Märṭulä-Maryam, folio200r, Mäzgäb, MS. Däbrä-Marqos, folio21v.
[12] Gebrä-Häwaryat, MS. Yägwära Qwesqwam, 89, XVI, 23-25.
[13] Ibid.
[14] Ibid.
[15] Ibid.
[16] Däqiqä-Näbeyat, MS.Märṭulä-Maryam, folio200r, Mäzgäb, MS.Däbrä-Marqos, folio21v.
[17] Mäzgäb, MS.Moṭa Giyorgis.
[18] Daniel Gebrä-Häwaryat, MS.Yägwära Qwesqwam, 89, XVI, 23-25
[19] Ibid.
[20] Ibid.
[21] Ibid.
[22] Ibid.
[23] Mäzgäb, MS. Däbrä-Marqos, folios15r and 38v.
[24] Ibid.
[25] Ibid.
[26] Ibid.
[27] Ibid.
[28] Ibid.
[29] Daniel,Tarikä Nägäst Zä-Ityopya, MS.Däbrä-Wärq, 89,II, 11-33,III, 3-18,Girma, pp.36-37.
[30] Daniel, Tarikä Nägäst Zä-Ityopya, MS.Däbrä-Wärq, 89, III, 3-18.
[31] Ibid.
[32] Ibid, 89, II, 11-33.
[33] Ibid, 89, II, 11-33, III, 3-18.
[34] Ibid.
[35] Ibid.
[36] Ibid, Informants, *Mägabi* Säyefä-Selassè Yohännes.
[37] Ibid.
[38] Ibid.
[39] Ibid.
[40] Merid Wolde Aregay, "Society and Technology in Ethiopia, 1500-1855" in Journal of Ethiopian Studies, vol.17 (1984), p.131.
[41] Girma, "Ancient Customary Law of the Gafat", pp.54-56.
[42] Ibid.

⁴³ Ibid.
⁴⁴ Ibid.
⁴⁵ Informants, *Ato* Ayechelè Täräfä, *Mägabi* Säyefä-Selassè.
⁴⁶ Ibid, Girma, "Ancient Customary law of the Gafat", p.54-56.
⁴⁷ Besides the charters mentioned above other charters containing clauses regulating the relationship between *zèga* and *däbtära* include, Daniel, Arba'etu-Wängèl, MS. Bichäna Giyorgis, 89,II, 3-8, *Idem,* Tamrä-Maryam, MS. Gemja-Bèt Kidanä Meherät, 89,I,2-12.
⁴⁸ The biggest church foundation of the period is Däbrä-Marqos, built by King Täklä-Häymanot in the early 1880s.The king granted land to individuals and institutions practically throughout the region. In the church of Däbrä-Marqos alone 212 *däbtära* were established over its lands, Mäzgäb, MS. Däbrä-Marqos, folio24v. They operated their land by settling their subjects as we have seen in the previous chapter.
⁴⁹ Täklä-Iyäsus, "Yä Gojjam Tarik", pp.48 and 50.
⁵⁰ Girma, "Ancient Customary law of the Gafat," p.44-45, Almieda in C.F. Beckingham and G.W.B. Huntingford (eds.) "Almieda on Ethiopia" in Some Records of Ethiopia, 1593-1646 (London: Hakluyt Society, 1954), p. 54.
⁵¹ D. Crummey and Shumet Sishagne, "Land Tenure and the Social Accumulation of Wealth in the Eighteenth Century Ethiopia", pp.252-253.
⁵² Plowden, *Travels in Abyssinia,* p.137.
⁵³ Compare the following charters for example Daniel, Fekarè-Iyasus, MS. Yäwish Mika'el, 89, XVI, 9, *Idem,* Giyorgis Wäldä Amid, MS. Moṭa Giyorgis, VIII.22-24.
⁵⁴ Ibid. All the charters cited above made labor service charge upon the peasantry.
⁵⁵ R.Pankhrust, "A Preliminary History of Ethiopian Measures, Weights and Values" in Journal of Ethiopian Studies vol.7, no.2 (1969), p.137.
⁵⁶ Daniel, Tarikä Nägäst Zä-Ityopya, MS.Däbrä-Wärq, 89, II, 11-33
⁵⁷ See fore example notes No.14, 49 and 54.
⁵⁸ Daniel, Tarikä Nägäst Zä-Ityopya, MS.Däbrä-Wärq, 89, III, 3-**18.**
⁵⁹ _____, Gebrä-Häwaryat, MS. Yägwära Qwesqwam, 89,XVI, 17-19.
⁶⁰ Pankhurst, "A Preliminary History of Ethiopian Measures, Weights and Values", p.131.
⁶¹ Daniel, Gebrä-Häwaryat, MS. Yägwära Qwesqwam, 89, XVI, 17-19.
⁶² _____, Giyorgis Wäldä-Amid, MS. Moṭa Giyorgis,VIII.22-24_____, Fekarè Iyäsus,MS.Yäwish Mika'el,89,XVI,9.

[63] _____, Giyorgis Wäldä Amid, Moṭa Giyorgis, VIII.22-24.
[64] _____, Fekarè-Iyäsus, MS.Yäwish Mika'el, 89, XVI, 9.
[65] _____, Tarikä Nägäst Zä-Ityopya, MS.Däbrä-Wärq, 89.II, 11-33, 89, III, 3-18.
[66] R.Pankhurst, "Hierarchy at the Feast: The Partition of the ox in Traditional Ethiopia" in A.Gromyko and others (eds), *Proceedings of the 9th International Congress of Ethiopian Studies*, vol.3 (Mosco, 1986), pp.173-182
[67] Fantahun, "Gojjam, 1800-1855," p.49.
[68] Ibid, p.25.
[69] Ibid, p.44, D.Arnauld, *Douze ans dans la Haute Ethiopie* Vol.III, p.3.
[70] Hoben, *Land Tenure among the Amhara of Ethiopia*, pp.22-24, Crummey, *Land and Society*, p.11.
[71] Daniel, Tarikä Nägäst Zä-Ityopya, MS.Däbrä-Wärq, 89.II, 11-33, 89,III, 3-18.
[72] Ibid.
[73] Crummey, *Land and Society*, pp.126-129, Hoben, *Land Tenure Among the Amhara of Ethiopia*, p.4.
[74] Daniel, Fekarè-Iyäsus, MS. Yäwish Mika'el, 89, XVI, 9.
[75] Girma, "Ancient Customary law of the Gafat", p.73.
[76] Ibid, p.57
[77] Informants, *Ato* Aychelè, *Märigèta* Libanos, *Ato, Härägä*-Wäyen.

CHAPTER THREE

LAND TENURE AND THE REDISTRIBUTION OF LAND: PEASANTS, *ZÈGAS* AND LORDS AND THE STATE, 1874-1900

3.1 Land Grants During the Reign of Täklä-Häymanot: Lords, Zègas and Peasants in the Last Quarter of the 19th Century.

The last quarter of the 19th century echoed the days of Wälätä-Isra'el and *Ras* Häylu I in respect to land redistribution and the foundation of new churches and expansion of old ones. In fact, one of the most noticeable developments during Täklä-Häymanot's rule, one can observe, was the mass redistribution of land. Like in the preceding century his reign saw the establishment of religious institutions of exceptional size. Donations of land to churches appear to have greatly increased in the last quarter of the nineteenth century, probably more than ever before in the period under study. Much of King Täklä-Häymanot's (r.1874-1880s) energy was expended in the building and expansion of churches and monasteries.[1] Indeed Täklä-Häymanot went beyond what might be imagined by his predecessors in his land grants to religious institutions. The *däbtäras* of the preceding century or their descendants remained in control and ownership of their lands and new confiscations were made during this time. He bestowed so much landed property upon the churches and monasteries by turning over extensive lands from the peasantry to the former to the extent that the grant of his eighteenth century illustrious forbears could not even reach anywhere near the extent of his grants. He managed to give away extensive tracts of land within a generation (1874-1899). Emperor Yohannes IV (r.1874-1889) encouraged Täklä-Häymanot to give away land to churches and monasteries and he himself distributed land to some of them. He suppressed the *Qebat* (one of the religious sects) sympathies in the region.[2] What all this means is that churches and monasteries came to wield much more power and influence in the region in this period than during the preceding century.

Täklä-Häymanot's court was organized on the model followed by the central state. His court was studded much with titled people below that of king.[3] None of Täklä-Häymanot's predecessors in Gojjam had held any title higher than *ras*. His promotion to the status of king had correspondingly increased the prestige of the regional dynasty. He rewarded his followers by giving them land. The king himself owned landed property elsewhere scattered throughout the region consisting of numerous *rims* in small units as we will see below. Though there are hosts of secular small land grants to individuals the most important class of land that we find in our land documents as in the proceeding century was *rim* land.[4] Thus it is clear that the extent of the domain of the church considerably increased corresponding to the increase in power and prestige of the regional dynasty. The construction of new churches and the promotion of old religious establishments to *däber* status were marked by the distribution of *rim* land. Though some districts were annexed in northern Wälläga and new lands were acquired in Mätäkäl in the west, the social and political edifice was sustained by the resources drawn from internal sources. In other words this land redistributed to the church was primarily, as stated everywhere in this study, derived from the *restäñña*, not from conquered lands.[5] It is difficult to consider all the important and big land redistributions during this period. Thus I have set limitations to the material collected for the study. Only selected and representative charters with direct relevance for the theme of this study will be considered.

Wälätä-Isra'el's charter offered a direct precedent for many similar grants in the region particularly with regard to the principle of land division between the peasants and the landlords and other things. That this happened almost everywhere in the region is easy to show and is attested by many charters. Moreover, the charter seems to have provided the basic features around which the institution of *zègenät* and the rights and obligation of the *däbtära* and the *balärest* in the period on which this section of my study is focused would progressively take shape. Though there are some important exceptions, as a whole Täklä-Häymanot formulated charters in accordance with the practices of the time of Wälätä-Isra'el and *Ras* Häylu I.

We begin then with the first land grant document of Täklä-Häymanot. Probably the earliest important land grants by the king were given to the churches of Bichäna Giyorgis and Mängesto Kidanä-Meherät. Since the contents of the two charters are on the whole identical, discussion will be limited to the charter of Bichäna Giyorgis.[6] As I have just noted above Wälätä-Israel's charter served as a model and it was imitated in almost all charters. However the grants to Bichäna Giyorgis and Mängesto Kidanä-Meherät form exceptions to this. These charters represented one of the few anomalies with regard to the principle of land division between landlords and the peasantry since the division of the land between the two was not drawn on the model of the charter of Moṭa. The division of the land between the *restäññas* and the *däbtäras* was carried out on the principle of half for the *restäñña* and half for the latter. As in the earlier period the term *däbtära* in this period was used to refer to clerical and secular social elites who owned land from the church. Much of the lands given to the church appear to have belonged to king Täklä-Häymanot and his wife Laqäch Gäbrä-Mädhen, and members of the aristocratic class. Of the people categorized by the scribe as noble the names of Laqäch and her husband are entered against many villages and plots of land. The woman held chiefly *rim* lands. It is interesting to note here the fact that half of the lands of the *restäñña* in some of the villages given away for the church are wholly recorded as belonging to the secular nobility, both men and women, at the time of land division between the *däbtäras* and the *restäññas*. There are also other village lands recorded as *rim* land held almost entirely by the nobility with some sprinkling of the religious class.[7]

The echo of Wälätä-Isra'el's charter is contained in this document with regard to the judicial and administrative powers of the *däbtäras* over their *zègas*. Although the *däbtäras* might have used hired labor to operate their lands we know very well that they chiefly employed *zègas* for cultivating their lands. The extent of the jurisdiction of *rim* owners over their land and the *zègas* to the exclusion of the government officials is clearly known. The methodology adopted in this chapter as in the preceding chapter is to proceed in the accounts and explanation of the dynamics of the socio-economic relationships between lords and peasants and *zègas* by citing, when necessary, selected and pertinent sections from charters. Thus it is good to quote selected passages from the charter for the sake of better exposition and also in order to clear up any or a little of possible obscurity about *zèga* and the right of the *restäñña* and landlords.[8]

ቲበብቶና በእነቆር የተሰሩ መክንንት የቋሚ አየፍም እንቁት ይሁን፡፡በአዲስ አምባ የተሰሩ መክንንት ለአቃቢ ይሁን፤፤ በቀፈት የተሰሩ መክንንት ለሰአታት ቋሚ ይሁን፡፡በየሰምቢ የተሰሩ መክንንት

የባለዘይነግስ ቁሚ ይሁን፡፡በደንሳ የተሰሩ 9 በደልጎልማ ከተሰሩ የ3 መክንንት ያንጻፊኤ የጫኝ አየአጻዊ ሆህት ይሁን፡፡በደልጎልማ ከተሰሩ የ2 ሀይማኖት አበውኡ የ4 የጥራን ጠባቂ አየ8 መሪጌታ ይሁን፡፡ይሀንንም ሲሰሩ ንጉስ ተክለሃይማኖት እኩል ምድር የባለርስት እኩል ምድር ለደብተራ ይሁን ብለዋል፡፡ባለርስቱ እኩል መሬት ይዞ ያገሩን ታቦት ያጥባ፡፡አለቃ በሾመው ቂቃ ይዳኝ፡፡በ3 በዓል 33ጨው ለየደብሩ ይስጥ፡፡ደብተራው በእኩል ምድሩ ያሰፈረውን ዜጋ ይዳኝ፡፡ገበዝ የመስዋቱን ሀገር ይዳኝ፡፡የዚህ ሁሉ ይግባኙ ለመላከብርሃኑ ይሁን፡፡የዚህ የደም የይናፋ የሌባ ዳኝነት ለመላከብርሁኑ ይሁን፡፡በስራም ጊዜ የመስዋቱ ሀገር ቤተልሄም አየአለቃ ሀገር አምስትያ ያለቃቤትአ ደብተራው የተሰራበት ሀገር ደጀሰለም ይስራ፡፡ቤተክርስትያን አእቃቤትአ ቅጽር ሁሉም 1ሆኖ ይስራ ብለዋል፡፡ከበቸና ከገብያው 2ጨው ለቅዱስ ጊወርጊስ የቀረው ከገብያው የተገኘው ሁሉ 2እጁ ለባለ አልጋ ሲሶው ለመላከብርሃኑ ይሁን ብለዋል፡፡

The [revenue contributed by the] mäkwanent (lit. nobility) established in Beto and Enäqor should be the salary of the qwami (choir-men in duty) and for buying the fum-enqèt (charcoal).The revenue contributed by the mäkwanent established in Addis Amba shall be for the salary of the aqabi (grinder and water drawer).The revenue contributed by the mäkwanent established in Yäqäfät shall be for the salary of [those responsible to the prayer of] the Hours. The revenue contributed by the mäkwanent established in Yäsämbi shall be for the salary of those [who are responsible for composing the qenè], zäyenäges. The revenue contributed by the nine [mäkwanent] established in Dänsa and the revenue contributed by the three mäkwanent established in Dälgolema shall be for the salary of porters, antsafi (the one who arranges the interior of the church before mass), and atsawi-hohet (door keeper).The *revenue collected from those established over Dälgolema should be for the salary of the two readers of Häymanotä Abäw (Book of Faith of Fathers), four ṭeran-ṭäbaqi (?) and eight märigèta (instructors).*

While establishing this king Täklä-Häymanot said half of the land shall be for the balärest and half of the land for the däbtära. The balärest holding half of the land have to support the tabot of their respective parishes. They shall be judged by the çheqa appointed by the aläqa. On three holidays they have to pay three rock-salts for the various däber. The däbtäras shall judge the zègas settled over the half of the land. The gäbäz shall judge the land given for the support of Mass. The mälakäberhän shall constitute the court of appeal for all these. Judgment over cases of homicide, theft and adultery of this shall be for the mälakäberhan. In times of work the [peasants occupying the] land of the mäsewat (Eucharist) shall build the bethlehem (the building where the material for the Eucharist are prepared and where the utensils for it are kept) the one-fifth of the aläqa country shall build the house for the aläqa, and the land in which the däbtära are established in shall build däjäsälam (lit. gate of peace or main gate of the church). He (Täklä-Häymanot) said all should jointly build the church, the treasury house, and the enclosure walls. He said, of the total of the tax from the market of Bichäna two-rock salts would be for Qedus Giyorgis and after this deduction the remaining two-thirds would be for the king and one-third for the mälakäberhan.

Two points are for my purpose of special interest in this charter. The scribe referred to those who received half of the land of the *restäñña* from the church in collectivity and interchangeably as nobility or *däbtäras*. They were given half of the former lands of the *restäñña* over which they settled their subjects or their *zègas*. The following observation can be made from the quotation above. The first point that stands out explicitly from the above excerpt is the distinct nature of the right of the *däbtäras* and the *restäññas*. They were accorded right over separate pieces of land. They had no tributary relationship since their right extended over separate lands. Half of the land of the *restäññas* was transferred to the nobility and members of the religious class and the right of cultivation of the *restäññas* in their former half of the land is completely ruled out or excluded. They retained only half of their ancestral land. The nobility who were given half of the former lands of the *restäññas* settled their subjects or their *zègas* over it. The nobility had administrative and legal rights only over the *zègas* settled over their land. Unlike the *zègas*, the *restäññas* enjoyed complete freedom from the judicial and administrative authority of the lords to which the former were subjected. The peasants were given autonomy in their internal affairs. The *çheqa* was made responsible for the local affairs of the peasants. They would be judged by the *çheqa* though they did not have the right to elect or choose him as the church authorities controlled his appointment. The *däbtäras* were allowed to sit in judgment only over their *zègas*. On the whole the *restäññas* had a high degree of freedom in local self-rule and were free from any interference by lords on the half of their land.[9]

The second point that stands out in the charter is that the *zèga* class had not improved in their status as in the previous period. Features characteristic of the preceding century can still be discerned and found intact, though this charter is not drawn out on the model of Wälätä-Isra'el with regard to the division of the land between the *däbtära* and the *restäñña*. The basic rights and obligations of the *restäññas* and the *däbtäras* just referred to and to be discussed below had been a general practice a century earlier. In so far as the local administration and the administration of justice are concerned there was no difference from the earlier period. One of the strands of custom inherited from the preceding century is, therefore, the right of full administrative and judicial powers by the grantee in his/her *rim* land and over the people working it, the *zègas*. The document to some extent regulates the legal relationship between the *zèga* and the *däbtära*. This is the subject, which is also often given sufficient attention in other charters dealing with the relationship between the *zèga* and the lord. One area of striking consistency between the preceding century and the last quarter of the 19th century is the fact that the *zèga* ought not to have any other judge in civil cases than their individual lords and the immunity from interference by church or government officials in the socio-economic relationship between them was maintained intact. The charter gave the *däbtäras* virtually unlimited powers over their land and their *zègas*. However, another element of continuity from the earlier period is that though the individual *däbtära*s had acquired judicial authority the possibilities of recourse to higher courts were not completely ruled out. To rephrase it, crimes remained within the normal jurisdiction of the *aläqa* of the church as in the preceding century[10] though the extent to which the law afforded protection for the *zègas* against mistreatment by their lords is very hard to know. All this evokes a view that the *däbtära*s' judicial and administrative powers over the *zèga*s who lived on their lands were conventionalized. The *zèga* lived in his own dwelling and subsisted on the produce of his own labor though we can presume that the *zèga* class did not have any right of ownership over the land.

Another area of continuity or carry-over in practice or tradition from the earlier century, it seems, is that custom still gave the lords absolute discretion in determining the socio-economic relationships between the *zèga* and the *däbtära*. Although the scribe does record the judicial and administrative rights of the *däbtära* over the *zèga* and the area of competence of the individual landlords and church officials with regard to the administration of justice he is silent on the right of the latter to depart and the basis of economic agreement between them. The economic contract between the *zèga* and the lord was perhaps often merely a verbal one for which reason there is no record about the kind of economic arrangement in between the *zèga* and the *däbtära*. The only record the scribes were interested to keep are lists of villages and lands granted to the church, the tax and the tribute demanded from peasants and the names of the *däbtära* to whom specific fields of land were assigned, including their obligations.[11] However, it is not hard to envisage that the right of jurisdiction of the *däbtära* helped to concentrate all kinds of socio-economic power in their hands over the *zèga* cultivating their lands. It is important to note that though custom or tradition governed the socio-economic relationship between the *däbtära* and the *zèga* the former could still have an absolute discretion in the exploitation of their lands. The mere fact that the *däbtära* were given extensive proprietary right over their *rim* land means that they could do pretty much as they wanted or pleased with its exploitation and management, including planting anything that they saw it fit. In other words the *rim* lands of the *däbtära* would be run in the manner that the owner deemed best and the *zèga* would be forced to plant and tend and harvest a crop of the choice of his lord. *Rim* land was in effect an embryonic manorial system. Unlike the charter of Wälätä-Isra'el, which placed some limitations on the right of the *zèga* to leave the landlord, there is no such provision in the charter. The silence of the scribe on this subject too may be because of the general acceptance of the right of free mobility for the *zèga* which rendered its special mention in the charter un-necessary. Therefore, if the *zèga* was unhappy with his lord or desired to depart on other account, he had a right to move away. However, the reasons of this anomaly (the silence of the scribe on the right of mobility of the *zèga*) can not be established absolutely.

I may now pass on to considering the characteristic features of the obligations and the rights of the nobility holding *rim* land. The *däbtäras* enjoyed the largest portion of the revenue from their *rim* land while paying the wages of some priests and deacons for the purpose of which *rim* land had nominally been granted. Officials of different rank and status who received *rim* lands are listed. Their rank and status can be identified from the title they bear. The charter is indeed studded with officials of all kinds and almost virtually no person whose name is entered in the charter exists who does not bear a secular or religious title of which the most important include *lejj, bäjerond, azzaž, blatta, grazmach, qäññazmach, balambaras, fitawrari, däjjach, ras, negus, wäyzäro* and *abun*. Of the nobility two are the sons of Täklä-Häymanot, *Däjjazmach* Bäläw and *Ras* Bäzabeh. Three important females appear in the list, one of which is the wife of king Täklä-Häymanot. The remaining two are relatives of the king. The bishop Luqas is also listed as one among the nobility.[12]

It would appear that the obligations of the nobility were not commensurate with the privileges and the power they enjoyed. The immunities of the *rim* holders, the nature of their authority over their subjects and the services and dues attached to their estates are very clearly put in the charter. The document makes it clear that the grant to the *balärim* was in land and in return for the money which they contributed towards the pay of certain individuals in the church. This differs from the administrative and military *gults* in that the holder was under no obligation to serve the church in person but that it was sufficient to contribute money or other payments in kind towards meeting his/her obligation. For example five nobles, who included Laqäch, to whom lands granted in the parish of Enäqor, were made responsible for the support of the *qwami* whose duties are not specified and contributed money for the purchase of charcoal. Five nobles settled over the parish of Addis Amba such as *Emäytè Wäyzäro* Laqäch, *Azaž* Gäbru, *Däjjach* Wärqenäh, *Blatta* Kinfè, and *Bäjerond* Sahlu were made jointly responsible for the support of water drawers and grinders. Those responsible for the prayers of the Hours, readers of the book known as *Faith of Fathers*, etc. were paid by the nobility who were given lands in the parishes of Dänsa, Yäqäfät, Dälgolema and Yäsämbi.[13]

Thus the right to cultivate and use the produce from *rim* lands by the grantees, including noblemen and women, was contingent upon their payment of the salary for the church's personnel. This is a fine testament to the central argument in my thesis that the theory that the actual cultivation of the land given for the support of the church was vested in the *restäñña*, together with the assertion that land was in the effective occupation of the peasantry, would appear unrealistic since much of the needs of the church was met by the grantees who cultivated the land through their *zèga* and paid the salary of church personnel. Thus *rim* land and the need for the support of the church by the nobility seem to have given validity or justification and cover to the expropriation of the *restäñña*. It would appear that in practice the *däbtära* enjoyed an unqualified right over *rim* land. The peasantry had a complete acceptance or recognition of such a right of the elite. The charter does no even made the labor service of building church or repairing it a charge upon the *däbtäras* together with the *restäññas*. Thus the church authorities could not make any demands upon the *rim* holders unless there was an express provision in the charter. The *rim* land holders were granted exemptions from many of the dues and levies demanded from the peasantry, like levies for the maintenance of church officials.[14] A *rim* holder could appoint someone as his/her representative and exercise his/her judicial and administrative powers over the land and the people working it through him. He could preside over the court, which tried the *zègas* who were largely committed to their care. The *rim* land granted to the *däbtäras* appears permanent and a gift in perpetuity.

As I have already noted in the paragraphs above the holdings of the *restäññas* and the *däbtäras* were not interdependent for which reason the judge of the independent *restäññas* who were made to surrender part of their land as *rim* was usually the *çheqa*. Generally the peasant had the right to choose the *çheqa*, though his appointment needed the approval of the church authorities. But in some areas like in this charter such a right for the peasants was curtailed and there is a possibility for a far more direct intervention by church officials in local affairs of the peasants than in other areas where the right of peasants to elect their *çheqa* was respected. The charter states that the *çheqa* would be appointed by the *aläqa* (the *mälakäberhän*) of the church from among the inhabitants of the villages.[15] The fact that the *mälakäberhän* was given power to appoint the *çheqa* for the peasants under the church means he could appoint a person who would not take side with peasants vis-à-vis the officials or would not defend the right and interest of the former. What all this means is that he could not assume an independent position against the officials in guarding the interest of the *restäñña* since he did not owe his position to the latter.

The duties of the *çheqa* were as follows. The *çheqa* appointed directly by the *mälakäberhän* was to decide in cases of dispute among the *restäñña*. The *çheqa* could decide and try all civil and minor criminal cases in the villages regarded as within his competence. Exceptional cases on the other hand were brought before the court of the *mälakäberhän*. He was responsible for the general order of the village and reported cases beyond his capacity such as adultery, theft and homicide or serious disputes and disorders among the villagers.[16] He supervised and organized peasants for the repairing of the church and enclosure walls. The *restäññas* who were left holding half of their land were ordered to support their respective parish under the overall administration of the church of Bichäna Giyorgis. That the church of Bichäna Giyorgis had satellite rural churches can be easily inferred from the stipulation that "The *balärest* holding half of the land have to support the *tabot* of their respective parish." They were required by the charter quoted above to present three rock-salts on the three holidays to their respective parish churches.[17] How the *çheqa* was remunerated to defray his expenses and for his service is not stated by the charter. Probably he received some payment in kind or in salt-bars, the currency of the time, from the peasants holding their half land and undoubtedly he also would take a share of some income gained from the administration of justice. Probably he could demand labor service from the local peasants under his administration.

Some other points remain to be considered in the charter. Various regulations existed in the dealings with the peasantry under the *gäbäz*, the *aläqa*, and those holding half of their ancestral lands including their dealings with the building of churches and other matters. We will come back to some of the points in other charters which are identical in their content though some important differences exist with regard to the right of the *aläqa*, the *gäbäz* and the peasants under their administration.

Täklä-Häymanot continued to endow many churches and put all his energy into the building of Däbrä-Marqos church and the expansion of others. According to Täklè a total of 320 *däbtäras* were established concurrent with the construction of the church.[18] Another 260 *däbtäras* were also established over the land of Gemja-Bèt Kidanä-Meherät, at Däbrä-Marqos, at about the same time.[19] Moreover, the king lavishly endowed Abema Maryam church at the town of Däbrä-Marqos and a considerable number of people were settled over the lands given to the church.[20] There are several other land grants by Täklä-Häymanot to churches and monasteries and to individuals. Among the collection of the manuscript sources from this period, the *gult* register known as Mäzgäb, deposited at Däbrä-Marqos church, is a unique manuscript. It contains many documents of primary importance. The charters were entered in the 1880s and 1890s. The MS. has sixty-five folios. All but the first four folios and folios 63-65 are covered with *gult* records, sanctions, and other important property and historical notes. The bulk of the folios are used for recording the lands of Däbrä-Marqos church together with the names of the *däbtära* and a record of residential and agricultural land distribution and measurements. In addition to the *gult* grant to Däbrä-Marqos church the MS. contains copies of *gult* grants to many churches and monasteries by Täklä-Häymanot. Some of the *gult* documents contained in the MS. appear to have been added to it after its compilation. All in all the MS. forms an important source for the period. I must say that I have been singularly fortunate in having successful access to and being able to reproduce this MS.

Täklä-Häymanot had already begun giving out *rim* lands on a large scale immediately before the construction of the church of Däbrä-Marqos. The first of such mass distribution of land made by Täklä-Häymanot was the grant to the church of Gemja-Bèt Kidanä Meherät at Däbrä-Marqos. The *gult* grant to Gemja-Bèt is recorded in the MS. called Tamrä-Maryam belonging to the same church. It lists 260 *däbtäras* by name together with the specific lands allotted to them. The names of most of the prominent persons whom we met in the charter of Bichäna Giyorgis are also listed in this charter. Residential sites were also allotted together with the *rim* land to the *däbtäras*. The *däbtäras* were required to build houses in their residential plots so as to either live there themselves or settle their own people.[21]

Crummey and Daniel have investigated this charter. Though Crummey more than anybody else has done extensive work on land tenure and is a much better judge on such matters he presented a much different picture of the reality in his recent monumental work, *Land and Society*. Crummey argues that the *däbtäras'* right over the two-thirds of the land did not extend to the soil. The *restäññas* continued to enjoy the occupation and cultivation of the land but were liable to pay tribute to the church on the two-thirds of the land. He writes that he interviewed the clergy of the church recently which confirmed the tributary arrangement between the *däbtäras* and the cultivators at the time of the grant, "The Gemjabét clergy, when Daniel Ayana and I interviewed them in February of 1989, claimed both that this gave them the right to exact two-thirds of the produce of the cultivators in tribute and that, in fact, their tributary arrangements with the cultivators were by 'negotiation'."[22] This ambiguity could be cleared up quite easily. Though we can not assume that written documents do always describe action of prescribed norms a careful analysis of the charter allows us to draw a firm conclusion about the right involved in connection with the *rim* land given for the *däbtäras* contrary to Crummey's generalization in *Land and Society*. Indeed the nature and limits of the rights and obligations of the *däbtära* and the *restäñña* does not demand a very rigorous effort of understanding since they are clearly put in relatively unequivocal terms. It is usual for a stipulation to be included in charters that the *däbtäras* had the right to judge the *zègas* they had settled over both their *rim* land and their residential plots. In the charter of Bichäna there was no fresh redistribution of residential sites since the town was an old foundation. Hence it refers only to the *zègas* whom the *däbtäras* settled over their *rim* land. But in Gemja-Bèt there was the distribution of residential sites together with *rim* land over which the *däbtära* settled their subjects. Sufficient attention has been paid by the charter under consideration to the exact nature of rights of the *däbtära* and the *restäñña*. The charter obliquely mentions the *zègas* by adding the usual stipulation to protect the interest of the *däbtära's* judicial right to judge his/her subjects settled over his respective *rim* land and town plots.[23]

The important phrases in the charters are usually those which state that the division of the land between the *däbtäras* and the *restäññas* was on the basis of one-third for the *restäññas* and two-thirds for the *däbtäras* which applied to the soil and the usual sentence that the *däbtäras* are the judges of those settled over their *rim* land and *bota*. Crummey takes this to mean that the right was only to the tribute, not over the land itself. The important section presented in the charter, which contains the key sentences on the nature of the specific judicial, and property right reads as follows: "የነውር ኡ የደም ኡ የይናፉ ኡ የሌባ ዳኝነት አለቃ ሊቀጠበብት ሊዳኝ ነው፡፡በደብተራ ቦታና ሪም የሰፈረ በሌላ ነገር ቢጣላ ደብተራው ሊዳኝ ነው፡ ፡"- which literally means "[t]he judges in cases involving homicide, theft, scandal and adultery are the *aläqa* and the *liqäṭäbäbt*. If those settled over the *däbtäras' rim* and *bota* quarrel [against each other] over other matters than [homicide, theft, scandal, and adultery] the judges are the *däbtäras*."[24] This can hardly be confused as a reference to independent peasants since they often appear explicitly in official documents and charters under either of the following two names, *balagär* or *restäñña*. No charter in the study area shows that the *restäññas* were settled over the *bota* and the *rim* land of the *däbtäras*.

Moreover, there is no mention of dues and services, which the *restäññas* are required to provide or pay for the two-thirds of the land. Only the dues and obligation of the one-third of the land of the *restäññas* is stated. Instead the *däbtäras* were made liable to pay the salary of the church personnel specifically for holding two-thirds of the land. This provides strong evidence in support of the argument that ownership of the soil was vested in the *däbtära* alone over the two-thirds of the land. The way in which the charter of Däbrä-Marqos is phrased with regard to the judicial power of the *däbtäras* over the *zègas* settled over their *rim* land and *bota* and the phraseology of the charter of Gemja-Bèt Kidanä Meherät are almost identical, although the latter does not explicitly mention the *zègas*.[25] Although the sentence "those settled over the *bota* and the *rim* land" is not explicit or loosely phrased the section lends support to the central point in my argument that the phrase is an oblique reference to the *zègas* but by no means a reference to the *restäññas*.

As in the case of the charter of Bichäna Giyorgis the lay *rim* holders were simply obliged to contribute money for the *rim* land they owned, for inevitably the right to hold *rim* land was contingent upon the obligation to pay money in lieu of doing service and if such a service was not done the land would be forfeited. The land of the *baläsisso* or *restäñña* carried with it certain immunities. Exemption from the payment of tribute was granted to peasants holding one-third of their former lands in view of the fact that they had surrendered two-thirds of their former lands to the *däbtära*. However, the *baläsisso* could not escape the obligations of paying three sheep during the three principal feast days. In case the peasants had no sheep to give or in order to avoid disagreements over the size of the sheep a conventional price was fixed at the rates of three *amolès* per sheep. Besides, the presents of sheep during the three feast days the *baläsisso* were also expected to build the house of the *aläqa*. They were also required to contribute labor service in building and repairing the church and its walls.[26]

The three individuals in the church who greatly benefited from the various incomes of the church were especially those who held the offices of *gäbäz*, *aläqa* and *liqäṭäbäbt*. The *gäbäz* was the administrator and the judge of the *mäsewat* land. The *restäññas* retained the right of cultivation and paid a certain amount of the produce of their land in wheat and also their dues partly in cash. In other words the land would not be divided between the *däbtäras* and the *restäññas*. Peasants contributed the expenses in connection with the Eucharist, the candle and the incense needed for all the services. The *aläqa* and the *liqäṭäbäbt* were not allowed to interfere in the lands given for the maintenance of the *gäbäz*. Only the *gäbäz* and the *çheqa* under him were responsible for the local affairs of such lands. The offices of *gebezzena* and *çheqenät* appear to have been hereditary and concentrated in the hands of a few families, which could pass from generation to generation. The office of *gebezzena* was given to the descendants of a certain ancient family called Asbä-Dengel. The office of the *çheqa* was also made the preserve of certain families.[27]

By vesting the offices of *gebezzena* and *çheqenät* in themselves or their families the original grantees were able to benefit from the major portion of the revenue of the church from such lands. The *gäbäz* as a hereditary office could not be revoked easily. Since the *mäsewat* land was granted in perpetuity the office could pass from generation to generation unless the regional ruler reallocated the land for other purposes. In the great majority of cases the *gäbäz* and the *çheqa* under him were considered the natural judges and the local administrators of the villages in the *mäsewat* land and over the peasants occupying and cultivating the *mäsewat* land of the church. Criminal justice was placed outside the jurisdiction of the *gäbäz's* court over matters connected with the *restäññas*. There is also a provision for referring to the *gäbäz* the decision of all disputes between the peasants under the officials who were entrusted with the administration of villages paying dues in wood.[28] This was of considerable importance to the *gäbäz*. Tribute on these lands was fixed in the form of a certain amount of wheat and cash. The right to sit in judgment over the peasantry appears to have been a legitimate source of revenue. The *çheqa* had a right to the exercise of justice and a share of the income there-from, the judgment fee. The *gäbäz* was to receive from the peasants presents of sheep on feast days and collect tax according to the assessments fixed by the charter. The *çheqa* was responsible for its collection. The present was given usually during the three main feast days of the year and the due in wheat was probably demanded by the *gäbäz* at harvest time. The *çheqa* under the *gäbäz* would pay an appointment fee to the latter.[29]

Cases that came up for decisions between the *restäññas* outside of the competence of the *gäbäz* were to be referred to the court next above him presided by the *aläqa* and the *liqäṭäbäbt*. The *aläqa* and the *liqäṭäbäbt* of the church were given a privileged position. Often one-fifth of the total villages assigned to the *däbtäras* would be deducted and granted to both officials jointly. For example if the lands of ten villages were given for the *däbtäras* the two officials would get two villages. These villages were put directly under the administrative and judicial control of the two officials. These villages were allocated as remuneration for the offices of the *aläqa* and the *liqäṭäbäbt*.[30] The nature of the obligations of the peasants towards the two officials varied from place to place, as we will see below. Market levy was a source of considerable income. The peasants going to the market of Gemja-Bèt paid market fees for buying and selling produce or other articles of trade and when they appeared for litigation in the courts of the two officials. The revenue from the market levy at Gemja-Bèt was divided between the church and the regional lord. One-third of it went to the church and the rest for the regional lord. The portion that went to the church after the deduction of the share of the regional lord was to be further divided equally between the two officials and the church. The taxes from transactions in pepper, onions and all other market goods were to be divided between the regional government and the church on the basis of two-thirds for the regional lord and one-third for the latter. The two officials received half of the remaining one-third of the revenue from the market levy of Gemja-Bèt going due to the church. The judgment fee from the market was for the *aläqa* and the *liqäṭäbäbt*.[31]

Every office holder paid *mäšwamya* (appointment fee) graded according to the importance of the office and income therefrom. The *gäbäz* paid thirty rock-salts or *amolès*. The chief of the tanners, who was appointed by the two officials, was required to pay an appointment fee corresponding to his means. The tax on market was collected both in *çhäw* (salt-bar) and in kind. The collectors of the market tax in *çhäw* and kind would receive from both the two church officials and the regional government the amount of pepper and cotton that could be taxed from a taxpayer. The collector of market fees called the *blatèn-gèta*, was appointed by the church officials and had to pay an appointment fee. The office of collector was hereditary. The right to be appointed collector was hereditary, vested in the descendants of Asbä-Dengel, whom we have met above. The two officials, the *aläqa* and the *liqäṭäbäbt*, carried with them for the most part the rights of seigniorial authority. There was no court of appeal beyond them. They were the ultimate and supreme appeal judges not only over the *aläqa amsteya agär* (one-fifth of the land deducted from the village lands allotted to the *däbtäras*) under their private judicial and administrative control but also over all the lands of the church of Gemja-Bèt. They judged both civil and criminal cases and disputes within the one-fifth of the land put under their direct administration as well as certain other serious criminal offences which lay outside the capacity of the courts of the individual *däbtäras* and the *gäbäz*.[32]

The placements of one-fifth of the villages under the administration of the two officials carried with it permanent rights which made them immune from any kind of interference by the regional lord or even the emperor. The state could not revoke the assignments. The *aläqa amsteya agär* was attached in perpetuity to the office. In certain charters the land assigned to the two officials jointly was divided between the peasantry in whose land the officials would settle their people and assume direct responsibility of cultivation on the basis of land division in the charter. This is true for the charter under consideration. The village lands assigned for the two officials were divided according to the principle of one-third for the *restäñña* and two-thirds for the two officials. The peasants holding the *sisso* land after the deduction of two-thirds of the land carried certain immunities and exemptions from the payment of any form of taxes except very light labor service and gifts of sheep for the two officials during the three feast days. The charter required the *baläsisso* to build a house for the *aläqa* at Däbrä-Marqos but not in any other town. However, in some charters the peasants exchanged the deduction of two-thirds of the land for the obligation of paying tax, the payment of presents and the monthly wages of the two officials. This will be discussed below when considering the charter of Däbrä-Marqos church. The wages, stipends, and expenses of the two principal officials were not to be deducted from the revenue of the church since the revenue of the church was clearly separated from that of these officials. All the revenue from the one-fifth of the land went to the two officials.[33] Unlike the *gäbäz* and the *çheqa* they did not derive their influence from the hereditary possession of the office but from the overall position they held in the hierarchy of church officials and the administration of the land attached to their office. The criteria of holding such offices were not based on descent from certain ancient families. However, the *liqäṭäbäbt* was required to be a *rim* holder.[34] Probably they were also appointed because of their learning. They were allowed to enjoy temporary administrative and judiciary rights as well as the right to collect all of the churches taxes and tributes for their own benefit.

I now pass onto considering the land grants of Däbrä-Marqos which forms the most important church to have been established in the period following the shift in the political centre of the region into the area from Bichäna. The land granted to the church and the peasantry working over it had different forms of obligations and rights. The nature and the variety of the obligations that the peasants had to pay varied widely depending on the purpose for which the lands of the peasants was assigned by the charter and whether the land was divided between the *restäñña* and the *däbtära*. Generally peasants whose land was transferred on the basis of one-third and two-thirds paid only very light labor dues and presents of sheep on the three annual holidays whereas peasants who retained all their ancestral lands had to pay tribute, labor dues and monthly wages to the officials. The *baläsisso* and peasants under the direct administration of the *aläqa* and the *liqäṭäbäb*t were made responsible for repairing the enclosure walls and the wages of carpenters who fixed the gates, windows, etc. of the church.[35] This correspondence was literally to be found in every charter in the period and region under study. Charters including the one under consideration listed and defined three different forms of land constituted for different purposes which will be discussed below.

Some of the lands given to Däbrä-Marqos were located in different parts of the region, ranging from Ennäsè in the far eastern part of the region to Damot outside the study area. A great many of the villages were situated around Däbrä-Marqos itself, in the district of Gozamin, where the church formed one of the largest land owning institutions in the area. According to local traditions the town of Däbrä-Marqos and its church were founded on the ancestral lands taken by Täklä-Häymanot from the descendants of Mänqorär and Zäna, who were said to have been important Gafat founding ancestors in the area. The *rest* land of the children of Mänqorär and Zäna did originate with the inauguration of the village of Mänqorär which was renamed Däbrä-Marqos after the church of St. Mark that Täklä-Häymanot built. It was mainly the shift in the political centre of the region to Däbrä-Marqos area and the economic exigencies that caused the displacement of the descendants of Mänqorär and Zäna. However, the king made hereditary grants to the descendants of Mänqorär, Zäna and himself out of the holdings of the *restänña* to recompense for their loss.[36]

The assignments of new *rest* lands to Mänqorär and Zäna and Täklä-Häymanot in lieu of their *rest* used for the building of the town and the church were hereditary lands taken from the *restännas*. This shows the general and all too powerful control that rulers enjoyed over land. With the exception of Täklä-Häymanot and the descendants of Mänqorär and Zäna who were given many *rim* lands in and around Däbrä-Marqos, many of the *däbtäras* received and held town plots and *rim* lands who did not have common descent with the former. Täklä-Häymanot assigned himself land in the same way as the descendants of Mänqorär and Zäna to recompense himself for the loss of his ancestral lands now assigned for the building of the town and the church. His title to a portion of the *rest* land descended from the original commencement of the village by virtue of himself being born into the family of Mänqorär and Zäna. He was a distant descendant of Mänqorär and Zäna. This can be accepted quite confidently. In the genealogical list of Täklè (folio16 recto) we find Mänqorär and Zäna placed at the sixth generation from the founding ancestor of the Gafat people, Gozè, after he came to Gojjam. They were the great grandchildren of Gozamin, one of the most important founding ancestors of the Gafat people in Gojjam. Täklä-Häymanot is listed in the genealogy as one of the descendants of Gozamin. It is believed that the present district of Gozamin, where the town of Däbrä-Marqos is located, derived its name from him. Before its name was changed the locality around contemporary Däbrä-Marqos was known by the name Mänqorär. For receiving hereditary rights over most plots of land Täklä-Häymanot and other descendants of Mänqorär and Zäna were charged with the obligation of providing a banquet on Epiphany and to pitch the tent of the *tabot* in the nearby river on the occasion of Epiphany. Moreover, they received eight *rim* lands proportional to their holding in return for the obligation of paying the wages of four grinders and water drawers and four priests who served the main church.[37]

The *gult* register of Däbrä-Marqos church contains a detailed and minute record of the distribution and measurement of town land and in the case of one village the division of the land between the *däbtäras* and the peasants. Town lands at Däbrä-Marqos were parceled out into symmetrical strips and divided among the *däbtäras*. Residential sites in towns of the region were known as *shi gämäd*, literally one thousand ropes. The name bears testimony to the division of the town sites into one thousand strips, hence the name *shi gämäd*, so as to make apportionment fair.[38] The residential sites were measured out in strips and then these strips were assigned for the settlement of the *däbtäras* concurrent with the establishment of great churches. The division was carried out perhaps by mutual agreement of all the recipients. There is also evidence showing that the division of town plots among the *däbtäras* took into account quality. It seems that the extent and quality of town land a person could get varied in accordance with the rank of the recipient. In other words the size and quality of the land granted to an individual was determined by the nature and the importance of the service he or she would render the church as well as his/her rank. Accordingly, Täklä-Häymanot and his wife Laqäch Gäbrä-Mädehen and other dignitaries had the largest size of twon land. They were given choice sites for residence, very close to the church of Däbrä-Marqos, and other sites for gardens where probably they grew vegetables, and for corral.[39]

We do not know exactly how the assignment of the land to the *däbtäras* was communicated to the peasantry. One way of communication was perhaps through decree. Unfortunately there was no custom of setting down in writing a detailed description of the individual share of the *däbtäras* and the *restäñña* at the time of the actual division and measurement of the agricultural fields as a whole. Records of land measurement and distribution are rare. There is one such rare instance of a record of the actual division of land between the *däbtäras* and the *restäññas* held by the church of Däbrä-Marqos where measurement and distribution of land between the *däbtäras* and the *restäññas* was duly registered on the occasion of the transfer of two-thirds of the land of the *restäññas* to the *däbtäras*. Folios 60r to folio62r of the *gult* register of Däbrä-Marqos record the measurement and allocation of land between the *däbtäras* and the *restäññas* in a village called Wänqa.[40]

With the exception of Wänqa the actual division of the land between the *däbtära* and the *restäñña* is not registered with any accuracy. The scribes and the grantors and grantees did not trouble much to register the actual dimensions of the *rim* lands of the individual *däbtära* and the division of the land. All the transfer of the two-thirds of the land to the *däbtäras* in the village called Wänqa is recorded in the *gult* register. The village is listed among other villages given to the church of Däbrä-Marqos. The conditions leading up to the recording of the measurement and distribution of the land in the village of Wänqa alone is not known. Perhaps its proximity to the town was one factor. However, the mere fact that there was instituted an office called *çheqa-mägaräfya* (to be discussed below) for the supervision of land division between the *däbtäras* and the *restäññas*, and the survival of some records of land measurement and distribution indicate there was proper survey or measurement that would take place following the decree on the assignment of village lands to the *däbtära*. A total of thirty-five *däbtäras* were assigned the agricultural fields of the village Wänqa.[41] Fifteen of them are listed by name, including Emperor Yohannes. The unit of measurement of land that is met frequently in charters is called *yäçheqa-mägaräfya* (which literally means the knot of a *çheqa*) the exact size of which is difficult to establish. In the charter of Däbrä-Marqos one *yäçheqa-mägaräfya* is stated to be the equivalent of one *däbtära rim*.[42] Unfortunately the exact dimension of one *däbtära rim* is also not stated. Based on the interpretation of contemporary sources Joseph Tubiana writes the following about the dimension, "About the land itself: the complete *rim* consists of four *q[e]faf* and one *bota*. *The bota* (size unspecified) is the "living place" of the tenant. This implies that a house is built upon it. The *q[e] faf* are for cultivation. One *q[e]faf* usually measures 70 by 50 cubits [this does not seem exceedingly long for its breadth], an area of approximately 80.64hectars..."⁴³ A stick is mentioned as having been used during the land division and measurement at Wänqa.

As a general rule the measurement and transfer of land from the *restäñña* to the *däbtära* was supervised by the local *çheqa*. Moreover, some witnesses had to attend as a norm perhaps to serve as security against any possible future fraud. A certain *Agafari* Näṭäru served as witness in the case of Wänqa. For his service as witness he received two plots of land in Wänqa. In the document recording the division and the distribution of the land that took place at Wänqa trees and streams are mentioned repeatedly, serving as boundary marks and separating the holding of the *däbtära* and the *baläsisso*. The *çheqa* was entitled to get remuneration for his service of supervising the division of the land according to different arrangements set forth in charters. In most cases the *çheqa* received one or more plots of land from both sides and this land was called *yä çheqa-mägaräfya*. Sometimes, as in the case of the charter of Däbrä-Marqos, the *restäñña* retained the land due to the *çheqa* and agreed to meet the land claim of the *çheqa* by annual payment of *amolè*, which is also called *yäçheqa-mägaräfya*.⁴⁴

In the *rim* land registers the name of the *däbtäras* would be entered either jointly or individually, followed by the names of the specific lands. A *rim* land given to several *däbtäras* is registered jointly in the name of the joint holders and the names of individual *däbtäras* are entered where *rim* land was held individually. Whether the shares of individuals constituting one *däbtära* were delimited with each of the joint owners having a right to a specific share of the total *rim* land or not cannot be known.⁴⁵ The precise shares of the individual *däbtäras* are not clearly stated. Most charters registered the name of the individual *däbtäras* corresponding to the village lands with the size and limits not usually defined. The scribes were not interested in defining the exact dimension of these *rim* lands. Some subsequent minor redistributions and exchange of *rim* lands made among the *däbtäras* are entered in the register. The *däbtäras* exchanged one another's *rim* lands perhaps for the purpose of consolidating holdings.⁴⁶ It is very clear from the records of town land measurement and distribution that the size of the residential sites of the grantees corresponded to their rank and the importance of their service to the church. Probably the rank of a person to whom *rim* was given seems to have been given consideration in determining the size of the land to be granted, although this might not have been always true.

We have similar records of the division of town lands into many individual parcels of long and symmetrical strips at Däbrä-Eliyas, Yälämeläm Kidanä-Meherät, a church in the district of Libän and Gemjja-Bèt Kidanä-Meherät in Däbrä-Marqos.[47] In the case of the charter of Däbrä-Eliyas church the *däbtäras'* land was to be divided by lot and it was to be entered in the register against the name of each holder. The land charter of Yälämeläm Kidanä-Meherät included an injunction which recorded and ordered that if the *däbtäras* who were assigned town lands (which included kings Minilek and Täklä-Häymanot and emperor Yohannes) at Yälämeläm could not build a house over it within a set period it was to be restored to the *balärest*.[48] The dimensions of the strips of the allotments at Däbrä-Eliyas are said to be about eighty cubits in length and width. Its charter orders the *däbtäras* to see to it that the boundary between the strips was used for the access paths, especially so that the movements of people were not impeded as during funeral processions.[49]

Täklä-Häymanot delegated to the church of Däbrä-Marqos many functions and powers of the government including judiciary and administrative in the areas under its domain. There was no interference of the regional government in churches especially in the sphere of justice. The church exercised the highest levels of judiciary rights, chiefly exercised by the emperor and the bishop themselves according to the nature of the case. It was given the high sounding title of *mäle'eltä-adebarat*, chief of the endowed churches. For example the *lèba-adem* (thief catcher), *meslänè*, the *buta* and the *korè are* forbidden by the charter to enter or interfere in the land in Gozamin under the direct administration of the church of Däbrä-Marqos .The *buta* according the modern Amharic dictionary of Käsatè-Berhän was a watchman who informed officials about disturbances or thefts in an area by shouting in a loud voice. He had also the power to punish offenders by beating .The *korè* according to the Ge'ez dictionary was the regent or agent of the episcopate. The district of Gozamin was immune from the intervention of all these secular and religious officials.[50] The state hardly ever interfered in the affairs of the church, and even cases which were religious in nature were settled within the limits of the jurisdiction of the church of Däbrä-Marqos. Any religious dispute between the monasteries and churches of the region had to be brought to the court presided by its head.[51] In effect it would not be too much to say that the church appeared to have constituted a kind of state within a state.

The top of the documents recording all the provision and privileges to the church were authenticated by having the seals of the archbishop Pèṭros, the bishop Luqas, *eçhägè* Teoflos, Täklä-Häymanot and emperor Yohannes. These sanctions threatened any possible transgression of the provision by very frightening curses.[52] These sanctions were included so as to insure the implementation of the charters and to frighten those who might fail to heed the provisions and regulations of the charter. In short it was concerned with preventing disorder or dispute and served as a bar against individuals from making claims to lands to which they might have former titles but not any more after they were transferred to someone and after the state had legitimized the transfer.

The big percentage of the lands of the church was in the *rim* category. As we have seen so far, as of the eighteenth century *rim* came to be employed as the generic name for the agricultural fields which lay and clerical lords held from the church or on behalf of the church, its earliest known use in this sense in the period and region under investigation being the charter of Wälätä-Isra'el. There was considerable change in the latter half of the nineteenth century as regards to the extent of this land. In the last decades of the nineteenth century when the size of *rim* land was greatly increased *rim* had become by far the most common way by which noblemen and women as well as the religious class held their land. Turning large amount of *rest* land of the peasants to church land (*rim*) increased the size of *rim* lands. Prominent individuals from neighboring regions like *Ras* Mika'el, Minilek, Yohannes, etc., were granted *rim* lands in the study area probably so that prayers would be said for them. The rights of holding *rim* land were granted to persons alive at the time of the creation of the right and it was possible for it to pass by inheritance. However, *rim* land was also given to persons who were not alive at the time of the grant and had passed away a long time ago. Such grants were made for example to *Däjjazmach* Gošu, grandfather of Täklä-Häymanot.[53] One indication of the permanent nature of the original grant was that the *däbtäras* and their descendants did not demand a new order with every change in the political leadership of the region and the grant of the departed lord was generally respected by his successors. For this reason it was not necessary to obtain confirmation of the grant by his successors.

Rim land conferred considerable economic benefit upon the individuals with some social prestige as well as political power. The *rim* holders cultivated their *rim* lands through their *zègas*. I have already quoted the passage in the charter of Däbrä-Marqos containing the regulations between the *däbtäras* and the *zègas*, the *däbtäras* and the *restäñña* and the officials of the church.[54] Because of the great increase in the *rim* land held by persons in this period the *zègas* might have been as numerous as the *baläsisso* around Gozamin. They formed an important element in the overall social structure of the rural population, particularly around the district of Gozamin. The charter is very vague in setting the economic obligations of the *zègas*. It simply mentions the judiciary and administrative right of the *däbtäras* over the *zègas*. This is perhaps because of the fact that custom did not demand it and it was wholly the concern of the recipient of the *rim* land to determine it. I have discussed the major characteristics of the socio-economic relationship between them elsewhere and no particulars need be given here. The nature and scale of the rights and privileges of the *däbtäras* of Däbrä-Marqos church were as extensive as those of the church of Bichäna Giyorgis. By the operation of the immunity the *däbtäras* were able to escape or avoid from providing onerous labor service like repairing church buildings, entertaining guests, etc. Much of the economic burden rested on the *restäñña*.[55]

The *gult* register described in details the services and dues required of the *baläsisso*. They were permanently exempted from taxation and dues except labor dues and the payment of obligatory presents on the three annual holidays. The *restäñña*s holding one-third of the land were responsible for the payment of the wages of the carpenters and the repair of the enclosure walls, the building of the *däjä-sälam*, the one storey main entrance to the church. They were also expected to offer one sheep each on principal feast days. In almost all of the land charters it was stipulated that in lieu of the gift of a sheep its price, which was fixed at three *amolès*, would be paid, showing the existence of the general level of regularization or uniformity in the obligation of the peasants. The price of the sheep given as a present was standardized as a universal custom.[56] Though there is no direct empirical evidence to support it, it is possible to presume that the *restäñña*s who had lost a good part of their former *rest* lands would find it difficult to live on their reduced holding alone; hence they had to supplement their income by working for the *rim* holders. They would be subject to rents and labor services, even possibly could end up merged with the *zègas*.

The socio-economic relationship between the *restäññas* under the direct administration of the *gäbäz* and the *aläqa* and the *liqäṭäbäbt* is of special importance for us. Important offices have land attached to them by way of payment of *yäwär-qäläb* (monthly stipend). The monthly stipend of the offices of the *aläqa* and *liqäṭäbäbt* and the *gäbäz* as distinct from other offices were allotted on certain villages. Church offices such as those for Däbrä-Marqos appear to have been highly profitable. According to the list of lands referring to Däbrä-Marqos three are listed under the holding of the *aläqa* and the *liqäṭäbäbt* as the one-fifth land of the total villages listed. This is however a theoretical assumption and there was no deduction of one-fifth of the total land given to the *däbtäras* in terms of acres. They were given such extensive lands in view of their important service to the church. Besides receiving *rim* land the *gäbaz* and the *aläqa* and the *liqäṭäbäbt* were given cash (salt-bar) payments and obligatory presents and monthly stipend from the lands under their special administration as the recognition of the their high rank and the importance of their service.[57]

Next to the *däbtära* land the most prevalent form of village is the village allotted as Mass or *mäsewat* land. The criterion for holding the office of *gäbäz* was descent from Mänqorär, Zäna and afterwards from Täklä-Häymanot himself. The charter of Däbrä-Marqos church recommended that the *gäbäz* should not be elected from among men other than the descendants of the three *restäññas* just referred to. The office was given in perpetuity and it rotated among members of the three families once every three years, i.e. the office rotated among the descendants of the three families after every three years. As a *gäbäz* the king would enjoy the right to the office and the stipend that went with it for three years. He received the dues and contributions from the peasants under the *gäbäz's* administration. The lands given for the support of Mass or *mäsewat* were distinct from those of the *aläqa* and the *liqäṭäbäbt*. Usually the lands under the administration of the *gäbäz* were not committed for the settlement of the *däbtäras* or the *zégas* of the *gäbäz*. Although the *gäbäz* did not hold proprietary right over such lands and he had to confine himself to judging civil cases he would still exercise an immense power over the peasantry in the *mäsewat* land. The *gäbäz* had one-fifth of the judgment fee collected from cases involving homicide, adultery and theft.[58]

The *gäbäz* was allowed by the charter to use certain parts of the tax and tribute from the lands given for the support of Mass in lieu of monthly stipend and to defray the cost of administering such lands. The method of collection and the time limit for the payment of the dues is clearly set out. The *gäbäz* was given monthly stipends and obligatory presents of sheep on the three holidays by the peasants as remuneration for his services. Presents on festive occasions appear to have been the most fruitful source of income. The peasants had no labor obligation to the *gäbäz*. The building of the *eqabèt* or treasury house and the *bethlehem,* the house where the Holy Communion bread was prepared, was made the responsibility of the peasants within the *gäbäz*'s administration. Usually the annual land tax and the tribute in the lands given for the support of Mass were assessed in wheat.[59]

Generally, the peasants were required to pay tribute and tax according to the nature of the crops grown. However, in the lands given for the support of Mass the peasants were forced to plant part of their land with wheat even when the land might not be good for such production. It is not difficult to understand the reason for the assessment of tribute on the lands given out for the support of Mass being made in kind (wheat). Wheat was necessary for the churches special needs, particularly for the preparation of the bread of the Holy Communion. The custom of assessing tax in fixed amount of wheat should not be considered simply to have resulted from the dominant agricultural practice in a particular area or the nature of the soil. Indeed some villages which were noted as chief producers of wheat or as much noted for their production of other grains, or perhaps even not self-supporting in wheat grain, were arbitrarily assigned for the support of Mass and the taxation was assessed in wheat for the purpose of meeting the needs of the church. In such circumstances, the peasants were obliged either to buy the necessary amount of wheat due to the church or sow or grow wheat over parts of their holdings. This means that the environment or the nature of the soil did not wholly dictate what the peasants would plant on their land. The peasants had to provide the amount of wheat stipulated in the document, even in the event of failure of the crop of wheat, by exchange or any other means.[60] The unit on which the dues were assessed varied from area to area. Tax and tribute was not assessed by measurement of the land given for the support of Mass.

Individuals who were vested with the offices of *aläqa* and *liqäṭäbäbt* were given rights for a prescribed period and had only life rights. Persons who were vested with the two offices were obliged to leave or pass the administration of the lands attached to the two offices to whoever would be appointed to the two positions after the end of their terms of office. The taxes and tributes from such lands went to the two officials. Unlike the case of the peasants under the two officials of Gemjja-Bèt, the *restäñña*s under the *aläqa* and *liqäṭäbäbt* of Däbrä-Marqos were to meet the land claims of the two officials out of the produce of the land instead of transferring land. In other words the *restäñña* did not give away two-thirds of his land in the case of Däbrä-Marqos. In the case of Däbrä-Marqos the division of the land between the officials and the *restäñña*s was commuted to taxation paid per annum, presents on the three annual holidays, monthly stipends and labor dues.[61] This was mainly aimed at avoiding the assumption of the not always easy responsibility of cultivating their share of the land by the two officials. This might also have been owing to the fact that they were rotating offices. As stated above all of the taxation and tribute from such lands went to the two officials. A monthly stipend and a payment in kind and presents of three sheep on the three holidays and tax in cash per annum were levied on the peasantry which were paid in kind and cash for the officials at regular intervals i.e. on a monthly and yearly basis and as a norm coinciding with the principal Christian feast days. The unit on which the dues were assessed varied from area to area. The Däbrä-Marqos charter gives an indication of the kind of imposition to which the peasants under the two officials were subject. The assessment of the wages of the *aläqa* was made in certain areas by *gundo* (unit of measurement) of butter. One of the villages called Šabla, for example, paid ten *madega* of grain and six rock-salts per month, one hundred rock-salt per annum and three sheep on the three holidays.[62] Whether the obligatory presents of sheep, butter, etc., were levied per household or collectively and according to the means of the peasant cannot be known.

The *liqäṭäbäbt* and the *aläqa* could extract much from the peasantry under them by using their position in the administrative structure of the church. The *mälakä-ṣahäy*, the title of the *aläqa* of Däbrä-Marqos church, was the chief appeal judge of all the lands under the church's domain. The *aläqa* could take not only all the fines of the proceeds of justice brought to him from *yä aläqa amsteya agär* which were especially set aside for his maintenance but also received *rim* lands in the remaining four-fifths. He also derived income from other sources like appointment fees, market tax, *täzkar*(memorial services) all minutely set down in the charter.[63] It is impossible to cover all the important points that stand out in the charter within the limiting confine of few pages. We need to pass on to discussing other charters.

Täklä-Häymanot continued to issue a constant stream of charters down to the end of the nineteenth century. One of the recipients of his favor was the church of Däbrä-Eliyas to be discussed in the pages that follow. As mention has already been made elsewhere in this study, Täklä-Häymanot generally followed the precedent of his illustrious forebear, Wälätä-Isra'el, his great, great grandmother in formulating charters, including that for Däbrä-Eliyas church.[64] Emperor Yohannes was responsible for the first extensive grant to the church in 1874.[65] However, Däbrä-Eliyas gained in strength and wealth during the late 1880s when Täklä-Häymanot, lavishly endowed it with extensive lands. Around 320 *däbtäras* were given *rim* lands.[66] The charters for the church always contained provisions for the right to administer and govern the area. The charter laid on the church officials the responsibility for ensuring order and peace as well as administering justice in the lands given to it. Under Yohannes's charter if the case was beyond the knowledge of the *aläqa* it would be referred to the court of the king, *eçhägè* and the bishop according to the nature of the case. Criminal justice and religious cases were to be tried only by the court of Yohannes and the *eçhägè* or the bishop.[67]

However, all kinds of criminal and religious cases were put within the competence of the church officials and were settled at the church by referring to the *Fetha Nägäst*, which was an official and universally recognized reference for criminal and civil cases by the second charter. Under Täklä-Häymanot's charter the independence of the court of the church of Däbrä-Eliyas was increased and it was determined that crimes including homicide as well as other serious disputes were to be referred to the court presided by the *aläqa* of the church. Final appeal which was formerly reserved for the courts of the king and bishops were now assigned by Täklä-Häymanot to Däbrä-Eliyas. The king gave it the right to try all crimes including those reserved for the king, *eçhägè* and the bishop by the former charter. The church was given the judicial powers to exercise over its dependents on the same basis that the bishop and the emperor had earlier exercised.[68]

The *däbtäras* had completely appropriated the right of trying all kinds of civil cases in their *rim* land and over the people working it, the *zègas*. They were given such immunities from government interference in their relation with their *zègas*, immunities from payment of judgment fees in cases involving dispute over *rim* land boundary and other ordinary cases. However, they were not immune from the payment of judgment fees in cases involving theft, adultery, homicide, *sämbär* (serious beating) and also *wurered* (bet?).The reference to quarrels between the *däbtäras* over the boundary of their respective *rim* land points to the fact that their holdings were very specific and individual.[69] The holders of *rim* land were given full powers to decide all cases involving the *zègas* settled over their *rim* lands granted to them to the exclusion of the officials of the church or the provincial government, except criminal cases, "ደብተራውም ከደም አ ከይናፉ አ ከሌባ ዳኝነት በቀር በቦታው በሪሙ ያሰፈረውን ዜጋውን ይዳኝ" -which literally means that [t]he *däbtäras*, with the exception of cases of homicide, adultery and theft, shall judge the *zègas* whom they settle over their *rim* and *bota*."[70] This shows that the *däbtära*s' judicial and administrative powers over the *zègas* who lived on their lands were conventional.

Thus the *däbtäras*, who included noblemen and women, who might have derived very large parts of their wealth from their *rest* land enjoyed on many of their *rim* lands exactly the same legal privileges as on their *rest* land. There is no indication in this land grant document about the nature of the socio-economic relationship between the *zègas* and the *däbtäras*. Likewise no provision is made to protect the *zègas* against any possible maltreatment by the landlords. The silence of the charter under consideration about the socio-economic relationship of the *zègas* and *däbtäras* bears further witness to the complete acceptance by the regional government of the right of the *däbtäras* to determine what it should be. The granting or acquiring of the powers and rights stated above to or by the *däbtäras* over their land and people working over it are on a par with manorial or seigniorial rights. Such rights of the *däbtäras* over the *zègas* together with extensive transference of peasant property to the control of powerful individuals led to a condition or tendency of increasing manorialism.

Despite the scattered distribution or nature of *rim* lands the holding of certain individuals would undoubtedly make into quite impressive blocks of land if they were to be consolidated and aggregated together. Where possible the individual *rim* owners would naturally prefer aggregated or consolidated holdings instead of widely dispersed holdings. There are instances of exchange of lands between the *däbtäras,* though documents recording such exchanges are far less frequently met. For example King Täklä-Häymanot exchanged his *rim* land located at Wänqa with the *rim* land of a certain Abba Ejjigu found in a place called Abbäzaj.[71] Perhaps there was an increasing tendency towards the concentration of lands and a possibility of the existence of hosts of successful concentration of holdings. Among those listed in the charter receiving *rim* lands are high profile dignitaries, including from neighboring regions and those who had died a long time before, like *Däjjazmach* Gošu.[72] Why did Yohannes and Minilek hold plots scattered throughout the region and why were persons, dead a long time before, given *rim* lands? It seems that this did not arise mainly from the need to derive income therefrom, although they could also reward their *rim* lands in the region to whom they favored so that they would say prayers for them. It is apparent that high dignitaries and dead persons were also given land probably out of respect and the desire to perpetuate their name as well as to provide support for their *täzkar* or memorial services.

In almost literally all of the land charters of this period the names of certain individuals, particularly those of Laqäch and Täklä-Häymanot, are entered. Indeed there was a blatant self-aggrandizement by the acquisition of *rim* lands, especially by Täklä-Häymanot and his wife. They held parcels of land scattered at intervals over several hundred miles, almost literally across the entire span of the region.[73] Many other nobles acquired many *rim* lands here and there in almost all districts of the region. The king and his wife derived the income for their material needs from their *rim* holding. Laqäch exercised seigniorial authority over a number of widely dispersed *rim* lands. She was a lord after her fashion. The following document is a typical case that illustrates this fact,[74]

በጎርጎር 4 መገበርያ ስንዴ ሰጥተው ጉልትዎን እመይቦ ላቀች ሊዳኍ ሊቃኍ ዕሪም አድርገው ተቀብለውታል። ፈርደው ይግባኍ ከገበዙ ነው። ከገበዙ የጸነው ከድማህ ገነቱ ነው። የድማህ ገነቱም ይግባኝ

የደብሩ ፍታነገስት ነው፡፡ባላነጣ ግን ከሲሶው ከርስቱ
በቀር በሪምም ሊይደርስ ነው፡፡በዚህም ውል
አለበት፡፡ተገዝቶበታል፡፡ ማህበሩ ያውቃሉ፡፡

Emäytè Laqäch transferred her gult [land] in Gorgor and received it as rim [land], paying four mägäbärya of [wheat] for it. She shall judge and administer. She judges and the appeal [judge] should be the gäbäz. If one is not satisfied with the decision of the gäbäz the appeal judge is the Demah Gänät. The appeal judge of the Demah Gänät is the Fetha Nägäst of the däber. The adversary shall have no rights in her rim except in the one-third of his rest [land]. There is a pact for this. It is anathematized .The community [of the church] know this.

The size of the *rim* land in the above document was not perhaps small. Laqäch had the right to take part of the produce of the land and whatever pertained thereto to her. The charter concluded with the injunction that the rival or *balanța* should not obstruct or interfere with Laqäch over the two-thirds of the land. *Balanța* stands for the *restäññas*, two-thirds of whose former land is now being transferred as *rim* land to the woman. The charter ruled out the *rest* rights of the peasants over two-thirds of their former land. Here Laqäch transferred her secular *gult* land into *rim* land in which she was given large judicial and administrative rights over the two-thirds of the land of the *restäññas* the only obligation attached to the land being the payment of a certain amount of wheat for the support of Mass. She was given as good as manorial rights over her land. Besides the lands quoted in this document, her name was entered in the charter, showing her holding several *rim* lands. The land being given for the support of Mass, the *gäbäz* exercised some judicial authorities over Laqäch and matters that came for decision among those under her. Cases beyond the competence of the *gäbäz* were to be referred to the Demah Gänät. The ultimate appeal judge of the Demah-Gänät was the Fetha Nägäst, the standard reference book in the period.[75]

The *gäbäz* in Däbrä-Eliyas derived his power from a hereditary title to the administration of lands given in support of the Mass. The charter ordered that the *gäbäz* should be elected from among men who were born into the family of Dil-Assäma, a fifteenth century founding ancestor. The first church of Däbrä-Eliyas is said to have been founded by Dil Assäma, who was a man from Shäwa who crossed into Gojjam during the reign of Zära-Ya'eqob (r.1434-1468).[76] There is a threat of the imposition of fine and a threat of curse, which were usually meant to serve as a guarantee for the loyalty of the *restäñña* to the charter. The mere fact that the charters had to add the injunction against ejection might be taken as a witness to the possibility of the existence of trespass or derogation of the grant. However, although grant documents were open for contestation there is no record of peasant attempts to stop the realization of the charter as a whole. Perhaps the immunities put barriers against any attempt by the *restäñña* to oppose the transfer of their land to the *däbtära* and to seize the land of one another. This suggests an interpretation that either there was nothing the peasant could do about it or that this act of near virtual expropriation was considered by the peasantry as impossible to stop arising out of the subordination and helplessness of the peasants. It might also be because the transfer of peasant *rest* land to the *rim* holders had become so well established and a common practice that the peasants recognized the transfer of their land to the elite as normal.

This charter provided with much consideration for the security and rights of the peasants' holding over the remaining one-third of the land. It guarded the right of the *restäññas* as carefully as those of the *däbtäras*. The transfer of extensive land from the *restäñña* to the *däbtära* would bring sweeping rearrangements in the structure of the landowning class. Moreover, it would bring tremendous increase in the personnel owning land from the church or on behalf of the church, though the extent of concentrated holding would probably melt away after some generation of use. Yohannes's charter required the *baläsisso* to provide for the feast of the prophet Eliyas thirty *gan* of *ṭälla* and three thousand *enjjära* as well as two beef cattle for the feast of Christmas, two beef cattle for the feast of Easter and two beef cattle for the feast of the Assumption of St.Mary.[77] As in the days of Wälätä-Isra'el memorial services and banquets as well as income from funeral services, market levies, appointment and judgment fees formed useful sources of income and constituted special concerns of this charter. The amount of payment the charter asks for appointment fees varied with the wealth and the importance of the office as well as with the rank of the individual holding the office. This was a universal custom.[78]

3.2. The Land Grants of the Churches of Amanu'el, Ledäta and Däbrä-Gälila.

Some charters that are of considerable importance for this study remain to be discussed. One of such very significant and very intriguing charters is that of the monastery of Ledäta, in the district of Basso. This charter issued by King Täklä-Häymanot placed some three villages under its overall administration. It orders that peasants would be required to provide labor for a number of days yearly for cultivating the lands of the monks or the lands of the peasants which were transferred to the monks. The charter ordered that the *çheqa* and one of the officials of the monastery, the *liqäräd* (the *aläqa* or chief of those vigorous members of the monastery who were put in charge of working its land) should organize and supervise the peasants in the cultivation of the land in a fitting manner or "as the *çheqa* saw it fit." The peasants were ordered to accept the monks as their rulers possessing full powers of administration. The charter is very vague as to whose land it is referring to. It simply states that the cultivation of the land is the concern of the *çheqa* and the *liqäräd* according to their discretion and the responsibility of the peasants who were engaged in the actual farming of the land. The charter orders the peasants to transfer an unspecified extent of their land to one of the dependent parish churches of Ledäta and to spend a couple of days providing agricultural labor service.[79]

In the revised charter of the same monastery (this is a point I will discuss below) there is very definitive evidence that the original charter obliged the peasantry to transfer part of their holdings to the monastery. The original charter was revised after a quarrel between the monks and the peasants. One of the terms of agreement that led to the reconciliation of the monks and the *restäñña* was that the latter agreed to meet the land claims of the monks by the payment of the monthly stipend of the monks and annual taxes and agricultural labor services. The phrase that contains the key point in the revised charter concerning the terms on which it was probably granted first pronounce, "ሥራው ግን ስለመሬቱ ለውጥ ርስተኛው ለመነኮሳቱ የሚሰጠው ወርቅ የአመት ግብሩ 4 ወቂት ታላድ ኦ የወር ቀለቡ 02 ለዳን ኦ 02 ጨሎ ስልደት ኦ (ጨሎ የፋሲክ ኦ (ጨሎ የፍልሰታ-" which literally means that "the obligation for the exchange of the land, the *restäñña* shall give to the monks the annual taxes in gold, four ounces of gold and *alad* (?), the monthly stipend of twelve *ladan*, twelve rock-salts for Christmas, sixty rock-salts for [the feast of] the Assumption of St. Mary, [and]sixty rock-salts for Easter."[80]

Twice in the document there are words and phrases that say the *restäñña* agreed to meet the claims of the monks in land as according to the provision of the charter by paying the monthly allowance of the monks, working in the agricultural fields of the monks, their annual taxes and to meet their other labor obligations.[81] This suggests a possible existence of an on-going negotiation between self-perceived rights of *restäñña* and the church authorities. It appears from the original charter that the land tax was *erbo*, which literally means a quarter of the total produce, since it is stated that from the produce of the soil the monastery would get a half *erbo* the remaining half *erbo* going to the *restäññas*. However, *erbo* as used here appears a theoretical assumption or abstraction and it simply means that the produce of the land was being divided on an equal basis between the *restäññas* and the monks. The charter imposed compulsory labor services in which the labor of peasants was used for production activities on lands directly owned and exploited by the monks. The monks were themselves engaged in productive activities and cultivated their fields with their own hands but further needed to draft labor from the peasantry. If forced labor levied was used chiefly on agricultural production it took the form of the performance of cultivation on the estate of monks, called *hudad*. From these passages it would seem that forced labor did not usually take the nature of public works for the benefit of the officials and churches but also and mainly that of agricultural labor. It was levied per household and consisted of some days of labor by the peasantry. It involved the provision of a team of oxen free on some stipulated days of the year. Probably food was provided for the peasants on the day they provided the service but no other payment was made to them. Peasants were required to plough, weed and reap the crops of the monks without receiving any compensation on the lands directly owned and exploited by the monastery.[82]

As already alluded to, the peasants and the monks quarreled and it was this quarrel that provided the condition leading to the revision of the original charter of the monastery. The peasants managed to retain their lands and agreed to meet the land claims of the monks by the payment of annual taxes, obligatory gifts, etc., as indicated above. The amount of free agricultural labor service levied on the peasants was increased. Each peasant household was required to provide free labor, without payment, for a couple of days yearly. The revised charter demanded that the peasants provide free service from seven to ten days each year: one day for *gwelgwalo* (the preparation of the land immediately before sowing), one day for ploughing and sowing, one day for weeding, one day for reaping, one day for *wägäz* (the agricultural work of driving cattle, donkeys and mules round and round over the land being planted *tèff* to level it immediately before sowing), and threshing and transporting the harvest to the granaries. The charter stipulates that peasants had to provide these services irrespective of the wealth and the capacity of providing such a service. Poor peasants who might not even have had the necessary draught animals were not immune from providing the service of ploughing. The service of ploughing is made per oxen and amounts to only one-day free labor of a peasant yearly. The wealthy peasants who might have more than one team of oxen were not obliged to mobilize all of their team of oxen and hence they were required to provide only a pair of oxen.[83] The threshing and transporting of the harvest to the granary of the monks would probably take many days. Approximately the peasants provided seven to ten days of free agricultural labor services per annum. Besides the number of days stated the peasants might have been performing free agricultural labor service whenever required to the effect that the land of the monks was ploughed, sowed, tended, harvested, reaped, and threshed by their corvée labor alone. The monks could levy causal labor during harvest or sowing or reaping out of the provision of the charter.

 The charter boldly stated that the *restäñña* should spend their time according to the order of the monks. This is stated in the charter as follows "ባላገሩ መነኮሳቱ ባዘዙት ሊውል ነው-"which means "the peasants are to spend their time as per the orders of the monks." This shows that the peasants were instructed to give obedience to their masters in everything and they should spend their time according to the order of the monks. The *restäññas* could not transgress or contravene what the monks ordered them to do. A very heavy fine of fifty ounces of gold threatened any transgression of the regulation of the charter. The revised charter commanded the *restäññas* to regard the monks as in effect their lords or owners of their labor since it ordered them to obey the monks in everything. Monks provided seeds and the peasant draught animals, agricultural implements and the necessary labor starting from preparing the land through to the threshing and transporting of the produce to the granary of the monks.[84] Unlike the labor obligation of the peasants under other churches discussed elsewhere, those of Ledäta were required the performance of agricultural services every year especially during the crucial periods of sowing and harvesting.

In another land charter peasants were required to provide agricultural labor services throughout the whole year, at an interval of every two months. This grant was made, as usual, by Täklä-Häymanot to a monastery called Mäkanä Qedusan in Gozamin district. In this case the peasants were not only forced to hand over two-thirds of their land but also required to repair the church, build houses for the nuns and monks and provide presents of sheep on the three annual holidays as well as to plough the land of the monastery one day every two months.[85] Peasants under the monastery of Ledäta were obliged to provide on three unspecified days milk for the monks and customary payments of food and drink on certain occasions. The revised charter of Ledäta also ordered artisans (weavers and tanners) to work four days per annum on whatever the monks ordered them to do.[86] Unlike labor services provided for the non-agricultural work the charter specified the number of workdays the peasants had to spend on the fields of monks. The *restäñña* would approximately spend between five to ten days working and farming in the fields of the monks. Though the number of days of agricultural labor services demanded from the peasantry appears few it could make a difference to spend even a single day of the peasants working time particularly during the crucial farming and harvesting periods. Threshing, winnowing and separating the grain from the chaff and transporting the produce to the granary of the monks might have required the peasants to spend three to five days on this obligation alone beyond the number of days envisaged by the charter.

In addition to the peasants' liability to perform free labor on a fixed number of days per annum for agricultural work peasants were required to build churches. The extent of the labor obligation performed in building in nearly every charter is the same. Providing labor services on church buildings, enclosures, etc. and the payment of presents on the three annual holidays did represent the total of the obligation of the peasants to the monks. Free labor services of repairing and building churches, the houses of officials, and the enclosure walls happened at intervals of several years. After the first construction activities the church building and the enclosure walls may not have needed repair every year. However, when it demanded repairing it some times took several years and much money. For example it took three years to rebuild the enclosure walls of Moṭa Giyorgis church and a large sum of money for the payment of carpenters. This took place in the 1870s, in the early years of Täklä-Häymanot's reign.[87]

The last two charters remaining which are worth considering and special interest for the purpose of my study are the charters of the church of Amanu'el and the monastery of Däbrä-Gälila, both located in the district of Machakäl which Täklä-Häymanot lavishly endowed. Both charters contain provisions for adjusting the obligations of the peasantry to the possible kinds of mischance, which are not found frequently in other charters. Such consideration was made in the event of some calamity happening to the peasants that seriously damaged their economy. The charter of Däbrä-Gälila expressed it as follows "በሬ ሳለ በመልቻሙ ዘመን የተጻፈው መሥዋዕት እና መሺሚያ ዛሬ ዘሙኑ ሲኔል እኩል መሥዋዕት እኩል መሺሚያ ንጉሥ ይስጥ ብለዋል፤፤እኩልም ቢኣጣ ምድር ያወጣውን እርቦውን ይስጥ ብለዋል፤፤ The rough rendering of this is: "The king[Täklä-Häymanot] has ordered that on the occasion of bad times[the peasants and office holders] should only pay half of the total appointment fees and the dues for the support of Mass assessed(determined) whilst there was ox [and]in times of prosperity. He says if [the peasants] were short of paying half of the original assessment [in good times] they are supposed to pay a quarter of the produce of the land [in bad times]."[88] The existence of such injunctions though very rarely and at least in some of the charters itself are indications of the concern for the well being of the peasantry. The first of the two grants was issued for Gälila during the reign of emperor Yohannes, in 1874. A total of eighty-four monks and clergymen as well as hosts of noblemen and women were settled over the land given to the monastery. This charter grants immunity to the *restäñña* from payment in bad years of the full dues for the abbot of the monastery on the occasion of his appointment and the payment of wheat for the support of Mass. The charter prohibited officials from demanding the full dues which the peasantry had to pay in normal years. However, the charter did not necessarily confer immunity upon the peasants from all taxes but it implies a mitigation of the taxes in bad times. The charter states that if some natural calamity destroyed the necessary draught animals or oxen, the peasantry would pay half the amount of the original assessment of the dues and obligations demanded in times of prosperity.[89] To demand the full dues in bad years would have amounted to squeezing peasants to the last limit. This would suggest that there have been some attempts made to adjust tribute and taxes demanded from the peasants and to set maximum limitation on the rate of taxes in times of calamity. This is indeed a very good bar against exploitation of the peasants to the last degree without regard to their well being.

The land charter of Amanu'el church is of great interest. It is probably the last charter issued by Täklä-Häymanot. It was granted in 1899.The charter provides additional evidence about the existence of some concern for the well-being of the peasantry in some areas, if not elsewhere too. The charter offers further evidence to the argument that church *gult* land was essentially a right to the soil rather than a right to tribute. The division of the land was on the basis of two-thirds for the *däbtära* and one-third for the *restäñña*. It is stated in this grant document that the charter was drawn on the model of the charter of Däbrä-Marqos church and ultimately on the model of Moṭa Giyorgis church. One of the most important indications of the right of the *däbtäras* in the soil was that the charter states that if the *däbtäras* and the *restäññas* quarrel over land the judge would be the *çheqa*, "ደብተራና ባለርስት በመሬት ቢጣሉ ጭቃው ዳኝቶ ከአስቃው ይደርሳል-" which literally means; [t]he case arising out of dispute over land between the *däbtäras* and the *restäññas* shall be heard by the *çheqa* and it shall be referred to [the appeal judge], the *aläqa*." The payment of the *çheqa-mägaräfya* was made a charge upon the *restäññas*. The charter exempted the peasantry who were made to support Mass, candle and incense from the payment of their full obligation. Moreover those villagers who were given as the *yä-aläqa amsteya agär* (one-fifth of the *aläqa* land) were exempted the payment of their full dues if their economic standing could not allow them to meet the demands of the church officials for any reason as the evidence of the following lines from the charter show "...ይፖውም ሲጋኝ ጨውን ይስጥ፤ ሚያጣ ሲሶውን አስቀርቶ 2እጂ ዕርቦ ይስጥ፤ የስነዶውም ስርአቱ እንዲህ ነው."[90] The assessment of the dues and obligation of the peasants occupying the land given for the support of Mass was partly made in cash and partly made in wheat. Here the charter exempted the peasants from the payment of the tax in *çhäw* (salt bar) and allowed them to retain a third of the total amount of the dues originally assessed. The exigencies, which could lead for such a consideration, are not stated. The charter simply states that special exemptions from the payment of the total taxes and dues should be given for peasants on the grounds of their inability to pay. Presumably calamities both natural like the *Kefu-Qan* (1888-1892) and artificial and independent of the cultivator could lead to the reconsideration of the original assessment. Whether the church officials would be able to demand retroactively the dues and taxes missed after the passing of the difficult times or not can not be known.

Like in many other charters King Täklä-Häymanot is the greatest beneficiary from both grants. Besides receiving *rim* lands he concentrated the office of *gebezzena* on three individuals one of whom was himself. The office was to rotate among the three *restäññas*. Moreover, the king made himself the overall administrator and the supreme appeal judge for the monastery of Gälila. The office of *çheqa* was given to individuals bearing high titles like *fitawrari*. The king was probably the biggest landlord in the region in the period under study. He concentrated extensive land under the cover of *rim* and the office of *gebbezena*.[91] However, it would probably be unfair or a misrepresentation to suggest that the king was inconsiderate of the well-being of the peasants. The extent to which he felt responsible to the well-being of the peasantry is vividly evidenced in the two charters discussed above. The mere fact of taking into consideration the paying capacity of peasants entered in some of the charters he issued shows the existence of some concern for the well-being of the peasantry and is a fine testament to the fact that he was a realistic ruler.

The discussion above and in the preceding chapters shed great light on our understanding of the nature and the scope of the right of social elites with regard to land and the land tenure system. The study is based on original and primary documents which have not so far been used. *Zègenät* which is extensively discussed in this study suggests the inadequacy of our knowledge in certain fields such as class and the land tenure system. The discussion about this institution points to its high importance in the local social structures of Eastern Gojjam. From the forgoing one important consequence of this institution on land tenure system is self-evident. As we have seen *rim* land was held individually and exclusively. The beneficiaries of *rim* land had also the right to transfer their land through various means of conveyance including sale. Thus one concomitant result of the institution of *zègenät* is the development of private property and a very vigorous trade in land. Therefore, in addition to the tremendous increase in the amount of church land brought about by the Täklä-Häymanot there had been a not inconsiderable private and voluntary transfer or grants of land to churches and monasteries in this period. Side by side with property transfer to institutions there was a great number of property transactions horizontally among individuals. Such a focus of interest would surely be important and the next chapter is devoted to a discussion of the mechanism of property transfer and to exploring the motives of individuals in adopting certain modes of transfer.

NOTES

[1] Crummey, *Land and Society*,pp.212-214, Bizualem Birhane, "Adal Abba Tanna Nigus of Gojjam and Kaffa 1850-1901"(BA thesis in history, Haile-Sellase I University, 1971), p.53, Kindeneh Endeg, "A History of Dabra-Marqos Church at Dabra-Marqos Town"(BA thesis history, Addis Ababa University,1997),pp.9-14.

[2] Bahru Zewde,<u>A Modern History of Ethiopia</u>(London: James Curry,1990),p.48,Bizualem ,p.52, Crummey, *Land and Society*,pp.212-214, Richard Caulk, " Religion and the State in Nineteenth Century Ethiopia" in <u>Journal of Ethiopian Studies</u>,10,no.1(1972),pp.23-36.There had been a very bitter religious controversy between the big monasteries in Eastern Gojjam over relgion. Märṭulä-Maryam, Moṭa and Däbrä-Wärq were *Qebat* protagonists whereas Dima Giyorgis was the bastion of *Täwahdo* Habtamu, "A Short History of the Monastery of Marṭula-Maryam," p.15.

[3] Täklä-Iyäsus, "Yä Gojjam Tarik", pp.111-113.

[4] The largest record of church *gult* grants is contained in an MS. entitled Mäzgäb, deposited in the church of Däbrä-Marqos (folios5recto through to folio62recto). Täklä-Häymanot received many plots of land and his name is entered in all of the charters.

[5] <u>Ibid</u>, Crummey, *Land and Society*, p.10-11.

[6] Daniel, Arba'etu-Wängèl, MS.Bichäna Giyorgis, 89, II, 3-8,*Idem*, Nägärä-Maryam, MS. Mängesto Kidanä-Meherät 89,IX,?

[7] _____, Arba'etu-Wängèl, MS. Bichäna Giyorgis, 89, II, 3-8.

[8] <u>Ibid</u>. The Amharic text is full of technical terms .The terms like *femenqèt* that should be read as *fum-ençhät* is written as in the original text. The Amharic text reads as follows:

[9] <u>Ibid.</u>
[10] <u>Ibid.</u>
[11] <u>Ibid.</u>
[12] <u>Ibid.</u>
[13] <u>Ibid.</u>
[14] <u>Ibid.</u>
[15] <u>Ibid.</u>
[16] <u>Ibid.</u>
[17] <u>Ibid.</u>
[18] Täklä-Iyäsus, "Yä Gojjam Tarik", p.87.

[19] Daniel, Tamrä-Iyäsus, MS.,Gemja-Bèt Kidanä-Meherät,89,I,13-32,Crummey, *Land and Society* ,p.214.
[20] Mäzgäb, MS.Däbrä-Marqos, folio41verso to 43verso.
[21] Daniel, Tamrä-Iyäsus, MS. Gemja-Bèt Kidanä-Meherät, 89, I, 13-32.
[22] Crummey, *Land and Society*, p.214.However, Crummey seems to have shifted his level of analysis. In a recent paper on the subject of *rim* he does seem to have presented a position contrary to his former view, *idem*, "The Term *rim* in Ethiopian Land Documents of the 18th and 19 th Centuries", pp.72-74
[23] See note No.21 above
[24] Ibid.
[25] Ibid, Mäzgäb, MS. Däbrä-Marqos, folio 10r
[26] Daniel, Tamrä-Iyäsus, MS. Gemja-Bèt Kidanä-Meherät, 89, I, 13-32,
[27] Ibid.
[28] Ibid.
[29] Ibid.
[30] Ibid.
[31] Ibid.
[32] Ibid.
[33] Ibid.
[34] Ibid.
[35] Mäzgäb, MS. Däbrä-Marqos, folios 5r-14r.
[36] Ibid, folio5r, 7r to 7v, 10r.
[37] Ibid, folio 7r and 7v and Täklä-Iyäsus, "The Genealogy of the People of Gojjam", folio17r.
[38] Mäzgäb, MS. Däbrä-Marqos, folios29recto to34verso, 60recto to62recto.
[39] Ibid, folios 29recto and 34verso.
[40] Ibid, folios60recto to 62recto.
[41] Ibid.
[42] Ibid, folio10verso.
[43] Tubiana, p.59.
[44] Mäzgäb, MS. Däbrä-Marqos folio10verso.
[45] Ibid, folios5verso to10verso.
[46] Ibid.
[47]Daniel, Tamrä-Iyäsus, MS. Gemja-Bèt Kidanä-Meherät, 89,I, 13-32,___,Nägäst, MS. Yälämläm Kidanä-Meherät,89,XV,29-32,___,Wanna-Mäzgäb,MS.Däbrä-Eliyas,89,XVIII,9-31.

[48] _____, Nägäst, MS.Yälämläm Kidanä-Meherät, 89, XV, 29-32.
[49] _____, Wanna Mäzgäb, MS.Däbrä-Eliyas, 89, XVIII, 9-31.
[50] Mäzgäb, MS.Däbrä-Marqos, folio10verso, Käsatè-Berhän Tässäma, Yä-Amareñña Mäzgäbä Qalat (Addis Ababa: Artistic Printing Press, 1951), p.514, Kidanä-Wäld, p.526.
[51] Mäzgäb, MS.Däbrä-Marqos, folio14verso.
[52] Ibid, folio11verso, 12recto and 15recto.
[53] Ibid, folio9verso.
[54] Ibid, folio10recto.
[55] Ibid.
[56] Ibid, folio10verso.
[57] Ibid.
[58] Ibid, folio8recto to 9recto.
[59] Ibid, folio10verso.
[60] Ibid, folio8recto to 9recto Informants, Märigèta Gètè, interviewed (in Addis Ababa) on 18/1102, and Märigèta Libanos.
[61] Mäzgäb, MS.Däbrä-Marqos, folio9recto.
[62] Ibid.
[63] Ibid, folio8verso, 22verso to 23recto.
[64] Daniel, Wanna Mäzgäb, MS.Däbrä-Eliyas, 89, XVIII, 9-31
[65] Ibid, Abebaw, "A Short History of Däbrä Elias Church, 1874-1974", p.14.
[66] Abebaw, "A Short History of Däbrä Elias Church, 1874-1974," p.13.
[67] Daniel, Wanna Mäzgäb, MS.Däbrä-Eliyas, 89, XVIII, 9-31.
[68] Ibid.
[69] Ibid.
[70] Cited in Abebaw, "A Short History of Däbrä Elias Church, 1874-1974", p.26.
[71] Mäzgäb, MS.Däbrä-Marqos, folio15verso.
[72] Daniel, Wanna Mäzgäb, MS.Däbrä-Eliyas, 89, XVIII, 9-31.
[73] Ibid, Idem, Tamrä-Iyäsus, MS.Gemja-Bèt Kidanä-Meherät, 89,I, 13-32, Mäzgäb, MS. Däbrä-Marqos, folios5recto to 20verso, 39recto to 48verso, Idem, Arba'etu-Wängèl, MS.Bichäna Giyorgis, 89,II, 3-8, _____, Nägärä-Maryam, MS. Mängesto Kidanä-Meherät 89,IX,etc.
[74] Daniel, Wanna Mäzgäb, MS.Däbrä-Eliyas, 89, XVIII, 9-31.
[75] Ibid.
[76] Abebaw, p.24.
[77] Daniel, Wanna Mäzgäb, MS.Däbrä-Eliyas, 89, XVIII, 9-31.

[78] Ibid.
[79] Mäzgäb, MS. Däbrä-Marqos, folio15verso.
[80] Daniel, Wanna Mäzgäb, MS.Däbrä-Eliyas, 89, XVIII, 9-31.
[81] Ibid.
[82] Mäzgäb, MS. Däbrä-Marqos, and folio15verso.
[83] Daniel, Wanna Mäzgäb, MS.Däbrä-Eliyas, 89, XVIII, 9-31.
[84] Ibid.
[85] Besratä-Gäbra'el, MS. Däbrä-Marqos, folio110verso.
[86] Daniel, Wanna Mäzgäb, MS. Däbrä-Eliyas, 89, XVIII, 9-31.
[87] _____, Wängèl, MS. Moṭa Giyorgis, 89, IX, 3.
[88] Mäzgäb, MS. Däbrä-Marqos, folio39recto to 41recto.
[89] Ibid.
[90] Ibid.
[91] Ibid.

CHAPTER FOUR

PROPERTY AND MODES OF PROPERTY TRANSFER: INDIVIDUAL RIGHTS AND THE COMMERCIALIZATION OF LAND

4.1 Property and the Making of Property Documents

Before passing into internal information contained in the property documents, the question why and how they were written merits an equal interest, as this would allow us to address the larger issue of the concern and purpose of property transfer. The writing of property documents seems to be a result of specific historical processes. The period when property documents first come into common use and the use of writing for business dealings in land and other property can not be fixed with absolute certainty.[1] Generally, however, the earliest property documents in Eastern Gojjam date from the second half of the 18th century. Presumably when land acquired a negotiable value it led into a market in land and it was this property transaction through sale that apparently called for a careful system of recording. Thus the need for registration or record of property transaction seems to have arisen with the commercialization of land. Though it is very difficult to recapture the modes of operation of the traditional means of recording of land transactions before the literate habit of recording transfer was established, it seems that it was not able to cope with the conditions created by the vigorous trade in land and other properties. It is apparent that trade in land made it imperative to register business dealings in land.

There seems to have been a number of other factors at work behind the keeping of records. The record of land transactions could also be considered as a response to political conditions. The practice of buying and selling land started in earnest in the period known as the Era of Princes. The period was marred by incessant military conflicts.[2] The unsettled political conditions of the period together with the growing importance of money as the operative medium to acquire land title, which brought in its wake a new departure from the preexisting mode of access to land apparently, led to a confusion and proliferation in land titles. This in turn presumably rendered the traditional modes of recording transfers and deeds insufficient and unreliable. Therefore oral media (witness) could not afford security of tenure in a period characterized by incessant political and military disturbances. The acquisition of land through purchase might have created many openings and causes for a flourishing of land litigations and it was with the purpose of securing validity to purchased land that documents were made.

Some documents bear definite evidence from which we can draw firm conclusions about the salient features, which will enable us to understand the factors and principles underlying the making of records. Churches and monasteries had a well developed system or arrangement for recording property dealings in land and other forms of property so as to avoid confusion or conflicts of interests and reduce the scope of litigations. Charters laid down conditions and inserted clauses regulating the registration of deeds and transactions.[3] The administrative hand book of Däbrä Wärq also contains regulations suggestive of the provisions often contained in the charters and other church documents concerning the registration of deeds. It is stated in this manual that any important disposal or acquisition by inheritance or purchase would not be valid unless and otherwise supervised by the *mägabi* and another official of the church called *ambäras* (lit. head or guardian of an a*mba*, but its meaning in this context I have not been able to establish) and properly registered in the central registry of the church. Anyone could apply to register his or her dealings in land and his/her name would, on his or her application, be registered as owner upon the payment of one rock-salt as registration fee to the two officials, and as a remuneration for their service of putting boundary marks on the land which was the object of the transaction. Any important disposal by sale or inheritance would be registered in the central registry and the rule required the presence of the abbot and the officials upon payment of the necessary registration fee. Proper registration conferred upon the transacting parties validity of the deed, which it would not otherwise have had. Any disposal would not have validity and could not be recorded in the register of deeds without the presence of the abbot and the officials of the monastery. This explains why land transaction was commonly committed to writing.[4]

It seems that the presence of church officials was an imperative need in particular. Indeed there is no extant document which does not invoke and bear the name of church officials.[5] This was done probably to attain publicity and further validity to the transaction. All the witnesses and guarantors would give a certain degree of additional security and validity for the transaction in case of any adverse claim. In other words those present during the event to observe the transaction would be called upon by the court to bear witness to the validity of the document on the occasion of land dispute. However, the presence of witnesses alone could not guarantee security indefinitely and hence the need to put down in writing the transaction.

Any person at any time including a long time after the transaction had taken place could ask for and get granted the permission of church officials or the regional lord for his land transaction to be placed on the register. There are tangible proofs for this. One of the most interesting classes of such cases took place in 1899 when *Lej* Ṣämru Asägehäññ (whom we will meet towards the end of this chapter) pleaded for the registration of his land transactions in Däbrä-Marqos to King Täklä-Häymanot. Ṣämru and his father *Balambaras* Asägehäññ were actively engaged in the land market from the early decades of the nineteenth century to the end of the century at Märṭulä-Maryam and all of their property dealings were recorded in the different folios of the Registry of Deeds at Märṭulä-Maryam. Ṣämru demanded that all his holdings acquired through purchase and other means be recorded in Däbrä-Marqos too. And all of it was recorded accordingly by the permission of the king in a manuscript of Däbrä-Marqos called *Giyorgis Wäldä Amid* (folio 191r).[6] Another classic example is the will of *Wäyzäro* Sehin, daughter of *Däjjazmach* Ayo (governor of Bägèmder during the reign of Iyasu II).This will is recorded in Märṭulä-Maryam, Qäranyo Mädehänè-Aläm and Moṭa Giyorgis.[7] The recording of titles and land transactions served an important function by promoting a sense of security and reducing the scope of litigation. Purchasers ordered the careful recording of their property dealings in different places so as to reduce the incidence of the destruction of evidence and insure the security of their title to a purchased property by denying any accidental or other destructive occurrence providing loopholes for an adverse claim.[8] Therefore, the practice of recording transactions in many places at the same time was aimed at increasing the chance of the preservation of the documents so that the purchaser could use them as a proof or a reference in any future dispute to counter an adverse claim.[9]

In some areas fraudulent documents were registered. One such outstanding fraudulent document involving persons who bore high titles was discovered during the reign of King Täklä-Häymanot in a place called Däwaro around the monastery of Däbrä-Wärq. The case was referred to the court of Täklä-Häymanot and the fraudulent document was deleted after serious court investigation.[10] Several documents were also deleted in other areas following similar procedures or by the decision of the court.[11] In some instances it seems that to cope with and to avoid the problem of the registration of some defective documents transacting parties were asked in Märṭulä-Maryam to apply for registration to government representatives and get the signature or the seal of the government body before their transaction could be recorded in the Register of Deeds. Moreover oral testaments could also be registered after the confirmation of their validity by the father confessor. Some oral testaments that took place at moments of death were subsequently included into the Register of Deeds upon the application of individuals and only after the confirmation of their authenticity. Two oral testaments were recorded in the Registry ten and nine years after they were made on the approval of the father confessor and other people who were called upon to act as witnesses at the event in Märṭulä-Maryam.[12]

The charter of Däbrä-Eliyas too bears a provision which states that any important disposal of residential sites by sale and registration of deeds could take place upon the authorization and knowledge of church officials.[13] King Täklä-Häymanot appointed a certain *aläqa* Tägäññ as chief registrar of deeds for the church of Däbrä-Marqos. Tägäññ was given *rim* land to remunerate him for his services. As chief registrar Tägäññ was entrusted with the control and supervision of all land registrations. It is stipulated in the charter of Däbrä-Marqos church that the office was created for the express purpose of recording land transactions involving the *däbtära* and others and for a careful inventory of church properties.[14] In the influential charter of Wälätä-Isra'el, there is also a clause regulating the registration of transactions. All the *däbtära* were exempted from the payment of registration fees. Other transacting parties were required to pay a registration fee and a certain part of the revenue collected from such sources was used to remunerate the subordinate official or assistant of the principal *gäbäz* of the church.[15]

There is a tangible piece of evidence in the charter of Däbrä-Marqos that the Register was used as a reference for solving litigations or any dealings in property. It is noted in the charter that the Mäzgäb (Registry) should be kept in the treasury and anybody had the right to search in the registry for any registered document or any information on matters which required the evidence of the Registry. However, by no means could it be taken out of the churchyard for the purpose of reference to settle any dispute.[16] According to informants the Moṭa registry was not bound together since there were many applicants for the right of search of documents each day. Everybody had to pay some fee for searching recorded documents in the registry. To serve as many individuals as possible at a time the register was divided into many quires containing different number of folios.[17] This is exquisitely suggestive of the fact that the systems of tenure did not only envisage the transference of land by sale or other means but also that when possession was contested the population used those property registries to settle disputes.

4.2 Modes and Factors of Property Transaction

4.2.1 Sale and Redeemability of Land

I am principally concerned with analyzing and identifying the factors which determined the modes of property transfer. Moreover, the nature of the property right involving land will be defined with reference to the mode of property transfer. The discussion in this chapter is essentially based on two original manuscripts containing immensely important property documents. One of the manuscripts is called Däqiqä Näbeyat (lit. means the Minor Prophets) and also known as Yäwel-Mäzgäb (Register of Deeds) found at Märṭulä-Maryam. The second manuscript is found in the treasury of Moṭa Giyorgis church. There it is called Mäzgäb and is not bound together. The Register of Deeds at Märṭulä-Maryam is inventoried as G1-IV-16 by the Ministry of Culture. The writer has reproduced this manuscript. It measures 27x38cm. It has 264 folios. The first three folios and folios 193recto through to folio264verso are all property dealings. The margins of other folios are also covered with property documents. The binding is of red leather on wooden boards and in a distressed condition. Both manuscripts have highly developed marginalia recording many forms of land transactions ranging from will to charters of manumission, sales to gifts, inheritance to litigations and many other historical notes. Taken together the manuscripts form a useful treasure of many strands of customs with regard to property of all sorts. The second thing that makes these manuscripts exceptional is their volume. Many important documents are written in almost every important margin of these manuscripts. The folios are additions made at different times. In both the Registry of Deeds and the Mäzgäb of Moṭa the quires are irregular and the folios have different size and quality. The distance between the lines and the number of columns on each folio likewise differ in spacing. The Mäzgäb has five hundred folios and most of them measure approximately 40cm X 40cm. I have copied the land transactions contained in the 350 folios.[18]

The property registers describe the names of the transacting parties, the witnesses, the prices of the properties transacted, etc. They also record the location of the land being transacted in the framework of its locality and after the early decades of the twentieth century the specific date, month and year on which the transaction took place are also given. From the standpoint of the Märṭulä-Maryam and Moṭa documents sale, gifts, wills, inheritance-related bequeathals involving adoptions, inheritance and litigations were the major methods of acquiring or relinquishing of property rights. Below are given the main features of three of the modes of land transaction. Although a full range of the property dealings are recorded a good percentage of the transactions belong to sales of land and titles to land. Sales of land have been going on for over three centuries and land transactions or transfers occasioned by sale had preponderance than those by way of gifts, wills, etc.[19]

A very vigorous trade in agricultural land, residential or building sites and rural lands and houses together with gardens started in the towns in the mid-18th century and continued through to the 19th century. Land sale attained a very high degree of intensity in the 20th century. The necessary conditions for the development of a particular kind of market in land were the result of quite specific historical processes. What factors or combination of factors produced the practice of buying and selling of land? Crummey asserts that the revival of trade and the attendant urban growth of many towns along the trade routes made land around towns very dear. This in turn produced the practice of buying and selling land and other properties. The country had a strong commercial contact with Sennar, its northwestern neighbor, and the Red Sea area in the period under study. He further asserts that the growing insecurity of life in the period (late 18th and 19th centuries) increased the importance of towns with churches, which served as sanctuaries.[20] I do not have a priori objection to the point that urban growth was a useful source of wealth for landowners who gained cash through outright sale of residential sites. However, although Crummey speaks about the strong commercial link or activity between the Red Sea region and Ethiopia the custom of transferring land through sale was neither adopted as a result of foreign influence nor was it solely a consequence of the revival of trade. To begin with Märṭulä-Maryam where land transaction through sale had been going on at least since the second half of the 18th century right through to 1972 was not located along the major trade route in the period under study. It was found very far away from it. Secondly nobody took refuge in the monastery in times of difficulty and once during the Era of Princes it was plundered.[21]

The custom of transferring land through sale was induced by many complicated factors. Thus as a complement to Crummey's argument it is necessary to examine the possibility of other factors working behind sales. I believe that the eighteenth century brought a new definition of property rights in land. The necessary conditions that led for the creation of the market in land were individual proprietary right and what might be considered its corollary or concomitant, the right of free disposal. The category of land that we find in most of the documents recording transaction is *rim* land though *rest* land transfer is to be met frequently. As we have seen extensively in the previous chapters *rim* land was held individually and exclusively. Thus just as *zégenät* was instituted for fulfilling the special needs of the social elites and possibly caused by other socio-economic exigencies, land transaction was thus occasioned by certain conditions and to meet the demands of elites. Land sale was a response to a new trend in the growing commercial outlook of land and the presence of the absolute freedom of disposal, which, I believe, lay at the root of all business dealings in land.[22] The emergence of individual proprietary rights, the acquisition of negotiable value by land, the full recognition of the right of transferring land for cash and economic forces that might for long have been at work were some of the factors behind the transfer of right through sale.

It is logical to assume that under normal circumstances individuals would be disinclined to give up land, particularly *rest* land, willingly by sale unless sufficient conditions that warranted transfer by sale existed. In a not inconsiderable number of cases property was transferred because of the helplessly poor conditions of many individuals, as we will see below. Thus I have delineated the following factors that led men to choose sale as a means of transfer. Sale could take place a) when the market was good b) when the necessity to raise money to meet social and economic obligations arose c) utter desperation of individuals due to natural or artificial calamities like famine and pillage and last but not least and related to the third reason is d) crushing debt. Each of these factors will be discussed in their proper place in the pages that follow.

Many documents of the 19th century often acknowledge the widespread existence of large credit extended to many individuals and their bankruptcy because of burdens of debt. There are many reliable documents which show us that due to severe debts many individuals were left with no choice save to resort to the sad fate of transferring their land and residential houses to their creditors. This conclusion is supported by many documents, as we shall see in the pages below.[23] It is apparent that the worst case of loss to many people usually occurred in times of difficulty occasioned by some natural or man-made calamities. The desperately poor state of many people resulted in the dispossession of their ancestral heritage, including *rest* land in many instances, through sale and debt. That this was true throughout the nineteenth century is very easy to show since it is attested by many documents. Individuals who were forced to sell parcels of their residential sites and lands due to their helplessly poor conditions in times of difficulties usually made a desperate attempt to regain their land after the passing of the bad times. This explains much of the instability in some places particularly in the Moṭa area. The problem of land litigation in Moṭa was so serious and such a threat to civil peace that King Täklä-Häymanot was forced to intervene by writing a letter to the church authorities of Moṭa ordering them to take measure so as to reduce the scope of litigation. Consider the evidence of the following lines from a letter of Täklä-Häymanot to the officials of Moṭa Giyorgis church which provides a very fine example on the existence of sale induced by the deep poverty of many people.[24]

የተላከ ከንጉስ ተክለሃይማኖት ርቱአ ሃይማኖት ወልዱ ለቅዱስ ማርቆስ ወንጌላዊ ፤ ይድረስ ከመላከ ገነት ወልደጊዮርጊስ ከአለቃ ገብረ ኤልያስ ከማህበሩ

እንዬት ሰነበታችሁ ፤ ፤ እኔ እግዚአብሔር ይመስገን ደህና ነኝ ። ጥንት በቃ የወለተ እስራኤል ይብቃ ብያለሁ ። ቦታም የሽጠ ዕሪምም የያዘ በባሀር ደብዳቤ ይቁም ፤ ፤ በዚህም በጥንቱ አዋጅ አስነግሩ ፤ ፤ በክፉ ጊዜ እየሸጠ እየበላ ቀን ሲወጣ ቢይዝ ስለምን ትይዛላቸሁ ፤ ፤ ዳኛስ ትሆናላቸሁ ፤ ፤ አሁንም በእንዲህ ያለ ነገር ሁሉ በሸጠበት ይቁም ፤ ፤ አታስከስሱ ፤ ፤

This letter is sent from King Täklä-Häymanot, son of Saint Mark the Evangelist, Orthodox in his religion. May it reach to Mälakä-Gänät Aläqa Gäbrä-Eliyas, [and] the community [of Moṭa]. How have you been? I, thanks to God, am well. I declare, that [you] stick to the old custom, in accordance to the practice during the time of Wälätä-Isra'el. Let the selling or holding of bota or rim be determined in the baher däbdabè (the Central Registry of the church). To this effect reissue the ancient decree. Why do you adjudicate over cases when a person sells in bad times and use [the money] and reclaims in better times? As of now let the transaction remain binding. Do not allow litigation to proceed in such cases.

The letter attempts to regulate litigation. It also testifies that bad times brought about the impoverishment of individuals which in turn led to important business dealings in land. In such circumstances individuals would be ready to make their land available to pass through sale to distant kinsmen or simply to the highest bidder who might not have any blood relationship with the vendor at all. The letter allows such a confident statement on the presence of frequent sales induced by bad times. We have records of serious droughts during the governorship of *Däjjach* Tädlä Gwalu (r.1854-1867)[25] and the well known Great Ethiopian Famine (1889-1892). Such natural disasters as famines undoubtedly left people in a hopeless impasse and landowners would have no alternative save to transfer whatever property they had through sale to individuals who might have little or no connection with the land whatsoever so as to survive the disaster. It would seem from the evidence of this document that land transactions in bad times did not decline from the level of sale in prosperous times. Indeed buyers could be encouraged to act by dramatic decrease in the selling price of land during such trying days as the *Kefu-Qän*, which would provide a golden opportunity for buying land. Thus instead of a fall in the volume of transactions in the land market bad times could spur an active trade in land and this can explain the reason why the trade in land was active throughout the nineteenth century, since bad times were frequent occurrences in this century. Thus many people were faced with acute debt pressure in bad times or shortly afterwards and the most important motive for selling land might be the need to clear debts. From the consideration of the above document, it is easy to argue, that vendors were motivated to sell part of their land to clear debts or even to survive. Many lands were perhaps offered for buyers during bad times. Indeed to find a buyer was perhaps a very rare opportunity during the *Kefu-Qän* given the scale of the famine. It was with the purpose of mitigating the flourishing land dispute that brought a considerable burden on the judiciary and the concern for public order that induced Täklä-Häymanot to write the letter to the church officials of Moṭa Giyorgis ordering them to take measures.[26]

We can deduce from the evidence of the above letter that transactions in land through sale could not always be redeemed. Whether land transferred through sale would be reversed or not was determined by the terms of agreement signed by the parties involved in the transaction. In other words when land was sold the seller did not retain a right of redemption whether at its original price or any price unless and otherwise there was a provision to reverse the transaction. The original owner of land could lose his/her land permanently unless the purchaser was willing to resell the land back to the original owner. The holding of the new owner of the land could be either on the basis of terminable privilege or permanent, depending on the agreement between the transacting parties. The original owner or his close kinsmen had the right to repurchase any land sold if the purchaser happened to be willing to resell it. It is clear from the above evidence that many people who sold their land during the *Kefu-Qän* were determined and perhaps did as much as they could do to regain their land lost through sale by repurchase.[27] The deed of land transaction was very binding though it was open for contestation and disputation. What all this mean is that the rigor and working of the customary rule of property transfer might be tempered and even be ignored altogether according to the specific exigencies of the time.[28]

Sitting in judgment over land disputes seems to have been a very fruitful source of revenue for church officials. For that reason church official in Moṭa seems to have been ready to be judges in disregard of the provision of the charter of Wälätä-Isra'el. This was mainly because they wanted to collect money from the proceeds of justice.[29] In the manual for the officials of the monastery of Däbrä-Wärq, church officials were allowed to inflict or impose a fee of four rock-salts for judgment if the case was land dispute and if the plaintiff referred the case to top officials without respect to the hierarchy of courts. Everybody was ready to sit in judgment over land and other disputes.[30] The officials of the church seem to have introduced some detrimental innovations which might have brought some insecurity with regard to purchased land contrary to the rule regulating land transactions through sale in the charter of Wälätä-Isra'el. This was aimed, as mentioned above, at collecting judgment fees. The king ordered the officials to stick to the practice of the old days as in the days of Wälätä-Isra'el and demanded that the church officials issue a decree to this effect. Thus purchasers enjoyed a real security of tenure of the purchased land and the practice in the majority of the areas seems that the purchaser retained the purchased land permanently. The king ordered that to avoid prevailing confusion, which land transaction through sale could immensely contribute, every sale document should be entered into the *baher-däbdabè*, i.e. the Central Registry which was intended to give validity to the transaction.[31] Let us see the extent to which the evidence in the letter of Täklä-Häymanot can be supplemented by other documents. Let us consider the following class of cases contained in the Central Register of Moṭa Giyorgis.[32]

Document 1:

በመላክ ሰላም ክንፈ ሚከኤል በአለቃ ወልደጊዮርጊስ ሹመት የያሬድ ክብቶ የልጅ ልጅ እንግዳየ በርህቡ ጊዜ 4 ድርብ...አስምንት ድርብ ጢፍ ተበድራ በልታ ሶስት ጨው ጨምራ ገንዘብ የለኝም ብላ የኔን ቦታየንም ኡ ርስቴንም ሰብላታ ፈንታ ስትሸጥ መድኑ ኖሪህ ተሻለ ።። መሳክርቱ ረብዙ ሰዉች ስም ተዘርዝራል ፪።።

During the tenure of office of Mälakäsäläm Kinfä-Mika'el and Aläqa Wäldä-Giyorgis, the grand daughter of Yarèd Käbtè, Engedayä, having borrowed and consumed four dereb(unit of measurement of grain)...and eight dereb tèff including three rocksalts, [and] saying she has nothing [to pay], sold her bota and rest [land] to [the creditor] blatta Fäntä. The guarantor is Noräh Täšalä. The witnesses [many people are listed].

Document 2:
በመላከ ሰላም ክንፈ ሚከኤል በአለቃ ወልደጊወረጊስ ሹመት የኪዳነ ማርያም ሀይሉ ልጅ ሰው አገኘሁ አስር ድርብ ጤፍ ተብድሮ በልቶ ከእንዚህ ወልደጊዮርጊስ እሱም የሚከፍለው ቢያጣ ዋሱም ለእንዚህ ወልደጊዮርጊስ ደስታ የትኖሮ የገዛውን እኩሌታ ጨርሶ ሲሽጥ መድኑ ብላታ አየለ ኦ መሳክርቱ ረየብዙ ሰዎች ስም ተዘርዝራልሪ።።

During the tenure of office of Mälakäsälam Kinfä-Mika'el and Aläqa Wäldä-Giyorgis the son of Kidanä-Maryam, Säw-Agäññähu, having borrowed and consumed ten dereb tèff from Adgäh Wäldä-Giyorgis, and since he has nothing to repay [his debt], the [debtor] guarantor sold all of the remaining half of the land, the [other half] formerly bought by Dästa Yät-Noro, for Adgäh Wäldä-Giyorgis. The guarantor is blatta Ayälä. The witnesses are [list of many people]

Document 3:
በመላከ ሰላም ክንፈ ሚከኤል በአለቃ ወልደጊዮረጊስ ሹመት በተሰረቁት በሶስት አህዮች በዳኛ ረቶ መትቶ የበሬው ኪዳኑን ዕሪሞች ቦታውንም ልጁቱ ስትሰጥ አባትዮው ሰብሮ ሄዶ አጋፋሪ አሰግሀኝ ሲቀበል መሳክርቱ ረየብዙ ሰዎች ስም ተዘርጉራልሪ።።

During the tenure of office of Mälakäsälam Kinfä-Mika'el and Aläqa Wäldä-Giyorgis , [Agafari Asägehäññ] won the case involving the theft of three of his donkeys by the decision of the judges. The bota and the rim [lands] of the [thief] Bärèw Kidanu are transferred by his daughter to Agafari Asägehäññ,

141

> since her father had escaped breaking [the prison?].
> The witnesses for this [list of many people]

These are some classic and extant documents on the transaction of property as the result of debts incurred during the great famine and to liquidate debts. Usually the land transferred in this way is depicted as a kind of freehold property. In the cases of documents one and two, land was acquired by the new owners because of the failure of the original holders to repay the dept incurred. We can make the following observation from the documents quoted above. A desperately weak person who is considerably indebted could sell and pass on to the creditor his/her land. There is no mention of the debtors consulting their kinsmen while transferring their land through sale to creditors. Nor is there any provision for redeeming the land through payment of the debt by the debtors.[33] This shows that the owner when selling his land may act on his own without obtaining the consent of or even consulting any person with a strong stake in the land. This in turn is a fine testament to the fact that cash might have been fully as important as the right of birth as a mechanism for acquiring and of relinquishing land although birthright remained the most important mechanism for establishing holding.

There is an explicit mention of the time when debt was incurred in the case of the first document. The debtor, Engedayä, borrowed grain and three rock-salts during the famine (*Kefu-Qän*) when people were reduced to the worst level of misery and poverty. The person in the second document was also unable to repay his debt, incurred most probably during the *Kefu-Qän* since the transaction took place during the tenure of office of the same officials. That the two persons were desperately poor can be inferred from the fact that they were not able to pay the debt of some quantity of grain and in the case of the first document including three rock-salts which would have been very easy to repay in normal years. The resort to surrendering *rest* land and *bota* for liquidating or clearing up old debts is another testimony to the abject poverty of the debtor because the sale of *rest* for reasons of debt might have been considered as a slight on honor by the society. The reason for the transfer of land in the case of the third document is slightly different. The person was sued for stealing three donkeys and after investigation the court decided to transfer his *rim* lands and residential site. The person apparently broke out of prison and escaped for which reason his daughter transferred the properties stated above on behalf of her father; since she had no other means to pay his liabilities.[34] As indicated above none of the land transactions above provides a redeemable pledge. We can infer from these instances that land which was lost to strangers (non-relatives) through debt constraints would not be regained by the repayment of the debt and the debtors seem to have accepted the reality of the permanent surrender of their lands since there is no provision in the transaction above as to whether the land right would be reacquired again by the former holders by the repayment of the debt.

Engedayä who was substantially indebted and as in the case of Säw-Agäññähu had to resort to selling land for payment of old debts she had contracted during the *Kefu-Qän*. We learn that the transaction took place during or shortly after the *Kefu-Qän* since she had not yet recuperated from the famine to pay her old debt without resorting to the surrendering of her *rest* land. What all this means is that personal bankruptcy through debt and forced sales for liquidating old debts probably made for much more of the land transactions than the need for obtaining cash throughout much of the nineteenth and the early decades of the next century. The motive of individuals selling land is not usually stated or known from the documents recording such transfers. Though the reasons for the transfer of land in the great majority of land sale documents is not stated, we can assume that there was the widespread existence of financial constraints and deep poverty silently working behind those land transactions the reasons for transfers of which are not stated.[35] A forced transfer of land to a stranger might have meant permanent loss unless and otherwise a special provision or terms of agreement at the time of transfer were made for the return of the land to its original holder on the repayment of the debt, irrespective of the consent and approval of kinsmen.

It is impossible, however, to make a complete analysis of the nature of forced sale from details given in the above documents only. Hence the need for considering more cases. Personal ruin in debt and forced transfers of property indeed proliferated in the twentieth century. The Register of Deeds of Märṭulä-Maryam is full of many forced transfers of land and residential sites. There are also many documents recording inheritance-related bequeathals, which are drawn both as sale and bequeathal and mortgage notes because of debt. This fact testifies that forced sale was a frequent occurrence in many areas. In Märṭulä-Maryam many people died in debt and creditors sued the children of the debtors.

Consider the following examples found here and there in the different folios of the Register of Deeds.[36]

Document 1:
በመምህር ለእክ ማርያም አየለ በቁስገበዝ ኀይለማርያም ስጦታው በመጋቢ ጥሩነህ እንግዳ ሹመት አቶ በላቸው ውበቱ ይብሳና ማርያም አባቱ በሴ የሆነ ርስቱን በምስራቅ ይበልጣል አበበ መሬት ኦ ከምዕራብ የደምሴ ታረቀኝ መሬት መቻከል ያለውን የይዞታ ርስቱን ለአቶ ይበልጣል አበበ ሰማንያ ዘጠኝ ብር እዳ ስለአለበት ለመክፈል ስለአልቻለ ስለእዳው አውርሷል ። አቶ ይበልጣልም በርስቱ በዘይቀርብ የአቶ በላቸው ወገን በዘይቀርብ ቢጠይቁ ገንዘቡን ተቀብሉ መሬቱን ሊለቅ ነው ። ።

During the tenure of office of Mämher La'ekä-Maryam Ayälä, Qèsä-Gäbäz Häylä-Maryam Seṭotaw and Mägabi Ṭerunäh Engeda, Ato Bälachäw Wubätu bequeathed [portion of] his rest holding which descended from the founding father Bässè, located in Yebesana Maryam, to the east of Yebältal Abäba's land, west of Dämissè Taräqäññ's land, to Yebalṭal Abäbä due to the debt of 89 birr which he could not repay. If the relations of Ato Bälachäw demand to redeem the rest [land held for debt], Ato Yebälṭal would leave the land upon receiving his money (261v-262r).

Document 2:
በመምህር ፊላታምስ በቁስገበዝ ፈንታ ስዮም በመጋቢ ፈንታ ሹመት አየለ ደርሰህ ከመጋቢ ፈንታ እንግዳ ሰላሳ ስድስት ብር ከባላምባራስ ገሰሳና ከግዬለው ጣቃ ሀያ ስድስት ብር ተበድሮ ስለሞተ ፣ አየለ ደርሰህ ወራሽ ስለአጣ የጡቱን ስለብራቸው የእስጢፋኖስን ሀገር ወርሷል ። ። ወራሽ የተገኝ እንደሆነ መጋቢ ፈንታ እንግዳ ብራቸውን ተቀብለው ረመሬቱንሪሊመልሱ ነው ። ።

144

During the tenure of office of Mämher Filatawos, Qèsä-Gäbäz Fänta Seyoum and Mägabi Fänta Engeda, Ayälä Därsäh died after borrowing 36 birr from Mägabi Fänta Engeda and twenty six birr from Balambaras Gässäsä and Gedeyäläw Ṭaqa, [and] since Ayälä Därsäh had no heir, he (Fänta Engeda) have inherited his (Ayälä's) land in Esṭifanos. If an inheritor is to be found Mägabi Fänta Engeda would give back the land on condition of receiving his money. (232v)

Document 3:
በራስ ጉግሳ በራስ ማርያ ዘመን ፈታውራሪ ጓንጉል ርእሰ ርኡሳን ሆነው ገብረ ህዮት ኪዳኑ ተሹሞ ገንዘብ*ን* አጥፍቶ ቢሞት በመምህር ቢኖር ቀ በቄስ ገበዝ መስተሳልም ቀ በመጋቢ ወዳጅ በሲህ ዳኛ ተከሰው ልጆች ብዙ ከብት ሆኖ ይከፍሉት ቢያጡ የግራቤትን ቦታ ተፈጽመው ሰጡ ፤ ፤ ይህንንም ለኤልያስ ጣይቱ ለልጁም ፈትአውራሪ ጓንጉል ሰጡ ፤ ፤

During the reign of Ras Gugsa [and] Ras Maryä, while Re'esä-Re'usan Gäbrä-Hiwot Kidanu was appointed Re'esa-Re'usan [he borrowed] Fitawrari Gwangul's money and died in debt. His children were sued and taken to the court presided by Mämher Binor, Qèsä-Gäbäz Mästäsalem and Mägabi Wädaji and [since the payment of the debt] made in cattle is too many and the children having nothing to repay they gave their bota in Gerabèt, by swearing. Fitawrari Gwangul gave this (the bota) to his daughter Eliyas Ṭayitu. (195v)

All the three documents provide further confirmation that land could be seized for debts incurred to creditors and even years after the death of the debtors. When forced transfers occurred there was usually the stipulation made safeguarding the new owner from interference by heirs or relatives of the debtor. In the case of the two documents the seller retained a right of redemption at its original price. This means that the new holder's right in the land was only on the basis of terminable privilege since the document acknowledged that kinsmen had the right to repurchase the land lost through debt. This evokes the view that land disposed by sale for whatever reason was subject to a right of redemption by the relative of the vendor. If the debt is not repaid, however, the land remained as land alienated because of debt. However, the huge percentage of the forced land transactions including all the above transactions did not mention reversion to the original owner or his relatives. In only two rare instances, folio231r and folio248v do we find the right of redeemable pledges of land at work.[37]

Having nothing to pay, according to the decision of the court, the children of *Re'esä- Re'usan* Gäbrä-Hiwot, surrendered their *bota* for liquidating old debts which their father had contracted. And all of the debtors in the documents cited above did not have any choice but the sad fate of surrendering their landed property. All of the lands and the *bota* in the case of document three come into the holding of the new owners through debt though there is possibility of redeeming the land lost through debt.[38]

In one outstanding case a certain Ayalèw Bogalä had to pass "all of his father's (Bogalä Anbaw's) land" to his creditor called *Grazmach* Alämayähu Birru for incurring a debt of one hundred thalers. This note exists on folio243v.[39] In case of document two above the dead man's property failed to find an inheritor. Since the person had no children, there was no one from whom to take the money and many unsuccessful offers for inheritance were probably made.[40] Many debtors were not able to get out of crushing debt during their lifetime. The decisions of the court which are known to us were invariably executed and remained binding.[41]

Though there are different and contradictory sets of data giving details of sale qualified by the redeem-ability of transacted land, the general trend and the tone of sources is such that land was permanently lost to non- family members (strangers) without the remotest link with the land. Though there is a tradition that says that nearest relatives has the right to buy land or redeem land, documents show that this was not always true. To clarify the points raised with the right of preemption and with redeemable mortgage, we need to consider a few cases from the Registry. We can infer from many documents in the Registry of Märṭulä-Maryam that a deeply indebted person could sell and pass his land on to a person who had no link with the land at all. It is apparent that in the huge percentage of documents incorporated in the Registry creditors who had no link with the land whatsoever obtained possession and ownership through cash. To facilitate discussion I have quoted the following examples.⁴²

Document 1:
በመምህር ፀሀይ በቄስገበዝ ወልደእየሱስ በመጋቢ ጥሩነህ እንግዳ ሹመት ገሰሰ አብተው ለአቶ ከልቻይ ሺበሺ ስለሙቶ ብር እዳ የሰጠውን መሬት አንደኛ ከባላምባራስ ተመስገን ይሁን አዋሳኝ ያለውን ፤ ሁለተኛ ከአባ ሺጦ ገብረኪዳን አዋሳኝ ያለውን ፤ ሶስተኛ ከአድጓ ቢሰውርና ከረታ ቢሰውር ረአዋሳኝ ያለውን ፤ ሶስተኛውን ከፍሶ ጋሻ ከአቶ ከልከይ ሺበሺ መጋቢ ጥሩነህ እንግዳ ስለእዳ ተቀበሉ ፤ ፤ መድኑ ባላምባራስ ተመስገን ፤ ፤

During the tenure of office of Mämher Ṣähäy, Qèsä-Gäbäz Wäldä-Iyäsus and Mägabi Ṯerunäh Engeda, Kälkay Shibäshi [transferred the following lands] which he acquired due to the debt of one hundred birr from Gässäsä Abetäw, to Mägabi Ṯerunäh Engeda: one is [found]adjacent to Balamabras Tämäsgän Yehun's land, the second [is found adjacent] to Abba Šitè Gäbrä-Kidan's holding, the third is [found adjacent] to Adegäh Bisäwer and Rätta Bisäwers' holdings, and the third[sic] land from Fisso gasha.Mägabi Ṯerunäh Engeda received [these lands] from Kälkay due to debt. The guarantor is Balambaras Tämäsgän. (240r).

Document 2:
...በመምህር ላእከ ማርያም አየለ ፤ በቄስገበዝ ሀይለ ማርያም ስጦታው ፤ በመጋቢ ጥሩነዉ እንግዳ ሹመት አቶ አንተነህ ይልማ ጉባ አፊ ክርስቶስ የተክሉን ምድር ከምስራቅ የመምህር ከሳ ምድር ፤ በምዕራብ ወንዙ መከከል የሚገኘውን የአቶ ዋለልኝ አንተነህ መቶ ሁለት ብር እዳ ስዕለ አለበት ስለ ዕዳው ወንድሞቹ እህቶቹ እንዳይደርሱበት በስርአት ገዳሙ ህግ በተለየ አውርሲአል ፤ ፤

> *During the tenure of office of Mämher La'ekä-Maryam, Qèsä-Gäbäz Häylä-Maryam Seṭotaw and Mägabi Ṭerunäh Engeda, Ato Antänäh Yelma bestowed Täklu's land in Guṭa Afä-Christos located to the east of Mämher Kassa's land [and] to the west of the river upon Wäläleññ Antänäh due to the debt of 102 birr. His sisters and brothers are not to interfere. He has bequeathed it to him especially in accordance with the regulation of the monastery.*

In the case of document two the person ordered his siblings not to take back the land which the debtor disposed of to his creditor by a special bequeathal. This fact is further suggestive of the reality that disposal of land by sale for whatever reason may or may not be subject to a right of redemption by the original owner. Whether the land right be reacquired again by reversing the sale by repurchase or not was determined by the specific terms agreed upon at the time of transfer. *Ato* Antänäh had no means to repay his debt and resorted to bequeathal. However, the same document indicates the existence of the possibility that the siblings and other nearest relatives had the right to a say in the disposal of land of their close kin, for the document unwittingly acknowledges their right by the inclusion of the special arrangement denying them chance to further interfere with the exercise of the right of the new owner. Conversely the specific injunction that his siblings were not to interfere shows he could make any kind of final disposal of the land without consulting persons with strong stakes in the land. In the case of document one the person acquired a piece of land from the one who had himself acquired it earlier through debt. The land changed hands more than once for reasons of debt. Kälkay acquired the land from the original owner Gässässä Abetäw, who surrendered the land to repay his debt of 100 thalers. Finally Ṭerunäh Engeda acquired the land from the second owner through debt.[43]

This indicates the speed with which land was changing hands in Märṭulä-Maryam within the lifetime of an individual. If the debtor had a special affection and love for the non-relative to whom he had transferred his land because of credit stringency the land can be lost permanently. If a person wished he/she could transfer the land irrespective of the consent and approval of the nearest relative, the transfer would be valid and the new owner could pass a valid title to a particular plot of land to a creditor through sale or any other means. Many of the land documents are full of phrases specifically prohibiting contest of sale by anyone who might have a strong stake in the land.[44]

Like Kälkay, many people bought lands and houses but only to lose them subsequently, being heavily indebted themselves. There is one such note on folio 241v when a certain *Mägabi* Fänta Moññä lost his *därb* (one storey building) for the debt of 250 thalers.[45] He contracted the debt from the church of Märṭulä-Maryam and the *därb* was acquired by the church. There are also other similar notes where the church served as a money lender. One of such notes exists on folio 235recto.[46] In the absence of data to the contrary it seems safe to argue that the non-relative purchasers enjoyed security of tenure and had valid titles to purchased lands. In one instance, a creditor who received a plot of land for a debt of fifty thalers sold it for 89 thalers making for himself the net profit of 36 thalers, a very fine reward.[47] Many other people probably earned large income in similar ways. This was perhaps because the debtors contracted their debt during difficult times when the price of land was not high and because of the subsequent rise in the selling price of land which offered a favorable opportunity for the creditor to sell his land acquired through debt.

There are also many property documents that have similar contents as the above. However, enough has been said on the nature of sale induced by credit stringencies and the right of the original owner or his/her closest kinsmen in redeeming land lost through debt. From all the above considerations and discussions, it would be a serious mistake to consider that sales of land were predominantly produced by the good land market and that *rest* land could be acquired only by virtue of being born into the descendants of the original settlers. Other causes of sale were the need to meet social and economic obligations.

Individuals bought and sold land because, it is logical to argue, there was a modest degree of monetization of the economy. In all the charters of the 18th and 19th centuries considered in this study tribute and tax were collected from peasants both in kind and cash and there was a very clear tendency of transition to money taxes. Thus with little risk of distortion of the reality we can make the following conclusion: that although the buying and selling took place in a predominantly agrarian society the economy was sufficiently monetized, and one of the factors which might have promoted transfer of land and other properties was the necessity to raise money to meet social and economic obligations. There are some documents in the Registry of Märṭulä-Maryam that record the sale of land for the purpose of raising money for the payment of fees for funeral services and covering court expenditures. In the charter of Wälätä-Isra'el, quoted in chapter two the fee paid for funeral services was called *asäbä mäqaber*. Thus some of the factors that promoted transfer of land included funerals, taxes and court cases.[48] From the point of view of the Märṭulä-Maryam and Moṭa documents though there might have been other motives and considerations the factors listed above exhaust the conditions leading to the sale.

This was probably true for other areas in the region too. Buying and selling of land suggests concentration of land and its converse or reverse the process of disintegration of holdings. There were some families and individuals who were active throughout the nineteenth and the early decades of the twentieth century as buyers and sellers. However, before discussing the successful purchasers and sellers we need to explore other modes of property transfer. The story of the individuals involved in the buying and selling process will be told in its appropriate place below. We now pass to the second chief means of property transfer, inheritance-related bequeathals next to sale. It is together with will the second important method of acquiring or relinquishing land and right to land.

4.2.2 Inheritance Related Bequeathal Involving Adoption and Will

The causes for bequeathal are as many as the causes for transaction. Will stands out diametrically opposed to inheritance because, unlike the principle of will, it evokes the principle of property on the basis of equal division. To avoid generalizations we would rely on documents by citing them extensively and then analyzing. The earliest and the most important extant document is the will of *Wäyzäro* Sehin of which mention has already been made.[49]

Document one:
ዓለም በተፈጠረ በ ፯ሺ ከ፰፻፺፮ ዘመን፣ በዘመነ ዮሀንስ፣ በዓጼ ጎሉ መንግስት ዕመይቦ ወይዘሮ ስሒን የደጃዝማች አዮ ልጅ ቤትዎን ሲሰሩ ያቦንም የናቦንም ጉልት ለልጄ ለክንፉ ሒሩት ሰጥቻለሁ ፤ መስጠቴም [ምክንያቱ]ልጅ የናቱን ከብት

ይወርሳል እረሲ ግን ያላትን የሌላትን ከቆሽነት
ጀምሮ እስከ ምንኩስና ድረስ ጨርሳ ሰታኛለችና
ረነውሪ፡፡ ከወንድሞችዋ ዲቃሎች ቢኖሩ እርሲን
ደጃጸንተው ብትሰጣቸው ይውሰዱ እንጂ ዳኛ
ቢያወጡ ግን እርጉም ይሁኑ፡፡ እርሲ የተከለችው
ይተከል ኦ የነቀለችው ይነቀል፡፡ እርግማኔን ያፈረስ
ቢኖር ከባሊ ከልጇ ያመጻችውን ከብት ኦ 5)ታቃ
ወወወቄት ወርቅአ 0 በቅሎ የስናር ልጅ ወስጀባት
አለሁ ሰጥተዋት ይብሉ፡፡ መሳክርቱም ረየብዙሰወች
ስም ተዘርዝራልሪ፡፡...ይህን የፋቀ በስልጣነ ጲጥሮስ
ወጳውሎስ አውግዘናል፡፡

In the year of creation of the world, 7296, in the year of Yohannes, in the governorship of Emperor (sic) Gwalu, Emäytè Wäyzäro Sehin daughter of Däjjazmach Ayo ,establishes her house as follows, I have given the gult which I acquired from my mother and my father to my daughter Kinfu Hirut .The reason for my gift is that a child inherits his /her mother's cattle ,however, she(Hirut) gave me whatever she has from the day of my youth till the time I was shorn as a nun. If there are bastards from among her brothers they should beg her [for shares] and if she wishes to give them let they (Hirut's brothers) take. Otherwise if they sue her and take her to a judge let them be cursed. Whoever she disinherits let him be disinherited and whomever she establishes let him be established. If they violate my curse, they share [my property] upon the repayment of the cattle, the 500 ounces of gold and the ten mules she brought from her husband and gave me. The witnesses are [many people are listed]. We have cursed one who might delete this by the power of Pètros and Pawlos.

Document two:

በደጃዝማች ብሩ ደጃዝማችነት ኦ በፊታውራሪ
መርድ አለቅነት ኦ በመምህር ቢኖር ኦ በቄስገበዝ

ንሉ ኦ በትርሲቱ ሀይሉ ሹመት ፊትአውራሪ አስፋ በወርቅ ውሀ ወለተሔር ምድር ተወለዱ በናቱ ፤ ፤ መሳክርቱ ረየብሁ ሰዎች ስም ዝርዝር ተጸፋልሪ ፤ ፤ ይሆነንም ስትሰጥ በፍጽም በግይድ ነው ፤ ፤ ስትኖር ደስ ሊላት ስትሞት ተዘክር ሊያጹላት ፤ ፤ ደግሞ ብትክዳ አስፋ ተሰማ መድን ተቀብሲት ፤ ፤ መድኖችምረየብሉሰዎች ስም ዝርዝር ተጸፋልሪ ፤ ፤

During Däjjazmach Birru's däjjazmachenät, during the aläqenät of Fitawrari Assefa ,during the tenure of office of Mämher Binor ,Qèsä-Gäbäz Gwalu and[Mägabi] Terstitu Häylu ,Fitawrari Assefa is adopted by Wärq-Wuhä Wälätä-Hèr and she bequeathed all the land she acquired from her mother to him. The witnesses are [many people are listed]. She swears while giving this and it is binding. She shall be pleased in her lifetime and upon her death that he (Assefa) should provide a commemorative feast for her. Again lest she should change her mind Assefa Tässäma has received a guarantor. The guarantors are [many individuals are listed] (folio66r column three).

Document one is the only source known to me that gives the name of *Däjjach* Ayo's daughter. There is another property document recording the sale of Ayo's lands in Ennäbsè in the twentieth century.[50] He was a senior official during the reign of Iyasu II (1730-1755).[51] Ayo had many lands in the district of Ennäbsè, which made the core of the holdings of the monastery of Marṭula-Maryam.[52] The document on Sehin refers to the cause of the making of the will. Sehin passed her lands inherited from her father and mother on to her daughter, Hirut, out of special favor (for the support Hirut gave to Sehin). This will is calculated as much to institute Hirut as to disinherit the brothers of Hirut (who were probably children of Sehin by another father) in the matter of succession to the landed property. She felt deeply grateful for the assistance in money and other property her daughter gave her during her lifetime, in this case because of the gold she owed to her daughter and the mules and cattle she took from her. This will bears further testimony that a person could make a will depriving some children and one that ran against the interest of some of the children. The brothers of Hirut were excluded from the inheritance of the land of Sehin by the sanction that Sehin made by her curses. Moreover, Hirut is given right and empowered to displace and disinherit her brothers according to her discretion.

As indicated above the will of Sehin is a telling testimony to the point that children could be excluded from their father's or their mother's land though we may have to expect that the displacement of some sons and daughters from a right to equal share of the inheritance is not of frequent occurrence, since a compelling reason should exist for discriminating. What all this means is that could not satisfy all the children at one and the same time unlike the rules of equal inheritance. Descent and the right to inherit an equal share of property based on lineage were not always practicable. However, we can presume that wills could also be contested especially when it came to inheritance. The will of *Emäytè* Sehin clearly shows that wills could be contested and there was a difference between legitimate and illegitimate children, especially when the father or the mother refused to accept the illegitimate child and recognize him/her as his or her own. That the brothers of Hirut could contest the will is clearly shown in the document above because Sehin had given some consideration to the possible claims of Hirut's brothers. If Hirut's brothers laid claim to a share of the land and sued their sister challenging the will, they were required to pay back all that Hirut had given her mother. However, it is unlikely that they could pay back 500 ounces of gold and ten mules.[53] However, the important question is that to what extent were the orders of the testator turned into practice? This is the point we will come back to below.

There is a special mention in the will of Sehin about what might have been a very widely held view with regard to the general movement of property transfer. Sehin acknowledges that she owed her daughter five hundred ounces of gold, mules, and cattle which ought not to have been the case. However, transmission of property between siblings was common. Many individuals adopted their sisters or brothers over their property including land.[54]

In the case of the second document the woman called Wärq-Wuhä Wälätä-Hèr placed herself under the care of a certain *Fitawrari* Assefa Tässäma by bequeathing all her mother's land to him on condition that he provided for the woman in her lifetime. The woman had no children and was heirless. She adopted Assefa and transferred to him all the land she inherited from her mother. As the woman got older and no longer vigorous she transferred it to Assefa together with the responsibility of working the land and maintaining and providing for her. In effect, this constituted a form of old age pension security. The concern for the salvation of their souls in the next world and the provision of food, clothing and shelter in old age are the factors that made individuals choose such kinds of transactions. This sort of transfer sanctioned the dependence of the woman on the adoptee and the latter's obligation to treat her as if she were his biological mother. Assefa was also required to give a commemorative feast on the death of his adopter. The woman is given a right to be treated and cared for in a fitting manner during her lifetime in this world through this form of transfer. [55] The document is enigmatic about the obligation of the adoptee. To judge from evidence in other similar documents the obligation indicated above does not exhaust other forms of services that the adoptee had to give to the adopter (folio205v). Other obligations of the adoptee would include providing food to the people attending the funeral of the woman on her death and the payment of the fee for funeral services (*asäbä mäqaber*) which were exacted in the large majority of deaths. Commemoration of the deceased adopter by feasts and the saying of prayers over his /her grave by the living, all done with the purpose of expiating sins, were carried out at differing intervals. The adopter depended upon the adoptee to whom he has willed his land for the food, clothing and shelter.[56] The relationship established in this way between the adoptee and the adopter is that the former provided him with considerable assistance in times of old age and assumed direct responsibility for the cultivation of the land.

The document laid down the conditions on which the holding of the adopted Assefa depended. The woman was entitled to be clothed and fed in a satisfactory manner. His holding of the land was conditional upon certain contingencies. He could not evade the performance of the obligation stated in the document. However, his holding is made less precarious and could not be easily disturbed unless a sufficient condition existed which could lead to the invalidation of his holding. Assefa received many guarantors so as to not be displaced from the land of the woman without good reason shown.[57]

Another very important cause for the making of will and inheritance-related bequeathal involving adoption is debt. There are many cases of adoption produced for reasons of debt. Many people failing to pay back their debts resorted to bequeathing their land in lieu of the payment of their debt. In some of the documents we see that the entire property of the debtor was bestowed upon the creditors and in some of the documents creditors without any blood relationship with the debtor were adopted and treated as biological children and given to hold his/or her rightful share of the adopter's land along with the biological children.[58] Thus membership in a corporate group was not ascribed to birth only, since it could be acquired through various means including failure to pay back debts. This provides additional evidence against the general belief that right to land could be acquired only by virtue of descent and canon of descent. Thus bequeathal-related inheritance involving adoption was one of the mechanisms for mitigating or displacing the customary rule of inheritance. A completely strange person could be introduced into the corporate or lineage group with full right to a share of the ancestral land of the adopters. In the case of one document two women adopted a person and bequeathed a residential site and both requested their children not to challenge the inheritance. The bequeathal of land and the adoption in itself were due to the payment of twenty thalers for clothing and for maintenance. He was made immune from any other type of obligation towards his adopters.[59]

A woman, called *Wäyzäro* Terengo Kassa when drawing up such a deed found in folio 253r, inserted a clause intended to prevent any appeal for the right of share by her siblings and children. She states that the reason for the adoption was due to a debt of 100 thalers, which she contracted from one of her brothers, Embi'alä Kassa. Having nothing to pay him Terengo bequeathed all of her father's and mother's *rest* land, from any share of which the rest of her siblings are excluded. Even her children were not to challenge it. Children were given no say in the distribution of the property whatsoever. The deed fenced off the children with restrictions with regard to their mother's and father's land. The right to a share of the land of their mother was conditional upon the payment of the debt of their mother to the creditor.[60]

Another equally important reason which induced individuals to adopt someone seems to have been the desire to place one's own children in good hands or under the protection of influential persons. The other reason might have been to preempt legal challenges of one's holding, though this is not explicitly stated in the document. The greatest beneficiary of this process of adoption in Märṭulä-Maryam in the early decades of the twentieth century was *Ras* Häylu Täklä-Häymanot. One typical document exists on folio 226r where a certain *Fitawrari* Rädè adopted Häylu as his son and gave all his lands to him. At the end of the bequeathal a clause was inserted which stated that "ልጆችን ሩስ ባወቁ ለያሳድራቸው ነው-"which literally means-"the children should be under his (Häylu) care, to be provided according to his discretion".[61] Rädè himself was adopted by an individual who had bequeathed to him many lands, which he eventually disposed of to Häylu whom he adopted as heir.[62] Rädè's action can be explained in terms of the fact that adopting a person of substance was very advantageous. Most probably the anticipation of better remuneration was the commonest reason working behind adopting and being associated with a certain person of some social standing. It would also provide the children of Rädè, the adopter, with considerable assistance in times of need and to help them to have good positions by putting them under the care of Häylu, who governed Gojjam in the early decades of the twentieth century.

There is also a further set of factors that made men choose inheritance-related bequeathal that involved adoption as a mechanism of property transfer. One important factor in one document on using bequeathal as means of property transfer is, it seems, because of the fact that the children of the adopter were yet too young to assume direct responsibility for the cultivation of their father's land. The document conferred the ownership of the land on the adoptee. It also made the cultivation of the land the responsibility of the adoptee till the children of the adopter came of age. This is explicitly stated in a document on folio 222v. Under this bequeathal the adoptee was obliged to provide maintenance for the adopter as well as for two of his young children while holding all the land of the adopter. Thus the adoptee had the additional responsibility of caring for or looking after the children of the adopter until they came of age and for the adopter. However, whether the adoptee was not obliged to provide the adopter in times of old age and after the children had come of age or not cannot be known from the document since it lacked clarity and does not have such stipulation. Probably the adoptee would retain part of the land of the adopter and return the remaining land to children of the latter after they had become old enough to work it on their own. Besides the minority of his children who did not have the physical strength to work the land the rationale behind this particular document seems to be the desire to get rid of the not always easy responsibility for the tillage of the land that induced the adopter to choose it as the mechanism of property transfer. Such a transaction though explanation of it will not be attempted here might have some political and economic contexts.[63] Whether the children of the adopter would work under the adoptee after they had come of age or not would take back their father's land after giving part of it to the adoptee is not stated in the document.

The documents discussed above highlight the need to clarify the rights of the adoptee and the adopter by considering a few more cases. What would be the position of the adoptee if the adopter were to fail in fulfilling his /her side of the contract? What conditions warranted the exercise of the adopter's right of reversion? There are ample documents in the Registries of Moṭa and Märṭulä-Maryam to enable us to explore these issues. Evidence from many documents show that adopters retained until the day they died their rights to the land handed over to their adoptee. They could revoke their grant with the good reason shown on the part of the adoptee to warrant the action of adopters.[64]

Document 1:
በመምህር ፊላታዎስ ዑ በቄሰገበዝ ምትኩ ዑ እንገዳ በመጋቢ ፋንታ ስዩም ሹመት አይኔ ወለተማርያም ፊትአውራሪ አለሙ አሰጌ በተወለዱበት ሀገር ልጆች አንጥርያም ስላሉ ተመለሰላት ለአይኔ ወለተማርያም።

During the tenure of office of Mämher Filatawos, Qèsä-Gäbäz Mitiku Engeda and Mägabi Fänta Seyoum, the land of Ayenè Wälätä-Maryam, over which she had formerly adopted Fitawrari Alämu Assägè, is restored to her since the children of Fitawrari Assägè refused to provide for her. (231v)

Document 2:
በመምህር አስገሆኝ በቄሰገበዝ ደሳለኝ በመጋባ ፋንታ ሹመት ከሳ ሀይሉ አለቃ ሀይለ እየሱስን በወለዱበት ሀገር አለቃ ሀይለእየሱስ አልችልም ብለው ተወሲዶውን ለከሳ ሀይሉ መለሱ።

During the tenure of office of Mämher Asägehäññ, Qèsä-Gäbäz Däsaläññ and Mägabi Fänta, aläqa Häylä-Iyäsus has renounced the täwälido(lit. adoption) [and restored] the land over which aläqa Häylä-Iyäsus was adopted, to Kassa Häylu[the adopter], on account of inability.(226v)

Document3:
በመምህር ፀሀይ ፍላቴ በቄስገበዝ ላይካ ማርያም አየል በመጋቢ ታደስ እምሩ ሹመት እመት ምንታምር ፈለቀ በናቷ ባባቷ ሀገር ደስታ ይልማን ልጆችና ግራጌታ ተገኘ ይልማን አማረ ተመስገንን በአለፈው ዘመን ከዚህ ቀድሞ ወልጃቸው ነበር፡፡ እነርሱ የማይጠቅሙኝ ስለሆኑ ትውልዳቸውን ሰርዤ ትቼ ባባቲ በናቲ ሀገር አበሉ ዘውዴንና ከፋለ ደስታን ወልጃለሁ ፡ ፡ አውርሻለሁ ፡ ፡ እነርሱም ሊመቹኝ ሊጦሩኝ ነው ፡ ፡

During the tenure of office of Mämher Ṣähäy Felatè, Qèsä-Gäbäz La'ekä-Maryam and Mägabi Taddässä Imeru, [I] Emmät Mentamer Fäläqä had formerly adopted the children of Dästä Yelma, Geragèta Tägäññä Yelma and Amarä Tämäsgän, over the land of my mother and father. [However], since they (the former adoptees) can not be of use for me I have disowned them and adopted in their stead A[m]bälu Zäwdè and Käfalä Dästa over the land of my mother and father. They shall provide and behave well to me.

The rights transferred are without doubt rights in the land and the adoptees would retain them unless they broke important terms of their holding. Moreover, the adoptees would inherit and permanently occupy the land following the death of the adopters unless they broke or defaulted on fulfilling important conditions of their tenure in the lifetime of the adopters. The Registries of Moṭa and especially of Märṭulä-Maryam are full of documents with deeds similar to the above. Both documents quoted above show that the terms of agreement at the time of transaction could not be binding always. The adopter retained his /her rights in the land until the day he/she died. The land rights and duties of an adopted person are exactly the same as those of a biological son or daughter. We can infer from documents one and three that the adopter had full power to take over and reallocate his/her lands from the adoptee on the ground of non-fulfillment of the conditions of the agreement by the adoptee. From the first and the second documents we learn that the adoptee could be ejected after a reasonable notice to quit by the adoptee. We can presume that at the time that when the deed was drawn the intention of the adopter was to bestow permanent ownership and rights on the adoptee.

However, whether the terms of agreement or the provision of the contract would be practicable and remain binding or not were wholly determined by the subsequent action of the two parties. The documents quoted above evoke a view that the adoptee's holding rights were to be understood as being subject to the adopter's right of reversion and depended on the meticulous fulfillment of the obligation towards the adoptees. Documents one and three are noteworthy cases in which the adopter's right to revoke the grant they made to the adoptee and evict them worked. If the adoptee failed to fulfill some vital conditions of his/her holding the adopter could revoke his/her grant and evict him/her through the exercise of his/her reversionary right. The adoptee had to meticulously meet his/her obligations or the land he or she was granted would be subject to the adopter's right of re-acquiring. Whether the adopter's reversionary right would be exercised or not was determined by the behavior of the adoptee. To provide maintenance to the adopters was perhaps very heavy so that many people willingly applied to end the contract, as in the case of document two in order to escape from over-burdensome obligations. In document two the adoptee ended his right of holder over the land of his adopter upon his appeal to end his obligation of provision of support. In the case of document one the children of the adoptee refused to provide for the adopter and the latter transferred her land to new adoptees.[65]

However, adoptees could not be lightly disinherited and their right in the land could not be easily challenged unless things warranted doing so. The adoptee could claim damages and obtain an injunction in case where the adopter broke his or her side of the bargain. There are instances of this in the Märṭulä-Maryam Registry whereby the adoptee's right to hold the land of the adopter was contested. One such outstanding case involved the great grandfather of the researcher, Chäkole Däbrä-Sina. It occurred during the reign of Täklä-Häymanot. Through adoption Chäkole acquired ownership of the land of a certain Häylu Amaräch. However, following the death of the woman an adverse claim was made by a certain *Balambaras* Ayälä. Chäkole was sued by Ayälä and taken to the court of Täklä-Häymanot. Ayälä won the case on the ground that though Chäkole was adopted by Amaräch he was subsequently disowned by the woman. Chäkole was a very notorious litigant. He appealed to Emperor Minilek II in 1905/6 but the latter confirmed the decision of Täklä-Häymanot after several years of wasteful litigation (folio212v).[66] In another typical document a certain Țedu Şadal revoked the land from her adoptees but only to bequeath it to *Ras* Häylu, after adopting him. Häylu paid back the money the adoptees had given to Țedu Şadal at the time when she adopted them. In another document the adoptee refused to surrender the land granted them by adoption and the woman who adopted them had to sue them, and she won her case.[67]

The desire to avert any possible conflict between heirs was another consideration in the making of wills. There is considerable number of documents to support this argument. The judiciary was burdened with hearing cases of land dispute between siblings. Precise prescriptions of the respective holdings of the members of the household before the death of the parents served to prevent the quarreling over the division of the land of the ancestors. Let us consider the following typical documents to elaborate this point.[68]

Document 1:

በመምህር ፀሀይ ፍላቴ ዐ በቄሰገበዝ ላዕከ ማርያም አየለ ዐ በመጋቢ ታደሰ እምሩ ሹመት ረእኔሪመንግስቴ ገብሩ በምወለድበት ባባቴ ዐ በናቴ ሀገር ሁሉ ጥሩሰው መንግስቴ በልጆች እንዳደርስባቸው በተለየ አውርሻቸዋለሁ ።። ጥሩሰው መንግስቴ ስላልተመቸችኝ ከፈቃዴ ስለወጣች ሰርጒ ግን የአያቴን የአሰቡ የተመሩን ሀገር ጮቅማን ስጥቻታለሁ ።።

During the tenure of office of Mämher Şähäy Felatè Qèsä-Gäbäz La'ekä-Maryam Ayälä, [and] Mägabi Täddässä Imeru, [I]Mängistè Gäbru say that Țerusäw Mängistè shall not interfere in my children to whom I have bequeathed as special favor all the land [I have inherited from my]mother and father over which I have a birth right. [However], since

> *Ṭerusäw Mängistè has misbehaved and went out of my control I have given her Çheqema, which I acquired from my grandmother, Assäbu Yätämäññu. (254r)*

Document 2:

በመምህር ላዕከ ማርያም አየለ ቀሰ ገብዝ ሀይለ ማርያም ስጦታው ኡ በመጋቢ ጥሩነህ እንግዳ ሹመት አቶ ሙኔ አቻሉ በሚወለድበት እርስቱ ልጆቼ እንዳይጣሉ በተለየ ይቀዳች የይታክሶስንና የሱታፌን ሀገሩን ለአድማስ ሙኔ አውርሷል። በሌላው አገሩ በገዛውም እንዳይደርስ ለልጆች አውርሷል። በሰጠሁት ታረጋ ሁሉን ክጃለሁ።

> *During the tenure of office of Mämher La'ekä-Maryam Ayälä, Qèsä-Gäbäz Häylä-Maryam Seṭotaw [and] Mägabi Ṭerunäh Engeda, to avoid the quarreling of his children over [the division of] his rest [land] in which he has a birthright, Ato Munè Akalu bequeathed his lands of Yetaksos and Sutafè in Yeqändach to Admas Munè. He (Admas) shall not enter a claim to the rest of the lands including my purchased land which I have bequeathed to the rest of my children. If he demanded apart from that which I have given him I shall disinherit [him] totally. (261v)*

The purpose of both documents is to ward off any possible conflict arising out of the division of the property of the deceased as much as favoring some of the heirs. We can assume that this prescription of the transfer of exclusive property to heirs by the holders in their lifetime would help to avoid the quarrels and litigations which might arise in connection with the transmission of property. Both documents prescribe in advance the transfer of the property with the desire to avoid conflicts and tensions between the heirs over the property of the dying holders. Contrary to the general belief, it seems that children did not receive equal share to the lands left them by their parents. Although the two documents do not show their parents totally and formally disinheriting some of their children they do not show them enjoying equal rights of inheritance. In the case of document one the reason for the discrimination against one of the daughters of the will maker, called Ṭerusäw, is clearly stated. Mängistè Gäbru, father of Ṭerusäw, prevented her from making any demands to a share of his lands beyond what he allowed her on account of her misbehavior. The second testator's will is aimed against the interest of his son, Admas. He threatened Admas to disown him totally if he interfered in the inheritance of the other children, beyond the one allowed him by the will. Both documents certainly run contrary to widely held moral norms of equal inheritance of the conventional *rest* system of land. From these cases we can deduce that the heads of households had the power to disinherit their children. In complete contrast to customary law of inheritance some of the sons and daughters of certain households are excluded while the rest of the heirs were given special treatments. This allows us to make a far bolder statement that whether children of a person would get an equal share of their fathers' property or not was subject to their good behavior and discipline.[69]

Birth does not always guarantee the right of equal access to the land of parents. The above documents suggest that serious misconduct on the part of children could result in even total disinheritance by the father when he expressly made a testament before death. This indicates the degree of freedom of individuals enjoyed in distributing and disposing of their land. He could vest some of the land on certain or all of his children, conditional upon certain contingencies. It seems that there was no bar against the action of the father with regard to the right of allocating his lands amongst his children. Whether the will would be executed after the death of the testator or not can not be known from the historical record and we are left without any clear information on this point. In some documents the will makers inserted an injunction of curses to insure that their order would be respected. However, we do not know how effective this was.

The last noteworthy point to consider with regard to bequeathal involving adoption is the status of slaves. Our manuscript provides us with a relatively large number of documents with which to examine the legal status and property rights of slaves. Two contrary tendencies of enslavement, transactions concerning slaves and the converse manumission exist in our documents. The famous Täklä-Iyäsus, whom we have met at the beginning of this study, was also a slave .He was set free on the death of his master, *Däjjazmach* Yälèmetu Gošu, the uncle of

Täklä-Häymanot.[70] Three of the documents on slaves are about enslavement and transactions concerning slaves. In one instance a weaver called Bädelu Wubenäh sold himself or gave up his freedom and liberty, of his own free will, to a certain *Fitawrari* Tässäma and his descendants to serve under them as a slave because of the assistance he received from Tässäma during the Great Famine.[71] There is also a will regarding the disposal of slaves. This will exists on folio 227v. It represents the greatest disposal of slaves. The master called *Aläqa* Gobäzu disposed of about seventeen slaves. This document is at one and the same time a charter of manumission and the transaction concerning slaves between the old and new owners. Gobäzu disposed eight of his slaves by granting them to his kinsmen. The remaining nine slaves were "set at liberty", the document acknowledges. However, it also states that Gobäzu adopted a certain *Qäññazmach* Yemär Wändè and transferred all the nine "freed" slaves and his *rest* land to the latter. In effect slaves were simply changing hands although the document states they were "set at liberty."[72] The fact that they were associated with the *rest* land suggests that slaves were used as agricultural laborers.

Charters of manumissions illustrate the extent of the land rights of slaves. The technical terms employed in the documents to describe the action of freeing slaves were "ሁር ማውጣትን or "አርነት ማውጣት." The following conclusion can be drawn from the evidence contained in the charters of manumission in the Registry. Let us see each case. Masters could adopt their slaves in the same way as a free man or non-relative was adopted. In other words the modes or system of adopting a slave and a free person by adopters are identical. One outstanding charter of manumission is found in folio 231v. In this document a woman called *Emahoy* Yätämäññu Engeda set at liberty her slave, Talchäkolu, together with her children. Yätämäññu bequeathed all her *rest* land upon them and adopted them as her children with some obligations. The old woman demanded that her former slave Talchäkolu and her children whom she had now adopted as her children should offer a commemorative feast upon her death and arrange for her annual memorial services. However, the same document hinted that the liberty of Talchäkolu could also be nominal and a relation of her former master could put claim on her and her children. Lest someone should deprive them of their liberty after her death the woman invoked the cooperation of six people requesting them to prevent anyone from trying to deprive them of their freedom. The children of Talchäkolu were allowed to live wherever they liked.[73]

Another charter of manumission is found on folio 236v. The document records the liberation and the adoption of three slaves by a woman called Bäzabeši Kassa. Bäzabeši also adopted with right over her lands the grandfather of the researcher, *Blatta* Tägäñña Chäkole together with her slaves. The old woman Bäzabeši Kassa freed and adopted her slaves whom she had inherited from her husband *Aläqa* Rätta. In another will this same *Aläqa* Rätta passed onto his wife all his property (land and livestock) but in the same breath the document tells us that the woman bequeathed it very soon to a person called Asräs Yehun. The number of slaves freed and adopted by Bäzabeši was three and the researcher had personal acquaintance with two of them. One of them has grown very old and is still alive and the other had died a couple of years of ago. *Aläqa* Rätta demanded his wife through his will (folio226r) to set free his slaves upon her death and that neither his relations nor Bäzabeši's relations were to deprive them of their freedom. Masters usually adopted their slaves when they had no children of their own. However, slaves were also adopted by their masters even when their masters had children. Rätta and Bäzabeši had no off-springs and all their property was transferred to their slaves and to other people with no rights to their land. The will made the three slaves owners or inheritors of much of their former masters' properties.[74]

The last important document recording the adoption of slaves by a master worth considering is found on 227v. A certain Alämitu Getahun reinforced the oral declaration of her deceased husband, *Šaqa* Yelma Gošu, who freed his slaves whose number is not stated. When Yelma the head of the household was about to die he set them free by oral declaration, at which his father confessor was present. Later the father confessor bore his witness to the liberation of the slaves, when the oral declaration of Yelma was reconfirmed and a formal charter of manumission was put into writing. In this charter of manumission was inserted a special clause to safeguard the freed slaves from any possible challenge of the will. Alämitu protected her freed slaves by her curse against any possible reversal of the decision and re-enslavement by any adverse claim to control them. She warned her children not to interfere or deny or deprive them of their freedom by threatening an eternal curse to whoever disobeyed her charter.[75] From all these considerations we can learn that even slaves had a very large margin of opportunity to change their status and acquire *rest* land through adoption. Good behavior and dedicated service rather than the chance of birth would determine the status of slaves and their off-springs. Upon good behavior slaves had as equal opportunity to inherit their masters' property as the relation of their masters.

The third most important mode of property transfer was gift together with mortgage. The factors that induced people to grant land to individuals and institutions are as many as the factors that led to sale and bequeathal. All the factors that produced sale and bequeathal were at work behind gift and mortgage and hence it will not be repeated here for reasons of space limitation. Thus discussion is confined to the last important means of property transfer, litigation. We have seen at the beginning of our discussion in this chapter the circumstances leading to the making of documents and the recording of transactions. The registered documents recording land transaction were intended to serve as basis against any contest. This might have greatly reduced incidences of land litigations. Unfortunately, however, ruinous litigation was not permanently remedied and disputes over land rights and claims to offices are recurring themes in our documents.[76] Though litigation constituted one important mode of acquiring or relinquishing property the study does not describe this mechanism of property transfer for reasons of space. Going to the details would swell the study unnecessarily and enough has been written above about the modes of property transfer and the motives for selecting certain modes of property transfer by individuals. Having said all this it remains to show some trends in concentration of holdings and its converse, disintegration of holdings, by looking at some of the families actively engaged in land transactions. The general trend in the price of land will also be indicated in the pages that follow.

4.3 Land Concentration and the Reverse process of Disintegrations

Hosts of people including noblemen, peasants and the religious class were engaged in the land market. However, the general movement of land was towards the rich especially the noblemen, both clerical and secular, who constituted the overwhelming mass of purchasers. Thus some representative families are selected as models in order to generalize about the trends in land transfer and land price. One such important family of purchasers was that of *Däjjach* Birru. *Wäyzäro* Ajämè, grandmother of Birru, was active in the land market in Märṭulä-Maryam during the nineteenth century especially during the 1840s and 1850s. The land transaction that Ajämè entered spans the tenures of office of six church officials and her land transactions are recorded in the different folios of our manuscript.[77] This woman spent much of her money in the purchase of residential sites at the total price of 52 thalers. The purchase price of each of these sites ranged from between four to eighteen thalers. Three of the urban lands were bought from people who had themselves acquired them by purchase. On folio 194r there is a note, which shows that the woman was selling land she had earlier bought. The original purchase price was 13 thalers and it was resold for fourteen thalers. This fact is important in that it testifies to the remarkable speed of transfer of land. The first transaction of the land was probably made just a little earlier and Ajämè then acquired it. Then it was sold for the third time for fourteen thalers. Thus there were three owners of the same plot of land within one generation.[78]

We never hear of Ajämè in the second half of the nineteenth century. However, in the early decades of the twentieth century Ajämè's name is mentioned in a document recording the transfer of her lands which brought to an end her link with these lands. Ajämè's lands passed from ownership by her descendants into the hands of *Ras* Häylu in the early twentieth century. Häylu purchased this land from *Lej* Gošu at the price of one hundred thalers.[79] The document refers to simply one parcel of urban land which belonged to Ajämè. The identity of Gošu is well known. Two land transaction documents recognize him as *Däjjach* Birru's grandson and son of Mentewab, Birru's daughter.[80] We do not know how Gošu inherited it. Nor is it clear from the above note if the purchased land included the sites Ajämè had brought together through purchase. The transaction took place after the death of Ajämè and the lands that she had succeeded in bringing together through purchase during her lifetime were transferred to *Ras* Häylu. The purchase price of the land indicates the dramatic increase in the value of land; almost double the amount that Ajämè had paid for them. This does not exhaust the property dealings of Birru's family. Birru was one of the most interesting personalities of the last decades of the Era of Princes. He was the ruler of the whole of Eastern Gojjam. We find him and his mother, Wälätä-Giyorgis, and his daughter, Mentewab, engaged in land transactions spanning many generations.

Birru's mother joined the land market as both buyer and seller. Her attention was focused on buying urban property. Residential sites provided an especially important form of landed property in the period under investigation. There are many documents recording the many parcels of residential lands which the woman bought.[81] Wälätä-Giyorgis bought three parcels of homestead sites in the town, one for eighty-four rock-salts and another for seventeen thalers. She resold two of the homestead sites or lands she had bought. In one outstanding document found in folio193r there is a record of Wälätä-Giyorgis's transactions. She resold one plot of residential land for sixty rock-salts, the original price of which was thirty rock-salts. She resold it for double its original price, without even building a house on it.[82] Of course this is not the only document recording a building land being resold without constructing a house over it. Many of the residential sites which were dealt and re-dealt with and frequently recorded in our documents changed hands without building houses on them subsequent to their transfer from the original owner to the new holders. The explanation for this should be sought in either of the following ways. The first explanation may be that residential sites were not perhaps bought arising out of the need to build houses over them. Therefore, the buying and selling of residential sites in towns does not seem to have been dictated by the immediate need for them. The second important explanation it seems is that residential sites were bought as a device for saving and protecting money from plunder and confiscation given the unsettled political conditions and the accompanying tremendous disturbances of the 19th century. Thus residential sites were bought but only to be resold when the opportunity warranted. Moreover, homestead sites were sold and bought as a means of making profit. Yet we can not rule out the possibility that town lands were also bought for building purposes.

Gift formed another important part of the process by which Wälätä-Giyorgis acquired land. In folio 66 verso a certain Yäwq-Irsu Gäbrä-Sellasè gave half of his father's *rest* land to her, which she immediately passed on to her son *Däjjach* Birru. In folio 2v the children of a certain Kidan Sahlu gave half of their agricultural fields and residential sites to the same woman. In folio 193r we read of Wälätä-Giyorgis receiving all the *bota* and lands of two individuals called Kisadu and Laku. They transferred their property because of a crime they had committed. Wälätä-Giyorgis paid the legal fee to liberate them from imprisonment and in return took their land and *bota* since they were not able to meet the court expenditure. This much is known from the manuscript about the woman's land transactions.[83]

Birru added both urban lands and houses to the purchases of his mother and grandmother. One of his important purchases was a *därb* with its enclosure for two ounces of gold from a certain Adäy Wäldä-Kidan.[84] There are many purchase notes of Birru. Finally he was stripped of his governorship of Eastern Gojjam and met a violent death in 1868. All of his properties together with those of Ajämè and Wälätä-Giyorgis were apparently inherited by his daughter Mentewab. Birru's daughter Mentewab and her son *Lej* Gošu Wubenäh added nothing to the property of the family. Mentewab sold half of the *bota* which Birru had bought from Adäy for two thalers to two purchasers together with another plot of residential land that Birru had bought from a person whose name is missing in the document. The remaining properties which Ajämè, Birru and Wälätä-Giyorgis had bought were all disposed of by *Lej* Gošu. A *bota* which Wälätä-Giyorgis bought from a certain *Mägabi* Gwalu for seventeen thalers, probably in the 1840s, was resold for more than double its original price of thirty-five thalers, later in the early decades of the twentieth century. The last document we have involving Birru's family was a gift of pastureland that his grandson made to a certain *Mämher* Zäwdu so that the latter would pray for him. This represented the last document involving Birru's family and we never hear of them after this. Thus Mentewab and her son preserved none of the properties they inherited nor invested anything in acquiring other lands.[85] Only a few people seem to have succeeded in passing some of their urban properties to the next generations. However, it is important to investigate the case of two other families whose property dealings are kept in the record to enable us to enlarge the conclusions that can be drawn from these documents.

One very important family that was active throughout the nineteenth century and the early decades of the twentieth century was that of *Balambaras* Asägehäññ. Thanks to the record of the full range of property dealings that this family was engaged in it is possible to delineate the transfer of the property at every generation. There are about thirty property documents from the Registry of Deeds which involve

Asägehäññ's family. This might not exhaust or represent the total of the property dealings of this family. The documents provide us with a continuous record of the property dealings of this family over a span of three generations. Before the dramatic subdivision of property following Asägehäññ's death in 1890s there was a concentration of land in his family. The reverse process of disintegration began particularly after the death of Asägehäññ. He had eight children some of whom were active in the land market.[86] Two chronological vantage points suggest themselves from the record of the property dealings of Asägehäññ's family, the year 1899, which saw *Lej* Ṣämru asking Täklä-Häymanot to register his land transaction at Däbrä-Marqos, serving as dividing line. Prior to the 1899 transaction there was a concentration of holding but two decades later there was a dramatic disintegration of the holdings.

Asägehäññ was one of the extensive purchasers of land, especially residential land. Most of his purchases were *bota* and he spent sixty-four thalers and fifty salt bars on this. All the purchases were in Märṭulä-Maryam, with the exception of one sale document, which refers to the countryside. He resold only one of his purchased *bota*. On folio 84v there is a record of a gift of residential land by the church of Märṭulä-Maryam to Asägehäññ and on folio 2v there is a similar record of gift to Asägehäññ by a certain *Abba* Binor. On folio 84v four purchase notes of Asägehäññ are recorded. One of the lands purchased is said to have been located in the countryside and bought for three thalers which Asägehäññ resold later on to one Asägehäññ Nureleññ at the original purchase price. This is the only sale by Asägehäññ. Asägehäññ acquired most of his parcels of land through purchase at third hand.[87] He also purchased agricultural fields from two vendors, one of whom is named *Blatta* Andu Hodè, for fifty rock-salts. Andu-Hodè was one of the most important persons in the period, buying and selling actively and acting as a guarantor and witness to so many of the land transactions.[88]

Asägehäññ acquired his parcels of land through purchase from female and male vendors. One of the successful sellers of land from whom Asägehäññ purchased land is a certain Wäldä-Gäbru Tangut. We find Tangut's name in a number of documents as an important vendor. All in all Asägehäññ invested fifty eight thalers and fifty rock-salts on buying *bota* and agricultural fields, other than the land transactions he acquired through other means.[89] However, this certainly does not exhaust Asägehäññ's property dealings. This could be inferred from the fact that perhaps years after his death we read of his children passing residential lands their father had bought on to a certain Abetäw Negusè, according to the request Asägehäññ made before his death.[90] The original transaction note can not be tracked down in the Registry. There were probably many transactions of Asägehäññ which were not recorded at all. All the lands Asägehäññ had brought together were passed on to his children. We do not know how the *Balambaras* disposed of his lands. He did not make a will. He might have settled much of his land on his heirs before his death during his lifetime and only his house and some of the properties he owned remained un-disposed. We know from his granddaughter, Michu, presently residing at Märṭulä-Maryam, that he died accidentally in Gondär while on a campaign with king Täklä-Häymanot's army. This may explain why he did not leave a will.[91]

Following the death of Asägehäññ an irreversible shift towards the break down of his property started though some of his children, especially *Lej* Ṣämru, succeeded in accumulating land. Ṣämru joined in the land market as buyer and vendor probably while his father was still alive. The kind of property documents we have for Ṣämru are similar to those of his father. Ṣämru inherited a considerable part of Asägehäññ's property. He acquired most of his property before 1899 at the time when he applied to Täklä-Häymanot to get permission to register his land transactions and the lands that he inherited from his father. The rest of his property was acquired after 1899.[92] The methods of his land acquisition are very diverse: through sale, gift, inheritance, and bequeathal involving adoption.

The children of Asägehäññ succeeded in retaining their father's house within the family for one generation only, as we will see below. In folio 205v there is a document recording the purchase by Ṣämru of his father's house from his siblings. To judge from evidence in this purchase document Asägehäññ had eight children by three different mothers. Ṣämru represented one segment of the Asägehäññ's family and he bought his father's house for 102 thalers well after Ṣämru had established himself as buyer and vendor. He acquired the house through purchase from Asägehäññ's children.[93] The transfer of Asägehäññ's house occurred after his death and at later point in the course of life of his children. This can be understood from the fact that the purchase document is not included in the Däbrä-Marqos record in which Ṣämru's land transactions were recorded in 1899.

Ṣämru consolidated his residential lands by exchange. Like his father the church gave him *rim* lands. However, Ṣämru bequeathed his *rim* land, which he acquired through gift from the church, to Ras Häylu Täklä-Häymanot whom he also adopted.[94] He included in the document that his children were not to challenge Häylu. This is his only disposal of property to a person outside of his family. Ṣämru passed the rest of his property to his daughters whom we will meet below. These included Bähärditu, Tämäsgän and Mentewab Ṣämru. Only Mentewab added land through mechanism other than inheritance. Mentewab acted as a money lender and on her debtor failing to repay the debt he was forced to pass his ancestral land to her in the village of Yebesana a little distance southeast of Märṭulä-Maryam. This is the only acquisition of additional land to Ṣämru's property by Mentewab. Ṣämru made Bähärditu *aläqa*, main successor or inheritor of much of his property, and the rest of his property was divided among his children. Unlike the church title, *aläqa* here refers to the right given to part of the family property which is not subject to division. The process of the disintegration of Asägehäññ's lands was completed in a very dramatic way during the lifetime of his grandchildren, i.e. during the life of Ṣämru's children. In folio 227r there is a document recording the transaction of Ṣämru's daughter, Tämäsgän, who sold her portion of the residential sites she inherited from her father to Ras Häylu for a 100 thalers. Moreover, Tämäsgän resold the house of Asägehäññ that Ṣämru had purchased from his siblings at a price of 130 thalers to the same purchaser, Häylu, at the net profit of twenty-eight thalers. Another important disposal of Tämäsgän is found in folio 227r which records the transfer of a residential site which the woman inherited from her father through sale to Häylu at the price of 100 thalers. In folio 225r the daughter of Asägehäññ called *Wäyzäro* Däbritu sold her portion of the residential land that she inherited from her father for fifty thalers, again to Häylu. The extensive sale of Asägehäññ's children in the 1910s and 1920s brought them 380 thalers, many times more than Asägehäññ's and Ṣämru's purchase prices put together. Indeed a transfer on this scale and in such a short space of time from a single family to one individual (Häylu) is not to be met elsewhere in the Registers. Whether the descendants of Asägehäññ sold their town property in excess of their needs or not can not be known from the records. The process of the breakdown of Asägehäññ's town property was completed within the lifetime of his grandchildren. This is a very fine testament to the low degree of trans-generational continuity especially with regard to property.⁹⁵

What all this means is that concentrated holdings could not survive the life span of many generations. Perhaps the increase in land values provided incentive to sell land. Häylu was probably one of the richest persons in the country in the early decades of the twentieth century. Only rich persons like him could afford to buy land at any price and to whom individual owners were prepared to make outright sales. That explains why a great deal of Asägehäññ's family property went into the hands of new owners, in particular to wealthy and powerful people like Häylu who could readily afford to make large investments. Abdussamad in his doctoral dissertation on the economic history of Gojjam in the early decades of the 20th century has recorded the land purchases of Häylu in other parts of the region. Häylu also heavily invested his money at Märṭulä-Maryam on the purchase of residential lands, houses and agricultural fields in the surrounding villages of Märṭulä-Maryam. He acquired lands through all kinds of means, including gift and adoption. He invested a total of 1442 thalers on building plots, houses and agricultural fields. There are innumerable numbers of documents involving Haylu.⁹⁶ Thus, there was at one and the same time dispersal and concentration of holdings. Very few of the town and agricultural lands at Märṭulä-Maryam and its immediate environs remained unsold. Sale brought in at one and the same time new landowners and eliminated old ones. Similar typical families exist whose property documents are carefully preserved in the Registry.

Thanks to this record of land transaction one is able to explore the changes in land value over the time spread of eighty years, from about the 1840s to the 1920s. These particular documents compel a view that land value had increased tremendously over the century. The examples of the two families discussed above will have to suffice to draw conclusions about the history of land transfers and land values between the 1840s and 1920s. The series of documents of the families discussed above and preserved in the Registry show that the same pieces of lands were dealt and re-dealt with several times and there was constant change of land ownership. The record helps to argue strongly in favor of an increase in land value. Undoubtedly there was tremendous increase in the value of land between the 1840s and 1920s. As we have seen above some of the vendors sold land to *Ras* Häylu and to others in the 1920s sometimes at the net profit of double their original prices in the nineteenth century. Thus the process of fragmentation in the 1920s was spurred by the increase of land prices. Most of the sale documents do not tell the precise dimensions of the lands transacted, the reference frequently occurring in our records with regard to the size of land transacted being simply one land, a *bota*, etc. Other things being equal around a century later the same piece of land was sold at many times its original price in the 1840s.

The discussion above shows the degree of freedom of land holders in respect of user and transfer or alienation. What the historical record shows is that although the theory says that a person could not acquire exclusive and separate property right over a piece of land against other members of the lineage group in actuality individual members could acquire absolute ownership with rights of permanent alienation of their share of the ancestral land by sale or other means of conveyance including to aliens. The traditional canon of descent did not wholly limit individual rights to mortgage, sell or otherwise transfer the land under their occupation including alienation to non-relatives. By way of conclusion *individual members of the descent group could acquire the nature of absolute ownership over his or her portion of the lineage land with rights of alienating and selling.*

NOTES

[1] The earliest transactions in the Gondar region took place around the middle of the eighteenth century, see, Crummey, "Gonderine *rim* Land Sales: An Introductory Description and Analysis",pp.469-479.There is no provision for the transaction of land granted to churches and individuals in the earlier land grant charters, C.C.Rossini (ed. and trans.),*Liber Axumae*,vol.III, Corpus Scriptorium Christianorum Orientalium (Paris,1962).The alleged land charters for the Cathedral of Aksum by Aksumite Kings like Abrehä and Atsebehä,Gäbrä-Mäsqäl, etc. are not reliable or were written based on memory of the original charters. However, there are some documents recording land transaction in *The Land Charters of Northern Ethiopia*, edited and translated by Huntingford. Huntingford is of the opinion that the charters attributed to ancient rulers for the Cathedral of Aksum were committed into writing much later and was not based on extant documents but traditions.

[2] The earliest reference for land transaction in charters is the charter of Wälätä-Isra'el which I have discussed in the first and second chapters. It coincides almost exactly with *Zämänä Mäsafent*.

[3] Daniel, Gebrä-Häwaryat, MS. Yägwära Qwesqwam, 89, XVI.23-25.

[4] _____, Tarikä Nägäst Zä-Etyopya, MS.Däbrä-Wärq, 89, II, 11-33.

[5] Ibid.

[6] Giyorgis Wäldä-Amid, MS.Däbrä-Marqos, folio191recto.

[7] Daniel,Dersanä Mädehänè-Aläm, MS. Qäranyo Mädehänè-Aläm, 89,IV, 26-36,Mäzgäb,MS.Moṭa Giyorgis, and Habtamu, "A Short History of the Monastery of Marṭula-Maryam", appendix no. VI.

[8] Informants, *Wäyzäro* Michu Däsyaläw, interviewed (at Martula-Maryam) on 29/07/02, *Emahoy* Bäyänäch Tamrat, interviewed (at Mota) on 21/02/08 and *Ato* Ayänäw Tezazu. This seems to be the rationale behind Sehin and Ṣämru's documents recorded in different places though not clearly stated.

[9] Ibid.

[10] Mäzgäb, MS.Däbrä-Marqos, folio 47recto -47verso.

[11] See Däqiqä Näbeyat, MS.Märṭulä-Maryam, folio1v, and 212v, etc.

[12] Ibid, folio 235v, 232r-232v, 240v, 242r, 262r

[13] Daniel, Wannä-Mäzgäb, MS.Däbrä-Eliyas, 89, XVIII, 9-31.

[14] Mäzgäb, MS.Däbrä-Marqos, folio15recto.

[15] Daniel, Gebrä-Häwaryat, MS.Yägwära Qwesqwam, 89, XVI.23-25.

16 Mäzgäb, MS.Däbrä-Marqos, folio25recto.
17 Informant, *Abba* Abäbä Jänbärè, interviewed (at Mota) on 11/08/02.
18 Mäzgäb, MS.Moṭa Giyorgis, Däqiqä Näbeyat, MS.Märṭulä-Maryam. I was introduced to one of them on which this chapter is based during a fieldwork for writing BA thesis on the monastery of Märṭulä-Maryam.
19 Ibid.
20 Crummey, *Land and Society*, p.166.
21 Habtamu, "A Short History of the Monastery of Marṭula-Maryam", p.20.
22 The influential charters including the charter of Moṭa allowed the *däbtära* a right of free disposal of *rim* lands; see also the growth of the commercialization of land in Crummey, *Land and Society*, p.166.
23 See notes number 35,39,45,48 and 50 below.
24 Daniel, Wängèl, MS. Moṭa Giyorgis, 89, VIII, 31-36.
25 Mäzgäb, MS. Däbrä-Marqos, folio 49recto.
26 Daniel, Wängèl, MS.Moṭa Giyorgis, 89, VIII, 31-36.
27 Ibid.
28 Ibid.
29 Ibid.
30 Daniel, Tarikä Nägäst Zä-Etyopya, MS.Däbrä-Wärq, 89, II, 11-33.
31 See note number 29 above.
32 Mäzgäb, MS.Moṭa Giyorgis.
33 Ibid.
34 Ibid.
35 Ibid.
36 Däqiqä Näbeyat, MS.Märṭulä-Maryam, folios261v-262r, 232v, 195v.
37 Ibid.
38 Ibid.
39 Ibid, folio243v.
40 Ibid, folio232v and 195v.
41 Ibid, 205v, 195v, etc.
42 Ibid, folio240recto, 262recto.
43 Ibid.
44 Ibid.
45 Ibid, folio241v.
46 Ibid, folio238recto.
47 Ibid, folio254recto.
48 Ibid, folio189recto, 241verso.

⁴⁹ See note number 10 above, Däqiqä Näbeyat, MS.Märṭulä- Maryam, folio66r.
⁵⁰ Däqiqä Näbeyat, folio226r.
⁵¹I.Guidi, *Annales Regum Iyasu II et Iyo'as.Corpus Scriptorium Christianorum Orientalium, Scriptores Aethiopici,Versio, Series* Altera, vol. 6 (Paris,1912), p.48.
⁵² Informants, *Ato* Dässè, *Mägabi* Ayähu.
⁵³ See note no.49 above.
⁵⁴Däqiqä Näbeyat folios212r, 226v, 249r-249v.These folios contain documents recording bequeathals of property involving adoption between brothers and sisters. On folio folio212r a certain *Mämher* Eshätè adopted the son of his brother called Därsäh Eshätè and bequeathed all his property including his house, in 1897 E.C. On folio 226v a certain *Wäyzäro* Mentewab adopted her sister, Yäshihäräg and bequeathed all her property and *rest* land to her. Other folios contain similar documents recording the transmission of property among siblings.
⁵⁵ Ibid, folio 66recto.
⁵⁶ Ibid, folio189recto, 205 verso and 241verso.
⁵⁷ Ibid, folio66recto.
⁵⁸ Ibid, folio253recto.
⁵⁹ Ibid folio219recto.
⁶⁰ Ibid, folio226 recto.
⁶¹ Ibid.
⁶² Ibid.
⁶³ Ibid, folio222verso.
⁶⁴ Ibid, folio231verso, 226verso and 253recto.
⁶⁵ Ibid.
⁶⁶ Ibid, 212verso.
⁶⁷ Ibid, 213recto, 219verso.
⁶⁸ Ibid, folio254recto, 261verso.
⁶⁹ Ibid.
⁷⁰ Täklè, "Yä Gojjam Tarik", pp.86-87.
⁷¹ Däqiqä Näbeyat, folio195recto.
⁷² Ibid, folio227verso.
⁷³ Ibid, folio231v.
⁷⁴ Ibid, folio236verso, 226recto.
⁷⁵ Ibid, folio227verso.

[76] Ibid, folio1recto, 29recto, 86recto, 85verso, 110recto, 162recto, 162verso-163recto, etc.
[77] Däqiqä Näbeyat, folio1v, 2v, 127v, 193r, 194r, and 210r.
[78] Ibid.
[79] Ibid, folio221r.
[80] Ibid, 221r, 222r.
[81] Ibid, folio84v, 132r, 154r, 191v, 193r, 196r, 66v and 2v.
[82] Ibid, folio193r.
[83] Ibid, folios2v and 193recto.
[84] Ibid, folio193recto.
[85] Ibid, folio154r, 132r, 208r, 22r and 222r
[86] Ibid, folio205v
[87] Ibid, folios1v, 2v, 84v, and 84r.
[88] Ibid,folio84v,1v,25v,64r,93r,127r,194r,194v,198r and 199r.
[89] Ibid, folio2v.
[90] Ibid, folio214v.
[91] Informant, *Wäyzäro* Michu.
[92] Giyorgis Wäldä-Amid, MS.Däbrä-Marqos, folio191recto.
[93] Däqiqä Näbeyat, folio205v.
[94] Ibid, folio219r.
[95] Ibid, folios225r, 225v, 227r.
[96] Ibid, folios 218recto through to folio228v are full of documents recording Häylu's purchase and other forms of transaction. cf. for the extensive land purchase of Häylu see Abdussamad H.Ahmed, "Gojjam: Early Merchant Capital and the World Economy 1901-1935" (PH.D. dissertation, University of Illinois at Urbana-Champaign, 1986), pp.198-200.

CHAPTER FIVE

EXPLAINING ETHIOPIA'S ECONOMIC STAGNATION: LAND TENURE AND THE PROBLEM OF UNDERDEVELOPMENT.

The perplexing issue of agrarian crisis that afflicts Ethiopia so frequently and with a shocking intensity has helped to shift the focus of historical discourse to agrarian matters. The most evident sign of stagnation of the economy is the phenomenon of recurrent famine, a phenomenon that is almost becoming an inevitable part of normal life in the country, in the recent history of Ethiopia. Indeed no historical phenomenon and process has been as intriguing and stimulating for historiographical and scholarly debate as the problems of cyclical agrarian crisis and the resultant human catastrophe and economic retrogression.[1] Impressive arrays of variables, with differing analytical validity, are forwarded in explaining Ethiopia's economic stagnation in the agrarian historiographical discourse. The debate on the problem of economic stagnation is still going on and is far from being resolved. However, the trend of current historiography, some studies excepted, is to emphasize the material structure as the reason for the agrarian crisis and perpetual economic stagnation.

Certain of the basic issues raised in the recent agrarian historiography of Ethiopia may be examined in light of my findings. And it is with respect to agrarian matters in particular that the institution of *zègenät* is very illuminating. *Zègenät* will give one a firm and sufficient ground from which to discuss some of the problems of underdevelopment. It helps to clear up the path towards a sober understanding of the nature of the Ethiopian polity and the classic problem of underdevelopment. However, there is no space to repeat all of the main arguments outlined in the scholarly discourse. Thus since it is too difficult to summarize in a few pages all of the issues involved in the debate, I shall restrict myself to showing the major lacunae in the historiography on the subject based on the insights from my finding and to a relatively narrow question of the change in the agrarian structure in the twentieth century Ethiopia.

As has already been alluded to above, the emphasis of current scholarship on agrarian studies is that what to a great extent determined civilizations and the economic advance or retardation of countries is the nature of the material structure stemming out of the prevalent property and social relations of production. This is too evident in the recent agrarian historiography of Ethiopia. Therefore, the dominant assumption in the conventional agrarian historiography of Ethiopia is that the prevalent forms of material relations especially property relations have to a great extent determined the socio-economic trajectory the country took. One such strand of arguments has wanted the property system to be the reason for the low quality of life in Ethiopia historically especially for the period between the sixteenth through to the first half of the nineteenth centuries. This period was the time when the seeds of capitalism were sown and became full blown in Western Europe. In effect the study is a subtle attempt to explain the absence of parallel development in Ethiopia and why capitalism was not replicated in the country while it took place elsewhere in the west.

Merid, who is a proponent of this view, does this so forcefully. The period between 1500 and 1850 is viewed to have constituted one historic continuum during which the Ethiopian state was moving cyclically and "purposelessly." According to Merid, there was hardly anything of the sort, even the trends towards what could legitimately be called linear progression in the socio-economic trajectory of the country during this long historic continuum. The rhythmic rise and fall in the fortune of the state and the monarchy stemmed from the nature of the material structure.[2] Looking back from the end of the nineteenth century at the modes of the socio-economic operation of the Ethiopian state one can observe hardly any major break away from the forms of material structure and economic traditions in the country a century earlier. Thus, though the study under review does stop its analysis in the middle of the nineteenth century, it is possible to project the modes of the socio-economic operation of the Ethiopian state prior to 1850 discussed by the proponent of this to have applied till the end of the century.

Merid holds that there was neither individual private ownership in land nor a positive element in the tenure system of the country strong enough to destroy the structure of *rest*. The material structure encapsulated by *rest* is viewed to have been impervious of individualism since it was based on communal ownership and condemned Ethiopia to underdevelopment. Individualism is viewed to have been a necessary preconditions for breaking away from the feudal relations of production ultimately to give rise to capitalist patterns of production relations (though the study under review does not actually use the word capitalism). What all this means is that the communal base of land ownership less stimulated peasants for increasing productivity and the long term price of this communalism was the impoverishment of the country. "Because hard work had no lasting reward and communal ownership of land allowed little latitude for individualism the energies of people, particularly of the more enterprising ones, channeled themselves into socially approved activities which brought more respect than wealth."[3]

Gult too is taken to have dispirited inventiveness and effort for maximum production by the peasantry or the ruling class. Arguments and conclusions of this kind are based on a simple theory and the premise that *gult* does not involve ownership and property right in land. For Merid the extortionate ruling class, who controlled the Ethiopian peasants, was less interested in *what could be produced from the land* than *what could be extracted from the peasant* since there was no property owning by the social elite in the long history of Ethiopia through *gult*. According to the study by Merid, the *gult* system made the ruling class to involve themselves in a painful and destructive internecine struggle. "The *gult* system, the reverse side of the *rest* form of tenure, made out of the ruling classes ever hungry predators, always destroying the administrative institutions which they wanted to build."[4] All this is understood to have stemmed from the weakness of the property system. Of course, this is an orthodox argument in Ethiopian agrarian studies. Merid concludes his study with the following claim, "In the final analysis therefore Ethiopian society was one where emperors, noblemen, soldiers, peasants and traders were all insecure, a society where even the law of the jungle would seem fair and where individualism and the creativeness of which comes from it never took root."[5]

Though put in different terminologies the views of a number of other scholars on Ethiopia's economic stagnation under the imperial regime are essentially similar to the one outlined above. The traditional land tenure system is said to have continued to provide a stronger, more rigid barrier to the dissolution of pre-capitalist relations of production till the last days of the imperial regime. Though not denying the penetration of capitalism into the country in the last days of the imperial regime the proponents of one such a view represented by Cohen and Weintraub hold that the force exerted by capitalism was not strong enough to bring a breakdown of the structure or the framework of the peasant economy and the *rest* system of tenure. For instance *rest* is believed to have been a major bottleneck for commercial farming and providing bank services or mortgage because it was not individually held and hence could not be transferred out of the lineage. For all these reasons capitalist forms of production relations did not occur in Ethiopia especially in the northern provinces.[6]

Cohen and his coauthor Weintraub confidently hold that Ethiopia's failure to grow along capitalist lines is attributable to the forces of the nobility or the resistance by the upper classes that stood against change in the agrarian institutions. The nobility deliberately halted capitalist relations of production fearing that this would erode their material interest and lead to a possible social revolution, "[t]he answer is that decision makers know agro-technology causes social change, and that in many parts of the country the land tenure system inherited from the Ethiopian feudalism is bound to warp social change in ways ultimately threatening to the maintenance of the traditional polity and the landed economy."[7]

Unlike many other scholars who wrote on the subject Bahru Zewde emphasizes the existence of an evident trend in the transition towards capitalism which was set in train in the country in the early twentieth century. The agrarian structure in the southern half of the country was being transformed to a capitalist manner in a piecemeal fashion. Bahru has documented this evident movement in the direction of capitalism in connection with a theoretical discussion on the nature of the absolutist state that emerged in the early decades of the twentieth century. For Bahru the social formation, which Ethiopia was in since the early decades of the twentieth century to the last years of the imperial regime, is a mixture of feudalism and incipient capitalism.

In such categorization the picture that is evoked is the beginning of the erosion of feudal relations of production and the transition towards embryonic capitalism. He argues that a process of further and further privatization with the resultant concentration of land in the hands of few people was set in train in the twentieth century in the south. It is apparently, among other things, the phenomena of increased land sale, privatization and absolutization of tenure in the pre-Italo-Ethiopian and post-Italo-Ethiopian war that are stressed and presented as useful empirical material for explaining the development of capitalism and the rendering of the social formation as feudo-bourgeois, one between full-blown feudalism and nascent capitalism.[8] The emergence of an impressive albeit small scale mechanized agriculture and commercial farming in some parts of the south in the sixties has lent credence to the argument that the society was tilting towards capitalist patterns.

Adhana Haile, who has done the most detailed work on famine and the problem of famine causation to date, represents dissenting opinion to Bahru. He holds more or less the same position with Merid and questioned the validity of the argument of the emergence of the feudo-capitalist state in Ethiopia. He has pieced together the many strands of arguments that have sought to come to grips with the problem. Adhana has provided a detailed critique of a variety of views on the problem of Ethiopia's underdevelopment.[9] In view of its importance for my study this work needs to be discussed and reviewed in some detail. As mention has already been made the major premise of Adhana's study is that there was very little or no change in respect to the land tenure system in the last days of the imperial era from the former period (pre-war period) the only difference being that the state under Häylä-Sellasè had greater coercive capacity than ever before. Adhana emphasizes the remarkable continuity of the political and economic traditions of the Ethiopian polity, a tradition that was impervious or impermissible to economic change. The advance in military technology helped the imperial state to have greater coercive capacity and to make strong intervention into local situations. However, the imperial state did not cause the destruction of older social and economic institutions by using its greater coercive capacity.[10]

Adhana emphatically attacks the "feudo-bourgeos" as a concept, largely criticizing that the country was essentially feudal and its economic world basically that of peasant. He further contends that the process of some degree of privatization and the beginning of commercial agriculture in some parts of the country can not be regarded as a testimony that the Ethiopian society in early decades of the twentieth century was qualitatively different from the earlier period. He argues that without any analytical credentials to what it means scholars have often unjustifiably characterized the Ethiopian state as a blend of feudalism and capitalism, "[t]o call this society feudo-capitalist is, to emphasis relativity more than balance, surely to be pedantic. It was essentially peasant and feudal; and it is unreasonable to blame pre-capitalist property relations for having blocked capitalist development in agriculture and the country at large."[11] The changes that marked the last days of the imperial regime out from the previous period are limited to the level of patterns of surplus appropriation and the phenomenon of greater money use. Appropriation of agrarian surplus was converted from tribute in kind to taxes in cash in the post-war period. However, the view has it that the monetization of the economy and the greater coercive power of the state could not constitute an empirical basis to qualify and legitimately call the Ethiopian society and economy one evolving towards capitalism in as long as taxation did not bring fundamental change in the agrarian relations.

Adhana holds that "Ethiopia was, historically speaking, certainly much more closer to the world capitalist system now than at any time before, but to claim that that closeness had, during the 1900-1935[period], wrought "modern political economy" and a bourgeosification of "some elements of the feudalists in power" in Ethiopia is to mistake the phenomena of the use of money and the quest for it for "modernity" and a social process linked with capitalist development."[12] One important reason offered for seeing continuity in the agrarian and social relations of production and leading to a rejection of the existence of capitalism for Ethiopia by this study is the absence of well-developed land and labor markets in the imperial period. Despite its recognition of the existence of land concentration and land grabbing in the last days of the imperial regime the proponent of this view does believe that the mechanism of transfer was traditional and not impersonal, and hence cannot testify to the existence of capitalism. The economy and the society was essentially peasant and rural and there was little or no production and social relations along capitalist lines.

What is equally stressed and viewed is the static or unchanging structure of peasant economy and the minimal influence exercised by the world capitalist economy. Capitalist farming, where it existed, did not displace the peasant economy or break up the material structure of the country to make way to capitalist agrarian relations through the development of commercial ones. Local or internal socio-economic dynamics suitable to the birth and development of capitalism is believed to have been absolutely lacking. The country's economy was not integrated into the capitalist world economy; it simply "engaged with" (the phrase is Adhana's) the latter. Adhana adds: "It was not, as I understand it, in its [the country's] design to become capitalist, but it engaged with it and could not but carry the stamp of that engagement."[13] What is important from the point of view of my study is that the work under review squarely states that the property system had not caused any obstruction in the possible forward stride of the country's economy along capitalist lines. "In the country at large, even areas which had a social regime that looked like the European feudal system had remained pre-capitalist. These in themselves are sufficient proofs that the argument which suggests resistant pre-capitalist production property relations as the cause for lack of capitalist development of the country is misplaced for the imperial period of 1941-74."[14]

Adhana holds that the argument by scholars that the weakness of the property system retarded economic advance and capitalism has a historical wisdom and analytical validity for the period prior to 1941. To project the modes of operation of the property system of the bygone centuries to the last days of the imperial regime, according to this view, does not have any analytical validity for it to be of much help.[15] The study holds that the pressure from capitalism and its impact on the old patterns of agrarian and property relations was very minimal to break up the structure of the latter. "The truth is that, during the 1941 -74[period], these institutions [*rest* and *gult*] had not been subjected to capitalist pressures and stimuli."[16] The favorable conditions, which could have driven agricultural production into the patterns of commerce and differentiation, are not simply material relations. Instead the absence of urban based manufacturing and trading proposed by this view as one reason to explain the failure of Ethiopia to tilt towards capitalism makes a lot of sense. "In general, that which should stimulate and pressed on peasant economy for capitalist development (trade and manufacture based urbanization) was not only very weak even by the last year of the imperial state, but its structure was of an exogenous graft in character more than of an internal process of capitalist development."[17] Adhana makes a subtle proposition that any argument can hardly be convincing in itself to be of much help in analyzing the problem of Ethiopia's agrarian history unless it incorporates town centered trading relations and manufacturing in towns in the discussion.

Tekalign whom we have met in the beginning of the study writes in similar vein though he presents some dissenting opinions on certain issues to the established historiography. He has done an extensive work on the issue of land tenure focusing on southern Ethiopia especially the region of Shawa from a perspective contrary to the conventional historiography. The study under review presents a very *balanced judgment* on the problem of dispossession of the southern peasantry. It challenges the old conception of massive eviction of the peasantry. He has convincingly showed the discrepancy between documentary prescription and the reality on the ground. However, he shares many similar views with Adhana on the important problem of the change in the agrarian relation of twentieth century Ethiopia. He holds that despite the purported destruction of the old patterns of property relations the material structure remained essentially the same down to the last days of the imperial regime. Emperor Häylä-Sellasè is said to have been protectionist of the age-old property relations and put up strong opposition against land transfer through sale rather than working towards privatization and the intensification of capitalist forms of production relations. Tekalign explains the action of the emperor in terms of his interest to stop landed property from being *de facto* privatized and concentrated in a few hands to become political capital.[18]

However, Tekialign's own study show that restrictions on the alienation of land do not mean of course that there was not land transfer through sale. Several important consequences stemmed from the extensive imperial land grants. Without abandoning the view that the imperial land grants did not bring significant re-arrangement in the organization of production and in rural social structure, Tekalign argues the emergence of an extensive land transfer and trade in land in the regions he studied. The grants led to a fairly well developed land market in southern Ethiopia.[19] The following observations can be made based on Tekalign's study. First, an increasing number of grants of land by the state to individuals created the condition for class conflict between the rural population and the grantees. This is because though theoretically the land given out to individuals by way of grant was supposed to be government land in actual fact the land turned over to the holding of the beneficiaries of the grant came from the rural population.

The rural population defended their property at best they could to prevent it from falling into the hands of grantees. The grantees on their part tried to grab land from the former by creating every excuse and referring to the terms of the grant document but most importantly by manipulating the fluidity of the traditional land holding system. A large amount of land sale was effected through the working or mechanism of the traditional land tenure system than because of any new and conscious policy towards privatization. Therefore, Tekalign's view on the means of land grabbing by individuals during the last days of the imperial regime is essentially similar to Adhana. He is also among the major exponents of the thesis that there was not significant commercial farming and fundamental change in the forms of agrarian organization. He emphasized that most landlords grew their crops not according to commercial criteria but to meet their consumption demands. The forces of a commercial system of production on the Ethiopian economy were not strong enough to break down the peasant economy.[20]

As a whole the discussion above predominantly points to the fact that notwithstanding some minor differences most scholars, Bahru excepted, tend to explain the lack of economic dynamism in Ethiopia in terms of the weakness of the property system. However, this line of interpretation of the agrarian history of Ethiopia does not have empirical base. The study has amply demonstrated the fact that *rest* was not impervious to individualism. It did not rigidly operate against individual right. The material and insights from Eastern Gojjam present a serious challenge to this idea. The discussion on *zègenät* amply shows how inadequate is the argument that the property system especially *gult* and including *rest* was inhibitive of individualism. The property system can not fully explain the problem of poverty and underdevelopment. Though further research is undoubtedly necessary the discussion in this work clearly shows that the institution of *zègenät* seems to have worked closely akin to feudalist kind of terms or lines as it existed in Europe. In other words the socio-economic operation of the institution of *zègenät* can enable one to describe it justifiably as feudalistic, and the class interaction between landlords and *zègas* was in the nature of all relationships that can be called serfdom in Marxist historiographical tradition. Private or individual right was neither lacking nor negligible. Not only was there private property in land but also turning the *rest* holding of the peasants into individual holdings by the social elites created such rights.

Private property normally co-existed with communal ownership without interruption for quite a considerable time. To be sure, the communal character of *rest* might have imposed some limitations on the exercise of the right of individual members of the lineage group. However, though the researcher does not have the objection to the point that the lineage might have exercised some degree of influence on individual members of the descent group, it can not be interpreted as an absolute barrier to individualism or inventiveness and a handicap for economic advance. Moreover, the study has rejected the idea that *gult* was only tributary right. What all this entails is that the argument that sees the agrarian foundation of the state to have been a major bottleneck for the economic advance of the country and cause for its perennial stagnation has not much validity.

The argument that land especially *rest* could not be mortgaged is empirically wrong or at best partially holds true for only some parts of Ethiopia. Two reasons may be advanced to think to the contrary; first as, we have seen extensively in chapter four, individuals acquired and lost their land because of impersonal reasons like credit stringency, etc. In short there was proprietary right in land in the modern sense of the word. Second, there was full right/opportunity of alienation and acquiring of property in land by individuals through sale and purchase. The argument against the existence of private property and land sale loses sight of the evidence of extensive land sale and a well-developed land market in northern Ethiopia. This has all too often resulted in serious misunderstanding of whole historical processes. The parameters often cited to argue against or in favor of the existence of private property or not and thereby categorize the economic system as feudal or otherwise, are the lack of right to transfer land through sale or the concentration and acquisition of land through (impersonal) mechanisms like debt and mortgage. If the defining element and the yardstick to measure the degree of ownership right over land exercised by individuals is the presence of land sale, then it was a general practice in Eastern Gojjam from at least the second half of the eighteenth century. The argument that land (especially *rest* land) was un-saleable and the mechanism and system of concentration or acquisition of land when it did exist was traditional rather than impersonal can no longer, in my opinion, be sustained.

The vested interest of the ruling class in not allowing capitalist forms of property system also not only still less explains the problem of the origin of underdevelopment but has no empirical ground at all. It is both moot and misconceived. The historical record shows that if the opportunity arose the big nobility were keenly interested in agro-technology and they made a very bold start in commercial and mechanized farming in the southern parts of the country.[21] Therefore, the argument by Cohen and Weintraub that the ruling class blocked the introduction of agro-technology and a change in the agrarian institutions of the country by itself is not a valid argument if it cannot be shown empirically. Without such empirical base, the assertion that the feudal nobility blocked capitalist pattern of economic development is unconvincing.

Without risking contradiction in my argument the researcher concurs with one major premises of Adhana's study. What sounds valid in Adhana's study is that it does not, though on a different ground from the researcher, wholly place the failure of Ethiopia to develop capitalistically for the years from 1941 to the last days of the imperial regime on the weakness of the property system.[22] However, Adhana has moved only a little distance further from the conventional historiography on the subject of Ethiopia's underdevelopment. The view of the researcher is that the property system did not obstruct any possible forward economic stride of the country even historically and before 1941, since what is most often assumed to have been missing in the Ethiopian context for possible progress and economic dynamism, namely private property and a land market, were present in those times too. The phenomena of land sale, as has been discussed earlier, did not emerge as the result of some kind of foreign influence. It was wholly an Ethiopian affair. Despite a vigorous dismissal of all the views which hold the material structures of the country as the reason for the retardation of the economy in the post war period, Adhana has neither empirically nor analytically proved the proposition that lack of urbanization based on trading and manufacturing was the reasons for the failure of Ethiopia to break into capitalism. Thus with no documenting and proof how much the absence of urbanization based on manufacturing and commerce retarded the economy or capitalism in the Ethiopian context, then Ethiopia's economic retardation becomes inexplicable. Much work still remains to be done along this line.

The second major contention of Adhana's study is his emphasize of the static nature of the Ethiopian agrarian order. The researcher has not any dispute with the argument that despite the existence of very promising beginnings in agriculture along capitalist lines the society did not fundamentally move away from feudalism. To be sure there was little technical change in agricultural production and labor organization. The cultivation technique remained static in most parts of the country. However, the lack of change in technical forces of production alone offers a very flimsy empirical base for describing the agrarian relations as static. Unless one wants to be pedantic hardly any compelling empirical material could be found to prove the argument against the existence of capitalism or at least the trend towards it. Adequate proof should be provided to argue otherwise. Adhana's interpretation sheds or loses its analytical wisdom in so far as he emphatically argues in favor of an unchanging agrarian order and against the existence of "capitalism" or the trends towards it. The earlier agrarian order did not continue to exist unvarnished well into the last days of the imperial regime including in the northern provinces. Therefore, despite the existence of some points of convergence and divergence between Adhana's work and some of my major premises the historical record urges one to be cautious of his contentions and about accepting it without some reservations.

Bahru's emphasis that the two ancient agrarian institutions (*gult* and *rest*) continued to work in northern half of the country and that part of Ethiopia escaped the experience and fate of the south in the imperial period[23] tends to telescope an older agrarian practice of the north into a view that it was a historical phenomenon that occurred only in later times and only in some areas. The primary agrarian processes in Eastern Gojjam discussed in the preceding chapters are similar in many ways to those of southern Ethiopia in the late 19th and 20th centuries. My own view is that although the process of privatization might have been speeded up in the twentieth century with increasing penetration of capitalism to the country it was not wholly without precedent. Given the multiplicity of *rim* land grants to churches in the second half of the nineteenth century we cannot even guess at how much land was held in *rest*. The pattern of relationship that came to be established between landlords and tenants in the southern half of the country in the twentieth century is reminiscent of the eighteenth and nineteenth centuries relationships between lord and *zèga*.

The tendency to privatization, towards the direct personal control of land, therefore, was not wholly a twentieth century phenomenon and not only in southern parts of the country. Although the absolutization of the political power of Häylä-Sellasè is said to have gradually changed in certain kinds of private and capitalist property relations particularly in the southern half of the country and in the last days of the imperial regime[24] similar processes seems to have occurred in Eastern Gojjam in the preceding centuries. It is justifiable to push back in time the precedent historical processes and the property system that developed in southern Ethiopia in the later days of Minilek II and Häylä-Sellasè and to argue for it has taken place in eighteenth century Eastern Gojjam though in different political and international contexts. Nor was the phenomenon of land concentration wholly unknown prior to the twentieth century. The cycle of concentration and disintegration of holdings started from early times and continued right down to the twentieth century.As extensively discussed in this study there was no legal restriction imposed on individuals to alienate their proprietary rights in land including *rest* and the land market continued unabated in the study area right down to the end of the imperial regime. Of course the land tenure system legalized land transfer. Tekalign's own study shows that imperial land grants had a tendency to increase privatization and informal commercialization of land. Therefore, one concomitant development of imperial land grants in the post-war period is a land market.[25] If we are to believe that concentration of land and the existence of private property were the essential pre-conditions for the development of capitalist forms of production relations, capitalism was therefore potentially nascent a century before in Eastern Gojjam. It was not land sale and privatization that was missing for capitalist patterns of development.

Though a full blown capitalist pattern of developments did not exist there are indications that its potentialities were not absolutely lacking even in the north including Eastern Gojjam. We have seen the prevalence of agrarian relations akin to serfdom for the study area. There had also occurred large redistribution of landed property and concentration of revenue and land in the hands of some individuals. *Ras* Häylu II of Gojjam proceeded to a private appropriation of land in the Märtulä-Maryam area and elsewhere in the region. It is not surprising; therefore, that he was probably the first to adapt to the possibilities of "capitalism" oriented towards commerce as well as handicraft production in Gojjam. He was a budding capitalist and consummate merchant *par excellence*. Häylu took all or a considerable part of the total revenue from his ancestral province of Gojjam. One study has aptly concluded that "Gojjam as a whole belonged bag and baggage to Räs Häylu."[26] His unscrupulous grabbing of land and love for money has become almost proverbial. He did not scruple to grab money at every opportunity and from sources that could have been considered shameful in the eyes of the public at the time: peasants, *prostitutes*, merchants, *invalid beggars* and others.[27] Sufficient accumulation of wealth enabled him to make a bold venture in business. He turned this massive wealth appropriation into urban assets and invested in many kinds of commercial activities. The most important of these pertained to hotel business; taxi business, a cinema hall, etc.[28] He had also under him extensive land in the province and also owned cattle.

Other important evidence, which points to the penetration of an incipient form of "capitalism" in the study area, is the "workshop" that Häylu organized in Däbrä-Marqos for the production of handicraft goods. The feudal element in the organization of the process of production is less visible. The presence of a very strong supportive empirical material tempts one to argue that a nascent "capitalist" line of development had asserted itself in that region no matter how immature it was. We may marvel how much more capitalistic than feudalistic was the organization and the purpose of the production in these "workshops" if we observe the evidence of the following lines by one of the artisans (Täklä-Iyäsus) who was a contemporary observer of those workshops organized by Häylu[29]:

ከዚህ በኋላ ሁሉም ቄርጥ አወቀ፡፡ ከዚህ በኋላ ደግሞ በመጠጫው መቅረት ቢአዝን በሰራተኛው የባሰ መከራ መጣበት፡፡ በንቱሱ ጊገርዜ በሱም በሹም በሹም አንጥረኛው ብሩን በቁጥር ወርቁን በሚዛን ነፍጥ ሰሪው ማረሻውን ገሶውን አራቢ የቡውን ተምቤቱን እ'ተቀበለ ከቤቱ ደጃፍ መስሪooያ ጎጆ ስርቶ ምሺቱ እንጨት እዉሀ ስትሄድ ቤቱን እየጠበቀ ስትመለስ አረረ ገልብጮዉ በሰለ አዉጮዉ እያለ ከ ምሺቱ ጋር እየተዳራ ሲርበዉ በዚዚያቱ እዬበላ ስራዉን ሲጨርስ በየአልደረባዉ ያገባነር፡፡ ደጃች ስዮም ግን ያንጊዜ ምሸዋ ደንብ ይሁን ብሎ ሰራተኛዉን ሁሉ አደባባይ አስብቶ በዮሙያዊ ያሰራዉ ጀመር፡፡ ያንጊዜ ሕራዉን በአደባባይ ያደረገ ሰራተኛዉን ጠርጥሮ ገንዘብ ወዶ ነዉ፡፡ በንቱሱ ጊዜ ሰራተኛዉ እንደሻዉ ነበር፡፡ ግMጃ ሰራዉ የግምጃ ቅዳጅ ጠላፊዉ የሀር ስንባጭ አንጠረኛዉ የብር ቅላጭ የወርቅ ቁማጭ ነፍጥ ቆርቁሪ የብሪት ን□ች አናጢ የንጨት ጉራጅ... ይወስድ ነበር፡፡ ደጃች ስዮም ግን የንቱሱን ስርአት ነቅፎ ለሰሙ ማክፍያ ሁሉን በሹም ጠባቂ አደረገ፡፡ የግምጃ ትልታይ የእርብ ቅዳጅ ሰቡዳ መድህኒት መስፈያ ከሰራተኛዉ ዘንድ ለምኖማግኘት ቀረ፡፡

After all this everybody lost hope. Besides being saddened by the interruption of the service of drink, still more worse happened to the workers. During the time of the king [Takla-Haymanot] the blacksmiths used to receive measured quantity of silver and gold nuggets, those engaged in casting [repairing?] arms, spade, spear and plough and the spinners and the tanners received their respective material through their overseers and carried on their work in small huts they have erected at their own places. When their wives were out to fetch water and gather fire wood they look after their house. On the return of his wife he controlled such domestic chores as cooking dishes instructing his wife when the meal was ready to serve. He used to spend good times with his wife feeding when he felt hungry and submit his production when he finishes his work through his superintendent. However, Dajjach Seyoum rebuked/ disapproved the old system and ordered the workers to come out of their place on to the open space and made them work according to their specialization based on the custom of Shawa. The reasons why he transferred the place of work to open space were because of his suspicion of the workers and his love of money. In the days of the King the workers were free. [Moreover], craftsmen in the making of velvet cloth had the right to take slice (slit) of cloth; those engaged in embroidery could take shreds of silk, crafts associated with the working of gold and silver could take smelt ore of silver and broken piece of gold, those crafts associated with the work of repairing arms took broken pieces of metal, carpenters engaged in woodcraft could take chip of wood. However, Dajjach Seyoum, violating the rules established by the king [Takla-Haymanot], appointed overseers over the artisans to strictly control them for the despoliation of his name. No body could anymore aspire to get from artisans even splinter of silk as small as the size enough for wrap up of amulet.

The production was not entirely luxury goods but goods to raise money. Häylu turned the finished products of these craftsmen to cash through outright sale in the market. The organization of craftsmen by Häylu for production for the market is indicative of the fact that changes along "capitalist" manners were in train. This evidence should not have been neglected in the general discourse on the problem of Ethiopia's economic backwardness.

Unfortunately, however, it was not a long way off that the initial thrust for "capitalist" development and the fascinating beginnings in business by Häylu in Gojjam and Addis Ababa were cut short following his arrest in 1932. The early progress towards "capitalism" was brought to a halt in the country as a whole with the Italian invasion of Ethiopia in 1935/6.[30] Thus it was rather because of the vagaries of the political system that all too often denied the acumen of businessmen like Häylu time to progress along capitalist line than the absence of conducive elements in the traditional land tenure system. Though its extent is hard to know the practice of employing agricultural laborers is also attested in the sources and we cannot rule out the possible existence of a labor market in the region.[31] Moreover, some scholars have documented that the peasant economy did not work independently and peasants contributed to the market no matter how involuntarily they were forced to enter that market. To attempt to explain the country's failure to cut into capitalist systems of production relations merely in terms of the weakness of the traditional property system would lead us astray from the main issues. The causes of Ethiopian stagnation can not be entirely material cause. It must include other causes like political and religious ones and no doubt others.

The early trend towards further and further privatization and absolutization of tenure continued after 1941. The state also had come to have much coercive power and modern military technology strong enough to make a deeper intervention in the affairs of local society. It established a centralized apparatus to collect revenue destroying the intermediary personnel between the state and the peasantry. In an array of edicts Häylä-Sellasè swept away an age-old feudal privilege and rights with the aim of increasing his power and achieving fiscal centralization.[32]

Notwithstanding its embryonic character, capitalism and commercial agriculture was penetrating the countryside. In an interesting article, which surveyed the literature on the degree of commercial agriculture in Ethiopia Dessalegn Rahmato concludes that immediately preceding the 1975 Ethiopian turn to compulsive socialism rural capitalism had "evolved to a stage where it could be said that a form of incipient capitalism was emerging in the countryside."[33] A budding and quite successful rural agrarian capitalism was expanding rather rapidly in various parts of Ethiopia during the last years of the imperial regime. Some landlords started mechanized and commercial agriculture and produced for the market. Those landlords who could not afford to use more modern methods used their oxen and employed wage laborers to produce for the market. The turn to mechanization and modern methods of farming brought displacement and dispossession of tenants and peasant farmers in some areas especially in the province of Arsi. Therefore, rural capitalism generated further polarization and social inequality in some areas of Ethiopia. It attracted attention and was a subject of bitter criticism by individuals in the intellectual circle.[34]

The social and economic system was based on very deep inequality and this social inequality had apparently reached monstrous and later intolerable proportion to some individuals in the intellectual circle. Therefore, the intelligentsia opened a virulent and orchestrated campaign against the imperial regime and its ruling ideals. The land tenure system was singled out as one of the repositories or the root of the evils of the social system and it was a target of orchestrated attack from both radicals and reformists. Malaise in the economic and social conditions became clear in the last days of the imperial regime in particular. However, the beginning of discourse on the agrarian system of the country in intellectual circles can be traced back to the early twentieth century. The intellectuals raised the issues of social justice and economic advance and struggled to achieve both. They argued for reform in the agrarian relations to obtain rapid economic growth. Some stood against concentration of holdings and for the right to alienate property freely at one and the same time.[35]

The agrarian structure and the social arrangements that came to be known under the general rubric of *gäbbar* system were bitterly criticized. Some also exposed the evils of *zègenät* together with the *gäbbar* system in the most powerful language.[36] Though we cannot exactly know when it became obsolete and fell into disuse, the institution(*zègenät*)still existed in the early twentieth century. Perhaps it took many years to disappear and dragged on till much later time than the early twentieth century.[37] The *zègas*, we can now say, continued to be treated as inferior at least from the 18th century, when the term is met frequently in land grant documents and church manuals, till the twentieth century. We have seen that the *mäkwanent* and the *däbtara* constituted the highest stratum of the society. At the base of this social structure were landless *zègas*, *gäbbars* and the *restäñña*. One of the intellectuals of the early twentieth century described the harsh treatment and contempt that the nobility had towards the *zègas*, and the *gäbbars* as in the following terms for which not even a perfect English translation can fully capture the meaning and the powerful expression of these lines.[38]

> ገባርናቸ ዜጋዉን እነሱ በገዛእጃቸዉ እንደእ}ጨት ጠራርበዉ አንደ ግንድ ጆራርገዉ እንደጭቃ ጠፍጥፈዉ እንደሊጥ ለዉሰዉ አሞልሙለዉ አይን ጆሮዉን አንገት ከንፈሩን ቀርጸዉ እፍብለዉ ነፍስ የዘሩበት እና ያቆሙት ያስመስሉት ነበር እንጂ እዉነት እንደነሱ በእግዚአብሄር ፈቃድ የተፈጠረ እና እንደነሱ ተምልዶ አድን አርጀቶ የሚሞት አይመስላቸዉም ነበር፡፡

> "...It was as if the zègas, and the gäbbars were their own creation, and not, like them, God's creatures, as they shaped them into being out of mud, giving them eyes, ears, neck and lips, and finally breathing life into them." The vigor of the corporate institutions was still intact in the twentieth century. The agrarian or material foundation of big churches and monasteries was still maintained despite the erosion of a significant portion of their judicial rights. They put up a very strong resistance against measures that threatened to take away their material privilege.[39]

The government, though belatedly, came to appreciate the need to make intervention in peasant agriculture. The policy of helping poor peasants by providing agricultural input and agro-technology was incorporated in the government's Five Year Development Plan. Paradoxical as it may sound, the development incentives and intervention by the government aimed at first helping poor peasants ended up deepening inequality and promoting capitalist farming and big landlords. As indicated above, in the last days of the imperial regime eviction became widespread and it was about the same time that big landlords started a very bold venture in mechanized and capitalist farming in many parts of the country.[40]

The main criticism labeled against mechanization and commercial agriculture was peasant displacement and eviction. Mechanization entails land concentration and consolidation of holding. The land so acquired by landlords was taken from the poor peasant farmers who were made to lose their land. The peasants evicted in certain areas turned to wage laborers on the capitalist and commercial farms. However, most of them were not employed as wage laborers since agro-industry was not well developed which could have opened rich possibilities for employment of surplus agricultural labor. If the revolution had not disrupted the process, rural agrarian capitalism could have naturally expanded rather rapidly. Dessalegn projected that around half a million people would have been evicted and become landless by 1980s if the early trend to mechanization and commercial agriculture was not interrupted by the *därg*.[41]

Therefore, the slide towards capitalist farming was cut short with the outbreak of the 1974 revolution. The ruling class was not able to grasp the tempo of the social and political change in the country. Radical socialism and Marxism were incorporated into the discourse of the intelligentsia. The slogan "Land to the Tiller" became capable of winning many followers. Since the government and the radical intelligentsia had failed to reach at consensus on the issue of land and achieving social justice, violence became a received wisdom either to maintain the *status quo* or to bring change. Bloodshed was unavoidable and became an inexorable manifest destiny and Ethiopia was in a hopeless impasse between 1974 and 1977.[42] The revolution of 1974 swept away an age-old political regime and imperial dynasty. The impact of the revolution on agrarian organization is significant and Ethiopian society can be seen to have undergone significant changes with regard to agrarian relations. The old pattern of agrarian relations and the social relations arising out of this had become a thing of the past. Land was redistributed based on egalitarian principles after the 1974 revolution. Private tenure was abolished and land was held communally. However, the revolution did very little, or no, good for the peasantry and the country at large. The agrarian consequences of political change especially in northern Ethiopia can simply be labeled adverse or catastrophic to the peasantry.[43]

Equitable distribution of land simply means redistributing wealth and could not achieve economic advance. Though what should be grown on the land was left for a decision of the peasant the government had too tight a grip on the peasantry and heavily taxed the latter under many guises. Simply wrong built upon wrong with serious consequences on the peasantry. The *därg* confiscated urban people who owned land in rural areas. The impressive and promising initiatives in mechanized agriculture and commercial farming in various parts of the country especially in the south were stifled which in turn resulted in economic backslide. Talking in historical terms the *därg's* land policy had simply taken the country an extraordinary step backwards. A paper submitted to a graduate class of the Department of History aptly characterizes the *därg's* land policy and its achievements in rural Ethiopia to have simply and essentially been "equality of poverty."[44]

The land policy of the current regime is essentially similar to that of the *därg*. The 1995 Ethiopian constitution declares that land is publicly and government owned. There is a strong empirical support not to see or make virtue out of public and government ownership of land. The cyclical land redistribution that had been carried out since 1975 throughout the country has created a reign of insecurity in the mentality of rural communities. This state of condition is bound to immobilize peasants from making some attempt in increasing productivity and from developing their land. What the government should do now is to build up the confidence and trust of the peasants on their property and work to persuade them to use better seeds, use selective irrigation, etc. The government can establish peasant confidence by promoting private enterprises as examples.

Public and government ownership of land blocks the individualism and creativeness that usually comes from private property rights on land. Privatization of landed property and the right to free disposal of land helps to dispel the reign of insecurity among rural communities. It will also encourage consolidation and concentration of holding in the hands of some individuals through the development of land market. Therefore, promoting free market in land as a measure of consolidating holdings is a necessary condition for developing commercial and mechanized agriculture. Placing much authority in the hands of private owners has much wisdom and would naturally facilitate the development of rural capitalism side by side with trying to transform the peasant economy. Transforming peasant economy in turn entails introducing and intensifying agro-industry. Agro-industry would resolve any possible social and economic problems which rural agrarian capitalism may generate by giving work opportunities for peasants losing their land by being wage laborers.

NOTES

[1] Space will not be enough to list down all of the works on famine and underdevelopment but the most pertinent and representative studies on agrarian issues include Adhana Haile Adhana, "History of Selected Famines in Peasant Societies in Tigray and Wallo, Ethiopia 1941-74" (PH.D. dissertation, Department of History (AAU), 1996), Dessalegn Rahmato, *Famine and Survival Strategies: A Case Study from Northeast Ethiopia*(Uppsala: The Scandinavian Institute of African Studies, 1991), Kidane Mengisteab, *Ethiopia: Failure of Land Reform and Agricultural Crisis*(New York, Westport, London: Greenwood Press), Kurt Jansson et al., *The Ethiopian Famine*(London/ New Jersey: Zed Books, 1987), Mesfin Wolde-Mariam, *Rural Vulnerability to Famine in Ethiopia 1958-1977*(New Delhi: Vikas Publishing House, 1984), *Idem, Suffering under God's Environment: A Vertical Study of Predicament of Peasants in North-Central Ethiopia*(Berne: The African Mountains Association and Geographica Bernensia, 1991).

[2] Merid, "Land Tenure and Agricultural Productivity," pp.115-124, See also idem, "Society and Technology in Ethiopia," pp.127-143.

[3] Ibid, "Land Tenure and Agricultural Productivity," p123.

[4] Ibid, p.124. He writes in similar vein in his "Society and Technology in Ethiopia,"pp.139-140.

[5] Ibid, "Society and Technology in Ethiopia," p.143.

[6] Cohen, J. and Weintraub, D., *Land and Peasants in Imperial Ethiopia: the Social Background to a Revolution* (Assen: Van Gorcum & Co., 1975), pp. 15-17, John Markakis and Nega Ayele, *Class and Revolution in Ethiopia*(London, Review of African political Economy, 1978. Reprinted by the Red Sea Press, Trenton: 1986), pp.59-60

[7] Cohen, J. and Weintraub, D., *Land and Peasants in Imperial Ethiopia*, p.17.

[8] Bahru Zewde, "Economic Origins of the Absolutist State in Ethiopia," in *Journal of Ethiopian Studies*, Vol.XVII, Pp. 10-19. One scholar argues that the northern peasantry was impoverished because of incipient capitalism and the erosion of pre-capitalist relations of production, Lionel Cliffe, "Capitalism or Feudalism? The Famine in Ethiopia," *Review of African Political Economy*, No.1 (1975), pp.36-38. Mesfin also writes in similar vein, *Rural Vulnerability to Famine in Ethiopia*, pp.87-90. There is still another scholarship which also speaks about the beginning of

capitalism even in the north, Lundstrom, Karl Johan, "North-eastern Ethiopia: Society in Famine: A Study of three Social Institutions in a Period of Severe Strain," Research Report 34(Uppsala: The Scandinavian Institute of African Studies, 1976), pp.44, 55-57.
[9] Adhana, "History of Selected Famines,"pp.598-644.
[10] Ibid, pp.610,-612, 625-6 and 636-644.
[11] Ibid, p.628.
[12] Ibid, p.637.
[13] Ibid, p.644.
[14] Ibid, pp.625-626.
[15] Ibid, pp.628-633.
[16] Ibid, p.626.
[17] Ibid, p.628.
[18] Tekalign, "A City and its Hinterlands,"pp.239-257, 298 and 342
[19] Ibid, pp.259-263.
[20] Ibid, p.298.
[21] See also Dessalegn Rahmato, "Moral Crusaders and Incipient Capitalists: Mechanized Agriculture and Its Critics in Ethiopia," in *Proceedings of the Third Annual Seminar of the Department of History* (Addis Ababa: Addis Ababa University, 1986), pp.69-90.
[22] Adhana, "History of Selected Famines," pp.628-633.
[23] Bahru, "Economic Origins of the Absolutist State in Ethiopia," Pp. 10-19.
[24] Bahru, "Economic Origins of the Absolutist State," pp.10-24.
[25] Tekalign, pp.259-263.
[26] Bahru, "Economic Origins of the Absolutist State in Ethiopia,"pp.17-19, Abdussamad, "Early Merchant Capital in Gojjam and the World Economy,"pp.192-198, 203-206 and 214.This latter study aptly declares that "Gojjām as a whole belonged bag and baggage to Rās Haylu,"p.197.
[27] Täklä-Iyäsus, "History of Gojjam from *Ras* Häylu I to *Ras* Häylu II,"pp.137-140.
[28] Abdussamad "Early Merchant Capital in Gojjam and the World Economy," p.255, Bahru, "Economic Origins of the Absolutist State," p.18.
[29] Täklä-Iyäsus, "History of Gojjam from *Ras* Häylu I to *Ras* Häylu II,"pp.115-116.
[30] Bahru, *A Modern History of Ethiopia*, pp.144 and 152-176

[31] Täklä-Iyäsus for example speaks about the *arash* (the agricultural wage laborers) as distinct from *zèga* and other forms of farmers. See in Girma, "Ancient Customary Law of the Gafat," p.73. McCann also extensively discusses about rural wage laborers for Lasta and its surrounding, see "Households, Peasants and Rural History in Lasta,"pp. 252-258.

[32] Crummey, *Land and Society in the Christian Kingdom of Ethiopia*, pp.231-241, Bahru, "Economic Origins of the Absolutist State," pp.12-19, *Idem, A Modern History of Ethiopia*, pp.98-99, and 137-148. Tekalign, "A City and its Hinterlands,"pp.273

[33] Dessalegn, "Moral Crusaders and Incipient Capitalists,"p.69

[34] Ibid, pp.69-71 and 85-86.

[35] Bahru, *Pioneers of Change in Ethiopia: The Reformist Intellectuals of the Early Twentieth Century* (Addis Ababa: Addis Ababa University Press, 2002), pp.120-127.

[36] Afäwärq Gäbrä-Iyäsus, "Mädiwä Ébo,"in *Berhänena Sälam*, 1, 8, 29, Cited and translated by Bahru in *Pioneers of Change in Ethiopia*,p.121.

[37] Ministry of Interior to the Office of the Ecclesiastical Council (Mänfäsawi Guba'e Tsefäte bèt), a letter dated on 24 Magabit 1937.E.C. The letter records the defense waged by the big churches and monasteries and the people attached to them in Eastern Gojjam to preserve their traditional privilege like sitting in judgment of their *zèga*, etc. Whether in the sense used by the eighteenth and nineteenth century documents or not there is an explicit mention of the term *zègas* under the church personnel in this document. I am indebted to my colleague Wudu Tafete for this information. He kindly allowed me to reproduce this letter which he copied from the archives of the Patriarchate Office of the Ethiopian Orthodox Church.

[38] See note No. 36 above.

[39] See note No. 37 above.

[40] Dessalegn Rahmato, "Moral Crusaders and Incipient Capitalists,"pp. 69-86, Bahru, *A History of Modern Ethiopia*, 1855-1991, pp.194-195.

[41] Dessalegn, "Moral Crusaders and Incipient Capitalists,"p.85

[42] Crummey, *Land and Society in the Christian Kingdom of Ethiopia*, pp.244-252.

[43] Ibid, pp.247-48.

[44] Mengistu Abebe, "Which Kind of Land Reform for Ethiopia: The Debate Preceding the 1975 Land Proclamation," (A paper submitted to the Graduate Studies of the Department of History (AAU), June 1995), p.31

CHAPTER SIX

CONCLUSION

Notwithstanding the tremendous success registered by Ethiopian historiography in recent times and the enthusiasm and excitement of scholars in unveiling the Ethiopian past, many aspects of Ethiopian history still promise to continue as virgin land for a few decades to come. This is no less evident particularly in the field of social history than other aspects of Ethiopian history. Of course social history could be pointed out as one of the serious lacunae of Ethiopian historiography. Though there is a body of knowledge and scholarly works which have achieved the status of classics and established points of departure in the field of economic and political history, the social aspect of Ethiopian history suggests possibilities of new perspectives to what might be loosely considered orthodox in those areas of scholarly inquiry. This orthodoxy in political and economic history of Ethiopia has unconsciously made even local studies, whose findings clearly contradict principles and systems often stated as pan-Ethiopian and applying in all regions of the country in the past, to be timid. All too often, promising local studies has ended up with conclusions which conform to this orthodoxy mainly because arguments otherwise amounts to being foolishly daring.

As mention has already been made, social history provides a very exciting prospect for the development of Ethiopian historiography. Moreover, the resource to be had from this field will undoubtedly shed great light on other aspects of Ethiopian history. This partly arises from the nature of the sources for the study of social history. The social history of Ethiopia has to be teased out and come from sources which have very little value to study political and diplomatic history, sources which unlike elite documents throw light on lower levels of socio-economic relationship among the different layers of society. The study has chiefly used documentation generated by and coming from the church. It is the neglect of these sources that has resulted in the escape of some very important social and agrarian institutions from the attention of scholars. Indeed, one could not have missed the existence of such institutions as the one discussed in this study with only the least time and energy expended since it is stated in the most unequivocal terms and in some of the documents with almost unusual clarity. Moreover, a close analysis of these sources suggests an interpretation which can almost revolutionize our knowledge on certain fields such as class and land tenure system. The central theme of this study, *zègenät*, is one of such class or social institutions anchored in the agrarian base structure which has so far remained obscure and practically unknown in other regions of historic Ethiopia. This institution has a tremendous bearing on our understanding of the political economy of Ethiopia. Based upon the discussion in the preceding chapters one can conclude with several observations.

Zègenät had very old roots going back to at least the seventeenth century. This study has delineated the characteristics of the institution of *zègenät* from the study of 18th and 19th century documents. Land that was the main form of property in the past was the key point of interaction between lord and *zèga* and peasant. *Zègenät* has close affinity to serfdom. The term *zèga* was applied to landless and subordinated individuals working on the land of lords and under almost complete legal and socio-economic domination of the lords. Though the *zèga* class enjoyed freedom of mobility and the bond established between the *zèga* and the lord was not hereditary, the obligation of the *zèga* towards the lord had the hallmark of servitude. The state and social elites exercised a very firm control over land including *rest* land and over the labor power of the peasants. Indeed, individuals who constituted the *zèga* class in the seventeenth century had originally been independent peasants working on their own land. Lords also exercised far more direct control over craftsmen although there were independent artisans working in their own place. There were many artisan *zègas* working under the landlords and whose obligation towards the landlords was similar to those of the farmer *zèga*.

Any discussion of the socio-economic relationship between *zèga* and peasant and lord to be complete must include the way in which means of production was customarily transferred from generation to generation. Sale was the most dominant mode of property transmission. The factors and concerns that led men to choose a particular type of mechanism of property transfer were many, including debt. The purchasers and vendors were both from the highest reach and the lower layers of society. Before closing the study it remains to add a few things as a kind of postscript to what had been said and argued so far.

As pointed out above *zègenät* was very important institution in the local social structures of Eastern Gojjam. It also shows how inadequate is our knowledge of the land tenure system. It has a strong implication on the existing interpretation of the land tenure system. Any argument, which does not consult the evidence of *zèga*, can only be doubtful. The new category of *zèga* and the institution that it embodies deserve analysis to advance methodological understanding. Moreover, the institution is of prime importance for the classic problem of underdevelopment and to test the validity of the argument that says the land holding system has blocked the possibility of the country's development along capitalist line.

It would certainly broaden the discourse on the nature of the Ethiopian polity and the problem of underdevelopment to a certain level. The forms of agrarian organization embodied by *zègenät* should be given pride of place. We have to explore local records and our grasp of Ethiopian agrarian history and polity would certainly be inadequate in a work that does not look at evidence for *zèga* or *zègenät*. Just as *zègenät* throw light on the nature of agrarian organization in Eastern Gojjam it might shed valuable light on the nature of the Ethiopian state as well.

Though the desire for modesty urges me to tone down my judgment and language the researcher can not help writing that the discussion on *zègenät* shows the absence of perceptive understanding of the nature of the production and property relations in the past. The researcher believes that the forms of the agrarian relation in the country are least fully understood in the historiography. Tentatively the study would suggest that sources are reassuring that the agrarian history of many regions of historic Ethiopia share many similarities with those pertaining to Eastern Gojjam. The form of agrarian and social relations embodied in *zègenät* has, therefore, significance for re-defining a pan-Ethiopian agrarian order presently missing in the historiography on the subject. We have to privilege *zèga* in the historical research into primary agrarian processes to advance our methodological understanding.

Another conclusion that one can make based on the discussion above is that the property system did not inhibit the possible growth of the seeds of capitalism. It was not a deterrent to the economic development of Ethiopian society. The point at hand is that though the ground was favorable for development towards the European pattern, capitalism was not fully replicated in Ethiopia and why this was so is something which only future research has to unveil.

BIBLIOGRAPHY

Published Sources

Abdussamad H. Ahmed. "Peasant Conditions in Gojjam during the Great Famine, 1888-1892" in *Journal of Ethiopian Studies*. Vol. XX (1987):1-18.

------------------."Baso: A Commercial Entreport of Gojjam, 1841-1889", *Proceeding of the Fourth Seminar of the Department of History*. Addis Ababa, (1987):1-14.

------------------."Emperor Yohannes' Campaign in Gojjam, August 1888 to February 1889", *Journal of North-East African Studies*. Vol.13, no.1 (1991):1-7

Abir, M .*Ethiopia: The Era of Princes: The Challenge of Islam and the Reunification of the Christian Empire, 1769-1855* .London: Longmans Green, 1968.

---------------.*Ethiopia and the Red Sea: The Rise and the Decline of the Solomonic Dynasty and Muslim and European Rivalry in the Region.*London .Cass, 1980.

Alämayähu Mogäs. *And Eräñña, And Mänga*. Addis Ababa: Commercial Printing Press, 1989 E.C.

Arnauld, D.*Douze ans dans la Haute Ethiopie (Abyssinie)*.4Vols, Vatican City: Biblioteca Apostolica Vaticana, 1980.

Bahru Zewde. "Economic Origins of the Absolutist State in Ethiopia," in *Journal of Ethiopian Studies*, Vol.XVII, 1984.

----------------. *A Modern History of Ethiopia*. London: James Curry, 1990.

----------------. *Pioneers of Change in Ethiopia: The Reformist Intellectuals of the Early Twentieth Century*. Addis Ababa: Addis Ababa University Press, 2002.

Bairu Tafla.*AsmeGiyorgis and his Work: History of Galla and the Kingdom of Shawa.*Stuttgart: Steiner-Verlag Wiesbaden Gambh, 1987.

Buckingham, C.F.and G.W.B.Huntingford (eds. and trans.). "Almieda on Ethiopia", *Some Records of Ethiopia, 1593-1646.*London: Hakluyt Society, 1954.

Beke, C.T. *Letters on the Commerce and Politics of Abyssinia and Other Parts of East Africa* .London, 1852.

----------- "Abyssinia-Being a Continuation of Routes in that Country", *Royal Geographical Society* vol.14, London, 1844.Microfilm code 2/J/4.
-----------.*Diary of Journey in Abyssinia, 1840-43*, pp.1-76.
Blanc, Henry. *A Narrative of Captivity in Abyssinia.* London: Smith, Elder & Co., 1868.
Bruce, James. *Travels to Discover the Source of the Nile.* 5vols, Edinburgh: Edinburgh University Press, 1964.
Caulk, Richard. "Religion and the State in Nineteenth Century Ethiopia", *Journal of the Ethiopian Studies.*Vol.10, no.1 (1972):23-41.
---------------. "Territorial Competition and the Battle of Embabo", *Journal of Ethiopian Studies*, vol.13, no.1 (1975):65-88.
Cliffe, Lionel. "Capitalism or Feudalism? The Famine in Ethiopia," *Review of African Political Economy*, No.1 (1975)
Cohen, J.M. "Ethiopia a Survey on the Existence of a Feudal Peasantry," *Journal of Modern African Studies.* Vol.12 (1974):665-72.
Cohen, J. and Weintraub, D., *Land and Peasants in Imperial Ethiopia: the Social Background to Revolution*.Assen: Van Gorcum & Co., 1975.
Combes E. and Tamisier. *Voyage en Abyssinie, dans le Pays des Galla, de Choa, et d'Ifat.*3Vols, Paris, 1838.
Crummey, D. "Society and Ethnicity in the Politics of Christian Ethiopia during the *Zamana-Masafent*," *International Journal of African Historical Studies.*Vol.8, no.2 (1975):266-278.
-----------------."Gonderine *rim* Land Sales: An Introductory Description and Analysis" in Robert Hess (ed) *Proceedings of the Fifth International Conference on Ethiopian Studies.* Chicago: University of Illinois at Chicago Circle (1979):469-479.
----------------."Abyssinian Feudalism", *Past and Present*.Vol.89 (1980):115-38.
----------------. "Women and Landed Property in Gondarine Ethiopia", *International Journal of African Historical Studies.*Vol.14, no.3 ((1981):444-465.
----------------. "Family and Property amongst the Amhara Nobility", *Journal of African Histoty.*Vol.24, no.2 ((1983):207-220.
----------------."Ethiopian Plow Agriculture in Nineteenth Century", *Journal of Ethiopian Studies.*Vol.16, (1983):1-23.
Crummey, D.and Shumet Sishagne. "Land Tenure and the Social Accumulation of Wealth in the Eighteenth Century Ethiopia: Evidence

from the Qwesqwam Land Register", *International Journal of African Historical Studies* .Vol.24, no.2 (1991):241-258.

Crummey, Donald, Daniel Ayana and Shumet Sishagne. "A Gonderine Land Grant in Gojjam: The Case of Qaranyo Madhane-Alam", Bahru Zewde, R.Pankhurst and Taddese Beyene (eds.).*Proceedings of the Eleventh International Conference of the Ethiopian Studies* .Vol.1, Addis Ababa (1994): 103-116.

Crummey, D. *Land and Society in the Christian Kingdom of Ethiopia: From the Thirteenth to the Twentieth Century. Urbana and Chicago: University of Illinois Press, 2000.*

--------------"The term *rim* in Ethiopian Land Documents of the 18th and 19th Centuries" in Alessandro Bausi, Gianni Dore and Irma Taddia (eds). *Anthropological and Historical Documents on "rim" in Ethiopia and Eritrea.* Torino (2001): 65-81.

Dästa Täklä-Wäld. *Yä-Amareñña Mäzgäbä Qalat* .Addis Ababa: Artistic Printing Press, 1962.

Dessalegn Rahmato. *Agrarian Reforms in Ethiopia.*Uppsala: Scandinavian Institute of African Studies, 1984.

-------------------. "Moral Crusaders and Incipient Capitalists: Mechanized Agriculture and Its Critics in Ethiopia," in *Proceedings of the Third Annual Seminar of the Department of History.* Addis Ababa: Addis Ababa University, 1986.

-------------------. *Famine and Survival Strategies: A Case Study from Northeast Ethiopia.* Uppsala: The Scandinavian Institute of African Studies, 1991.

Donham, D. "Old Abyssinia and the New Ethiopian Empire: Themes in Social History", Donham, D and Wendy James (eds.).*The Southern Marches of Imperial Ethiopia: Essays in History and Social Anthropology.* Cambridge: Cambridge University Press (1986):3-48.

Ege, S. *Class, State, and Power in Africa. A Case Study of the Kingdom of Shawa (Ethiopia) about 1840.*Wiesbaden: Harrassowitz, Verlag, 1996.

Ehret, C. "On the Antiquity of Agriculture in Ethiopia", *Journal of African History.*Vol.20, no.2 (1979): 161-177.

Gäbrä-Sellasè.*Tarikä Zämän Dagmawi Minilik, Nigusä-Nägäst Zä-Ityopya.* Addis Ababa: Berhänena Sälam Printing Press, 1959.

Gäbrä-Wäld Engeda-Wärq. *YäItyopya märetenna Geber sem.* Addis Ababa, 1944.E.C translated and published by Mengesha Gessesse as

"Ethiopia's Traditional System of Land Tenure and Taxation". *Ethiopia Observer* 5(1962):302-39.

Gamst, F. "Peasantries and Elites without Urbanism", *Comparative Studies in Society and History.* Vol.12 (1970):373-392.

Getachew Haile and William Macomber (eds). *A Catalogue of Ethiopian Manuscripts Microfilmed for the Ethiopian Manuscripts Microfilm Library, Addis Ababa and for the Hill Monastic Manuscript Library Collegeville.* Vols.1-9, Collegeville, Minn: Hill Monastic Manuscript Library, St.John's Abbey and University, 1975-1987.

Girma Getahun. "Ancient Customary Law of the Gafat", *Journal of Ethiopian Studies.* Vol.xxx, no.2 (1997):28-88.

Griaule, M. *Abyssinian Journey.* London: John Miles, 1925.

Guidi, I. *Annales Regum Iyasu II et Iyo'as._*Corpus Scriptorium Christianorum Orientalium, Scriptores Aethiopici, Versio, Series Altera, vol.6, Paris, 1912.

Hoben, A. *Land Tenure among the Amhara of Ethiopia: The Dynamics of Cognatic Descent.* Chicago/London: 1973.

Huntingford, G.W.B.*The Glories Victories of Amda Seyon King of Ethiopia.* Oxford: Clarendon Press, 1965.

------------. *The Land Charters of Northern Ethiopia: Studies in Ethiopian Land Tenure.* Vol.1, Addis Ababa: Institute of Ethiopian Studies and Faculty of Law, 1965.

Käsati-Berhän Tässäma Häylä-Mika'el. *Yä Amareñña Mäzgäbä Qalat.* Addis Ababa: Artistic Printing Press, 1951.

Kidanä-Wäld Kiflè. *Sewasäw Wäges Wämäzgäb Qalat Häddis Nebabu Bägeez Fechew Bamaragna (A Book of Grammer and Verb, and New Dictionary.Geez Entries with Amharic Definions.* Addis Ababa: Artistic Printing Press, 19489E.C.

Kidane Mengisteab. *Ethiopia: Failure of Land Reform and Agricultural Crisis.* New York, Westport, London: Greenwood Press, 1990.

Leslau, Wolf. *Etymological Dictionary of Gurage (Ethiopic)* vol.III.Wiesbaden: Otto Harrassowitz, 1979.

Levine, D. *Wax and Gold: Tradition and Innovation in Ethiopian Culture.* London/Chicago: University of Chicago, 1965.

Lundstrom, Karl Johan. *North-eastern Ethiopia: Society in Famine: A Study of three Social Institutions in a Period of Severe Strain.* Research Report 34.Uppsala: The Scandinavian Institute of African Studies, 1976.

Mahtämä Sellase Wäldä-Mäsqäl. "The Land System of Ethiopia." Ethiopia Observer 1(1957):283-301.

----------------.*Zekra-Nagar*.2nd ed. Addis Ababa: Artistic Printing Press, 1962 E.C.

Mantel-Niecko, J. *The Role of Land Tenure in the System of Ethiopian Imperial Government in Modern Times*.Warsaw, 1980.

Marcaccini, Paolo. "Osservazioni Aerophotographiche sul paessaggio agrario nella regione del Ciocche (Goggiam, Etiopia)", *Rivista Geographica Italiana*.Vol.xxxv, Firenze: LaNuova Italia (1978):234-261.

Maydon, H.C. *Semen: Its Heights and Abysses*.London: H.F. & G.Witherby, 1925.

McCann, James. *From Poverty to Famine in Northeast Ethiopia: A Rural History, 1900-1935*.Philadelphia University: University of Pennsylvania Press, 1987.

-----------------. *People of the Plow: An Agricultural History of Ethiopia, 1800-1990*.Madison: University of Wisconsin Press, 1995.

Merid Wolde Aregay. "Political Geography of Ethiopia at the Beginning of the Sixteenth Century", *Accadamia Nazionale Dei Lincei IV Congresso Internazionale Di studi Etiopici*. Vol.1, Rome (1974): 613-631.

--------------." Society and Technology in Ethiopia, 1500-1855", *Journal of Ethiopian Studies*.Vol.17 (1984):127-47.

-------------"Land Tenure and Agricultural Productivity, 1500-1850", *Proceedings of the Third Annual Seminar of the Department of History*. Addis Ababa, (1986):115-29.

Mesfin Wolde-Mariam. *Suffering under God's Environment: A Vertical Study of Predicament of Peasants in North-Central Ethiopia*. Berne: The African Mountains Association and Geographica Bernensia, 1991.

-----------------. *Rural Vulnerability to Famine in Ethiopia 1958-1977*. New Delhi: Vikas Publishing House, 1984),

Pankhrust, R. "The Great Ethiopian Famine of 1888-92: A New Assessment," *Journal of the History of Medicine and Allied Sciences*. Vol. 21(1966):95-124 and 271-294.

----------------.*State and Land in Ethiopian History Monographs in Land Tenure*. Vol.3, Addis Ababa: Addis Ababa University Press, 1966.

----------------.*Economic History of Ethiopia, 1800-1935*.Addis Ababa: Haile Sellassie I University Press, 1968.

----------------." A Preliminary History of Ethiopian Measures, Weights and Values" in *Journal of Ethiopian Studies* vol.7, no.2 (1969):99-164.

----------------."Hierarchy at the Feast: the Partition of the Ox in Traditional Ethiopia", A.Gromyko and others (eds).*Proceedings of the 9th International Congress of Ethiopian Studies.* Vol.3, Mosco (1986):173-182.

Parkyns, Mansfield. *Life in Abyssinia, Being Notes Collected during Three Years Residence and Travels in that Country.* 2nd ed, London: J.Murray, 1868.

Perruchon, Jules. "Notes pour l'Histoire d'Éthiopie: Règnes de Ya'qob et Za- Dengel (1597-1607)," *Revue Sémitique* 4(1896):355-363.

Plowden, W.C. *Travels in Abyssinia and the Galla Country.* London: Longmans, Green, and Co., 1868.

Rey, C.F. *In the Country of the Blue Nile* .London: Duckworth, 1927.

Rossini, C.C. (ed. and trans.). *Liber Axumae.* Vol.III, Corpus Scriptorium Christianorum Orientalium, Paris, 1962.

Rubenson, Sven. *King of Kings Tewodros of Ethiopia.* Addis Ababa: Haile Sellase I University, 1966.

--------------. *The Survival of the Ethiopian Independence* .Addis Ababa: Kuraz Publishing Agency, 1976.

"Selä Abun Nägär Kä A'emero Gazzeṭa Yätägäläbäṭä" *Brehänena Sälam* No.10, (March10, 1927): 78.

Shiferaw Bekele. "The State in the *Zamana-Masafent,* 1769-1853: An Essay in Reinterpretation", Taddese Beyene, R.Pankhrust, and Shiferaw Bekele (eds.). *Kasa and Kasa: Papers on the Lives, Times and Images of Tewodros II and Yohannes IV, 1855-1889.* Addis Ababa: Institute of Ethiopian Studies (1990):25-68.

-------------."Reflections on the Power Elite of the *Wara Seh Masfenate,*" *Annales d'Ethiopie* .Vol.15 (1990):155-79.

---------------."The Evolution of Land Tenure in the Imperial Era", Shiferaw Bekele (ed.).*An Economic History of Modern Ethiopia 1941-74.* Dakar: Codesria (1995):72-142.

Taddesse Tamrat.Church and State in Ethiopia, 1270-1527.Oxford: Clarendon Press, 1972.

----------------."Ethnic Interaction and Integration in Ethiopian History: The Case of the Gafat", *Journal of Ethiopian Studies*, vol.21 (1988):121-154.

----------------."Processes of Ethnic Interaction and Integration in Ethiopian History: The Case of the Agaw", *Journal of African History,* vol.29, no.1 (1988):5-18.

----------------."Ethiopia in Miniature: The Peopling of Gojjam", *12th International Conference of Ethiopian Studies,* vol.1, Michigan State University (1994):951-962.

Zänäb. *Yä-Tewodros Tarik.Amharic Text Published as the Chronicle of King Theodore of Abyssinia* edited by Enno Littmann .Princeton, 1902.

Yältyopya Qwanqwawoch Ṭenatena Meremere Ma'ekäle-Ethiopian Languages Research and Study Centre, *Amareñña Mäzgäbä Qalat (Amharic Dictionary.* Addis Ababa: Artistic Printing Press, 1993 E.C

Yohännes Gäbrä-Egziabher. *Mäzgäbä Qalat Tigereñña Amhareñña (Ethiopian Dictionary Tigrigna Amharic.* Asmara: Artgraphic Eritrea, 1948-49.

Unpublished Sources Dissertations and Theses

Abdusamad H.Ahmed. "Trade and Politics in Gojjam 1882-1935", MA thesis, Department of History, Addis Ababa University, 1980.

-----------------. "Gojjam: Early Merchant Capital and the World Economy 1901-1935".PH.D.dissertation, University of Illinois at Urbana-Champaign, 1986.

Adhana Haile Adhana, "History of Selected Famines in Peasant Societies in Tigray and Wallo, Ethiopia 1941-74" .PH.D. Dissertation, Department of History (AAU), 1996)

Bizualem Birhane. "Adal Abba Tanna Nigus of Gojjam and Kaffa 1850-1901".BA thesis in History, Haile-Sellase I University, 1971.

Fantahun Birhane. Gojjam, 1800-1855.BA thesis in History, Department of History, Haile Sellase I University, 1973.

Habtamu Mengistie. "A Short History of the Monastery of Martula-Maryam, 1500-1974".BA thesis in History, Addis Ababa University, 1998.

Kindeneh Endeg. "A History of Dabra-Marqos Church at Dabra-Marqos Town". A thesis History, Addis Ababa University, 1997.

Mengistu Abebe, "Which Kind of Land Reform for Ethiopia: The Debate Preceding the 1975 Land Proclamation," A paper submitted to the Graduate Studies of the Department of History (AAU), June 1995.

Merid Wolde Aregay. "Southern Ethiopia and the Christian Kingdom, 1508-1708, with Special Reference to the Galla Migrations and their Consequences".PH.D. Dissertation, University of London, 1971.
Seleshi Mengiste. "A Short History of the Monastery of Dima Giyorgis".BA thesis in History, Addis Ababa University, 1998.
Tekalign Wolde-Mariam. "A City and its Hinterlands: The Political Economy of Land Tenure, Agriculture and Food Supply for Addis Ababa, Ethiopia.PH. D .disserataion, Boston University, 1995.

Manuscripts

Manuscripts found at the Institute of Ethiopian Studies, Addis Ababa University.
Arba'etu-Wängèl, MS. Bichäna Giyorgis, 89, II, 3-8.
Dersanä-Mädehänè-Aläm, MS.Qäranyo Mädehänè-Aläm, 89, VIII, 11-18.
Dersanä Mädehänè-Aläm, MS.Qäranyo Mädehänè-Aläm, 89, IV, 26-36.
Fekarè-Iyäsus, MS.Yäwish Mika'el, 89, XVI, 9.
Fetha Nägäst, MS.Yäwish Mika'el, 89, XVI, 6-9.
Gädlä-Giyorgis, MS. Dima Giyorgis 89. XIV.8-9.
Gebrä-Häwaryat, MS. Yägwära Qwesqwam 89, XVI.23-25.
Gebrä-Häwaryat, MS.Yägwära Qwesqwam, 89, XVI.23-25.
Giyorgis Wäldä-Amid, MS.Moṭa Giyorgis, VIII.22-24.
Mazgaba Se'el, MS NO.7,IES.
Nägärä-Maryam, MS. Mängesto Kidanä-Meherät 89, IX.
Nägäst, MS.Yälämläm Kidanä-Meherät, 89, XV, 29-32.
Tamrä-Iyäsus, MS., Gemja-Bèt Kidanä-Meherät, 89, I, 2-32.
Tarikä-Nägäst Zä-Ityopya, MS. Däbrä-Wärq, catalogued as II.11-33; III.3-18.
Tarikä-Nägäst Zä-Ityopya, MS. Däbrä-Wärq, II.11-33; III.3-18.
Wängèl, MS. Moṭa Giyorgis, 89, IX, 3-6.
Wanna-Mäzgäb, MS.Däbrä-Eliyas, 89, XVIII, 9-31.
Other Manuscripts found in various places
Besratä-Gäbra'el, MS.Däbrä-Marqos
Däqiqä Näbeyat, MS.Märtulä-Maryam, The Researcher has reproduced the Original Manuscript.
Giyorgis Wäldä-Amid, MS.Däbrä-Marqos
Mäzgäb, MS.Moṭa Giyorgis

Mäzgäb, MS. Däbrä-Marqos, A Copy of the Original Manuscript is in the Possession of the Researcher.

Täklä-Iyäsus Waqjera. "The Genealogy of the People of Gojjam."A Copy of the Original Manuscript in the Possession of the Researcher.

--------------------. "The Genealogy of the People of Gojjam", Incorporated in Yäzämän Tarik Matäraqämya, MS. National Library, 527.

------------------. "Yä Gojjam Tarik", MS. IES.No.254.

FSS PUBLICATIONS LIST

FSS Newsletter

Medrek, now renamed BULLETIN (Quarterly since 1998. English and Amharic)

FSS Discussion Papers

No. 1 *Water Resource Development in Ethiopia: Issues of Sustainability and Participation*. Dessalegn Rahmato. June 1999

No. 2 *The City of Addis Ababa: Policy Options for the Governance and Management of a City with Multiple Identity*. Meheret Ayenew. December 1999

No. 3 *Listening to the Poor: A Study Based on Selected Rural and Urban Sites in Ethiopia*. Aklilu Kidanu and Dessalegn Rahmato. May 2000

No. 4 *Small-Scale Irrigation and Household Food Security. A Case Study from Central Ethiopia*. Fuad Adem. February 2001

No. 5 *Land Redistribution and Female-Headed Households*. By Yigremew Adal. November 2001

No. 6 *Environmental Impact of Development Policies in Peripheral Areas: The Case of Metekel, Northwest Ethiopia*. Wolde-Selassie Abbute. Forthcoming, 2001

No. 7 *The Environmental Impact of Small-scale Irrigation: A Case Study*. Fuad Adem. Forthcoming, 2001

No. 8 *Livelihood Insecurity Among Urban Households in Ethiopia*. Dessalegn Rahmato and Aklilu Kidanu. October 2002

No. 9 *Rural Poverty in Ethiopia: Household Case Studies from North Shewa*. Yared Amare. December 2002

No.10 *Rural Lands in Ethiopia: Issues, Evidences and Policy Response*. Tesfaye Teklu. May 2003

No.11 *Resettlement in Ethiopia: The Tragedy of Population Relocation in the 1980s*. Dessalegn Rahmato. June 2003

No.12 *Searching for Tenure Security? The Land System and New Policy Initiatives in Ethiopia*. Dessalegn Rahmato. August 2004.

FSS Monograph Series

No. 1 *Survey of the Private Press in Ethiopia: 1991-1999.* Shimelis Bonsa. 2000
No. 2 *Environmental Change and State Policy in Ethiopia: Lessons from Past Experience.* Dessalegn Rahmato. 2001
No. 3 *Democratic Assistance to Post-Conflict Ethiopia: Impact and Limitations.* Dessalegn Rahmato and Meheret Ayenew. 2004

Special Monograph Series

1. *Lord, Zega and Peasant: A Study of Property and Agrarian Relations in Rural Eastern Gojjam.* Habtamu Mengistie. 2004

FSS Conference Proceedings

2. *Issues in Rural Development. Proceedings of the Inaugural Workshop of the Forum for Social Studies, 18 September 1998.* Edited by Zenebeworke Tadesse. 2000
3. *Development and Public Access to Information in Ethiopia.* Edited by Zenebeworke Tadesse. 2000
4. *Environment and Development in Ethiopia.* Edited by Zenebeworke Tadesse. 2001
5. *Food Security and Sustainable Livelihoods in Ethiopia.* Edited by Yared Amare. 2001
6. *Natural Resource Management in Ethiopia.* Edited by Alula Pankhurst. 2001
7. *Poverty and Poverty Policy in Ethiopia.* Special issue containing the papers of FSS' final conference on poverty held on 8 March 2002

Consultation Papers on Poverty

No. 1 *The Social Dimensions of Poverty.* Papers by Minas Hiruy, Abebe Kebede, and Zenebework Tadesse. Edited by Meheret Ayenew. June 2001
No. 2 *NGOs and Poverty Reduction.* Papers by Fassil W. Mariam, Abowork Haile, Berhanu Geleto, and Jemal Ahmed. Edited by Meheret Ayenew. July 2001
No. 3 *Civil Society Groups and Poverty Reduction.* Papers by Abonesh H. Mariam, Zena Berhanu, and Zewdie Shitie. Edited by Meheret Ayenew. August 2001

No. 4 *Listening to the Poor.* Oral Presentation by Gizachew Haile, Senait Zenawi, Sisay Gessesse and Martha Tadesse. In Amharic. Edited by Meheret Ayenew. November 2001

No. 5 *The Private Sector and Poverty Reduction [Amharic].* Papers by Teshome Kebede, Mullu Solomon and Hailemeskel Abebe. Edited by Meheret Ayenew, November 2001

No. 6 *Government, Donors and Poverty Reduction.* Papers by H.E. Ato Mekonnen Manyazewal, William James Smith and Jeroen Verheul. Edited by Meheret Ayenew, February 2002.

No. 7 *Poverty and Poverty Policy in Ethiopia.* Edited by Meheret Ayenew, 2002

Books

1. *Ethiopia: The Challenge of Democracy from Below.* Edited by Bahru Zewde and Siegfried Pausewang. Nordic African Institute, Uppsala and the Forum for Social Studies, Addis Ababa. 2002

Special Publications

- *Thematic Briefings on Natural Resource Management. Enlarged Edition.* Edited by Alula Pankhurst. Produced jointly by the Forum for Social Studies and the University of Sussex. January 2001

New Series

- **Gender Policy Dialogue Series**

No. 1 *Gender and Economic Policy.* Edited by Zenebework Tadesse. March 2003

No. 2 *Gender and Poverty (Amharic).* Edited by Zenebework Tadesse. March 2003

No. 3 *Gender and Social Development in Ethiopia.* (Forthcoming).

No. 4 *Gender Policy Dialogue in Oromiya Region.* Edited by Eshetu Bekele. September 2003

- **Consultation Papers on Environment**

No. 1 *Environment and Environmental Change in Ethiopia.* Edited by Gedion Asfaw. Consultation Papers on Environment. March 2003

No. 2 *Environment, Poverty and Gender.* Edited by Gedion Asfaw. Consultation Papers on Environment. May 2003

No. 3 *Environmental Conflict.* Edited by Gedion Asfaw. Consultation Papers on Environment. July 2003

No. 4 *Economic Development and its Environmental Impact.* Edited by Gedion Asfaw. Consultation Papers on Environment. August 2003

No. 5 *Government and Environmental Policy.* Consultation Papers on Environment. January 2004

No. 6 *የግልና የጋራ ጥረት ለአካባቢ ሕይወት መሻሻል (የሶሜን ሾፕ ገበሬዎች ተሞክሮ)* Consultation Papers on Environment. May 2004

No. 7 *Promotion of Indigenous Trees and Biodiversity Conservation.* Consultation Papers on Environment. June 2004

- **FSS Studies on Poverty**

No. 1 *Some Aspects of Poverty in Ethiopia: Three Selected Papers.* Papers by Dessalegn Rahmato, Meheret Ayenew and Aklilu Kidanu. Edited by Dessalegn Rahmato. March 2003.

No. 2 *Faces of Poverty: Life in Gäta, Wälo.* By Harald Aspen. June 2003.

No. 3 *Destitution in Rural Ethiopia.* By Yared Amare. August 2003

No. 4 *Environment, Poverty and Conflict.* Tesfaye Teklu and Tesfaye Tafesse. October 2004

Other Educational Materials

- Environmental Posters
- Environmental Video Films
    - የከተማችን አካባቢ ከየት ወደየት?
    - ውጥንቅጥ፤ ድህነትና የአካባቢያችን መጎሳቆል

www.ingramcontent.com/pod-product-compliance
Lightning Source LLC
Chambersburg PA
CBHW021403290426
44108CB00010B/366